Stalinism ... into stone

COMMUNISM AND
BRITISH INTELLECTUALS

COMMUNISM AND
BRITISH INTELLECTUALS

by

NEAL WOOD

NEW YORK
COLUMBIA UNIVERSITY PRESS
1959

Library of Congress Catalog Card Number: 59-13519

An extended version of certain sections of the introductory chapter has been published in the *Political Science Quarterly* under the title "The Empirical Proletarian: A Note on British Communism".

Manufactured in Great Britain

TO RED AND CODY

Unless philosophers bear kingly rule in cities, or those who are now called kings and princes become genuine and adequate philosophers, and political power and philosophy be brought together, and unless the numerous natures who at present pursue either politics or philosophy, the one to the exclusion of the other, be forcibly debarred from this behaviour, there will be no respite from evil, my dear Glaucon, for cities, nor I fancy for humanity....

Plato, *The Republic*

Scientist and artists, examine with the eye of genius the present condition of the human mind. You will perceive that the sceptre of public opinion is in your hands; seize it, therefore boldly. You have the power to bring happiness to yourselves and to your contemporaries, to preserve posterity from the evils we have suffered and are suffering still.

Henri Comte De Saint-Simon,
Letters From an Inhabitant of Geneva to His Contemporaries (1803)

Philosophy cannot be realized without the abolition of the proletariat, the proletariat cannot abolish itself without realizing philosophy.

Karl Marx,
A Criticism of the Hegelian Philosophy of Right (1844)

CONTENTS

PREFACE

THE LIMITATIONS OF this survey—apart from the defects of my own analysis and synthesis—are the limitations of "social science" with its abstraction of human experience. "Man" in social science tends to be less of a concrete individual of flesh and blood who feels, thinks, and acts, than an artifice that "behaves". If there is no escape from abstraction, at least some of its excesses can be avoided. But even if I have succeeded in this, what remains can at best be only an intimation, never a revelation, for the "ultimate explanation" of the appeal of communism is forever concealed from rational enquiry in the minds and hearts of many diverse individuals.

An important motive in my writing has been a continual concern with the problem of wisdom and the exercise of political power. If political philosophy is to be written in and for the present scientific age, such a problem will be of paramount consideration. In his approach to the human predicament the political philosopher will have to deal with the impact of science upon society and government, with the intellectual in politics, and with many related questions. I hope that I have been able to furnish a fraction of the grist for the mill of such philosophy.

The term "intellectual" has been employed in the following pages in a very unscientific fashion. It is, perhaps, a concept just as useful and meaningful as "class" and just as difficult to define precisely. The intellectuals whom I discuss are chiefly men of literature and science who have been articulate about man, society and nature, and who have left a written record of their thoughts. The expression, "communist intellectual" does not necessarily indicate a person who is or has been a member of the Communist Party, but may refer to anyone who over a period of some time has publicly expressed his sympathy for communism and communist ideas.

This study is not an "inside story" or exposé of communism. My treatment is aimed at a critical but sympathetic understanding. Whenever possible I have talked with the actors in the scene that I portray. Their observations have often been used as part of the raw material upon which my own judgments have been based, although I have refrained from acknowledging my great debt to them in order to spare them possible embarrassment. In a study of this kind, there is every likelihood of omission, error, misinterpretation, and faulty judgment. Naturally, I assume entire responsibility for such flaws, and hope that the reader will bring to my attention any that he may discover.

To the Trustees of the Rockefeller Foundation I am greatly indebted for a grant that enabled me to spend two fruitful years in England, from 1955 to 1957, thereby making this book possible. For their wise counsel and constant support I wish particularly to thank Professors Julian Towster and Norman Jacobson of the University of California, Berkeley. Others at Berkeley who did so much to advise and to encourage were Professors Eugene Burdick, Peter Odegard, Sheldon Wolin, and Dr. Caesar Grana, now of the University of Chicago. My only regret is that the manuscript did not profit from the perceptive criticism of the late Professor Lloyd Fisher, to whom a few owe so much. At the beginning stage of thought and research Dr. Hannah Arendt of New York offered many valuable ideas, and Professor Samuel Beer of Harvard University made a number of very useful suggestions. The final draft was read and helpfully criticized by Professor Herbert Deane of Columbia University.

In England I was fortunate to benefit from the knowledge and guidance of Mr. Nöel Annan, Provost of King's College, Cambridge; Mr. R. N. Carew Hunt of St. Antony's College, Oxford; Mr. Hugo Dewar of London; and Professor Michael Polanyi of the University of Manchester. Mr. Victor

Gollancz, my British publisher, aided in making this a better book than it might have been. I greatly appreciate permission to use the Cambridge University Library, the Reading Room of the British Museum, the British Library of Political and Economic Science, the Marx Memorial Library, and the Library of Transport House. Their staffs were unfailing in their courtesy and assistance. I am also obligated to countless others who were so generous in such various ways. A very pleasant stay in Cambridge was in no small part due to the kindness of Professor D. W. Brogan of Peterhouse, of the Censor and Tutor of Fitzwilliam House, and of Mr. V. F. Wick.

I am deeply grateful to my wife and son to whom this volume is dedicated. The typing of many drafts, and the unflagging cheerfulness and patience with what at times must have been a trying husband and father, only hint at their real contribution.

NEAL WOOD

Mount Vernon, New York
March 29, 1959

INTRODUCTION

CHAPTER I

INTRODUCTION

A DISTINCTIVE FEATURE of our age is the participation
of the intellectual in the "game of political passions". So
wrote M. Julien Benda over thirty years ago in his brilliant
analysis of the modern epoch, *La Trahison des Clercs*. One
need not accept M. Benda's concept of the intellectual as a
mandarin to appreciate his suggestion of a major development in history. Nowhere is the phenomenon more apparent
than in the relation of the intellectual to socialism. The way
was opened by the bourgeois literati of the eighteenth
century who, armed with the weapons of reason, science, and
progress, attacked the "old unity" of the traditional aristo-
cratic society. Some, like Mably, Morelly, and later Saint-
Simon and his followers, inspired by the vision of a new
socialist unity, turned these same weapons against bourgeois
individualism as well.

In the second half of the nineteenth century these political
passions were organized into the modern, centralized
political party. War against the bourgeoisie began to be
waged by socialist participation in the electoral and parliamentary process. Discontented intellectuals, bringing
theories and slogans, and organizing and administrative
ability to the youthful movement, soon came to the fore in
the ranks of its leadership. To list only a few is to bring together a host of illustrious names: Marx, Engels, Bakunin,
Lassalle, Proudhon, Bernstein, Kautsky, Luxemburg, Liebknecht, Adler, Vandervelde, Hyndman, Jaurès, Longuet,
Molkenbuler, Plekhanov, Lenin, Trotsky. The degree of
participation of intellectuals in the socialist leadership varied
from country to country. At one extreme was British Labour,
largely manned and led by workers. Only recently have intellectuals figured as Labour Party leaders. At the other

extreme were the Russian opposition groups, the Social Revolutionaries, Social-Democrats, Legal Marxists, and Economists—almost entirely in the hands of dissenting members of the bourgeoisie and aristocracy.

Marx was one of the first socialists to delineate the role of the intellectual in the socialist movement. He believed that the "head" of the emancipation of mankind is philosophy, while its "heart" is the proletariat. True philosophy could be realized only with the abolition of the proletariat and conversely freedom for the proletariat would depend upon the realization of philosophy. At the decisive moment in history, when the great majority had become the wage slaves of a minority of capitalists, a segment of the bourgeoisie, in particular the ideologists—writers, artists, scientists, etc.—who had been able to transcend their class-bound outlook, would place their skills at the disposal of the proletariat. In the language of the Platonic "Allegory of the Cave" it is the man of learning who first escapes from the den of obscurantism to discover the *summum bonum* and who is then able to return to release the captive audience from their chains, leading them forth into the light of the real world. The ideologists must be completely committed to the proletarian cause, leaving behind all bourgeois prejudices. Because of their understanding of the general direction of the movement of history and the role of the proletariat as the bearer of reason and progress, they would join the most enlightened workers to form the Communist Party whose basic task would be the conversion of the masses into a self-conscious, organized, militant class.

But in practice the new partnership between worker and intellectual was not completely harmonious. In the beginning intellectuals were welcomed with the greatest friendliness by their working-class patrons. However, as the movement matured and as the intellectuals began to compete with the proletarians for power in the recently organized parties, the original cordiality receded before an ever growing distrust. Representative of this change is the remark attributed to August Bebel: "If a bourgeois wants to join you, look him over closely; if he is an intellectual, twice as closely." [1] Intellectuals became scapegoats for many of the difficulties and setbacks suffered by the socialists. They were accused of being both reformists and fanatics. Charges of untrustworthiness and uncontrolled individualism were made. Naturally, there was some truth to these accusations. By upbringing and outlook, the bourgeois intellectual has always been something of a non-conformist. Moreover, his dogmatism, his impatience with the practical details of a subject, his contempt for the parochialism of his proletarian comrades, and, most obviously, his bourgeois manners and speech set him apart, and did little to endear him to the workers. Some of the trouble stemmed from a lack of understanding. The workers frequently forgot that the intellectual became a socialist, not usually from motives of self-interest, but for idealistic reasons. Often he joined at great personal sacrifice and loss of social position, turning his back on many of the "plums" of bourgeois life. The increasing friction between worker and intellectual soon had consequences at the organizational level. At least one important motive of the syndicalist movement was the desire on the part of working-class socialists to free themselves from the leadership of the intellectuals and the bourgeoisie. Sorel called upon the proletariat to end the leadership of the intellectuals, and Edouard Berth of the *mouvement socialiste* described Social-Democracy as a "half-bourgeois philosophy", and the proletariat as the pawn of bourgeois intellectuals.[2] A similar reaction accounted in part for the origin of the I.W.W. in America.

An undercurrent of "anti-intellectualism" appears in the

---

[1] As quoted in Golo Mann, "The Intellectuals 3. Germany", *Encounter*, Vol. IV (June 1955), p. 45.

[2] Robert Michels, *Political Parties: A Sociological Study of the Oligarchical Tendencies of Modern Democracy*, trans. from the Italian by Eden and Cedar Paul (London: Jarrold, 1915), p. 313; G. D. H. Cole, *A History of Socialist Thought* (London: Macmillan, 1953–1956), Vol. III, "The Second International 1889–1914", Part I, pp. 383–384, 389, Part II, pp. 732–735.

thought of Lenin, although it is necessary to be precise about its nature in order to avoid misunderstanding. Lenin was treading solid doctrinal ground and realistically confronting the fact of the non-existence of a Russian proletariat when he stressed that revolutionary consciousness could be brought to the workers only from without—by bourgeois ideologists like himself. Nevertheless, he was acutely sensitive to the pedanticism, dilletantism, indecisiveness, and anarchistic tendencies of many bourgeois intellectuals. He objected to the bourgeois who remained a bourgeois after entering the party, and resisted the discipline that was the requisite of a competent revolutionist. No distinction between worker and intellectual must exist in the Russian Social Democratic Party; all must be revolutionists. Organization and discipline would rid the movement not of the workers, but of the undependable among the "professors" and "schoolboys". To the socialist worker, graduated from the hard discipline of the factory, would fall the task of curbing the anarchism of the bourgeois intellectual, and thereby safeguarding the party life of collective action. Because of this elementary faith in the worker, Lenin felt that the differences between Bolshevism and Menshevism could be reduced to simplicity itself: the one was proletarianism: the other, intellectualism.

A more pronounced hostility to the intellectual with far-reaching consequences for Russia and the world emerged during the bureaucratic stage of the communist movement under Joseph Stalin. The Council of People's Commissars of 1917, the first Soviet Government, consisted of fifteen members: eleven intellectuals and four workers.[1] Trotsky recollected that a few years later he was the only member attending a meeting of the Political Bureau who could speak fluent French.[2] What happened in the interval to the revolutionary intellectuals, the "emigrés", as Stalin called them, who

[1] Isaac Deutscher, *Stalin: A Political Biography* (London: Oxford University Press, 1949), pp. 176–177.

[2] Leon Trotsky, *Stalin: An Appraisal of the Man and His Influence*, edited and trans. by Charles Malamuth (New York and London: Harper, 1946), p. 395.

had suffered the deprivations of Siberia, who had plotted and prepared abroad, and who had returned to captain the seizure of power in 1917, can be explained by the emergence of the new bureaucratic breed whose embodiment was Stalin.

A duel for power between Trotsky and Stalin, the "literary" and the "practico", ending in the defeat and banishment of the former, was to presage the complete elimination of a distinguished group of intellectual revolutionaries from the directorate of the regime. Among the most prominent were Zinoviev, Kamenev, Bukharin, Radek, Krestinsky, and Rykov. When it was apparent that Lenin was dying, Stalin, Kamenev and Zinoviev formed a triumvirate to prevent Trotsky from succeeding his master. Although Trotsky possessed the enthusiastic support of intellectuals and students, he had lost the backing of many workers by advocating and instituting a number of unpopular measures at the end of the Civil War. His policies of conscription, of the direction of labour, of the introduction of socialist emulation and production drives, and his desire to transform the trade unions into organs of the state were hardly designed to win the applause of the masses. Furthermore, after the death of Lenin in April 1924, Stalin as Secretary General of the Party initiated a number of special membership drives, the famous "Lenin calls", resulting in an increase in size from 472,000 members and candidates on January 1, 1924 to 801,804 the next year, the largest gain between 1920 and 1930.[1] Of greater importance than the number, however, was the social composition of the new candidates. From 1920 to 1924 the working-class composition of the party remained approximately stable at about 44%. An average of 83.3% of the recruits for 1924 were of working-class origin. By 1929 the percentage of workers in the Party had risen to 61.4% and that of the intellectuals had decreased from 27.2% in 1924 to 16.9%. The significance of these figures is that Stalin had "packed" the party with men of his own kind. Many listed

[1] For membership figure see Merle Fainsod, *How Russia Is Ruled* (Cambridge: Harvard University Press, 1953), pp. 212–213.

as workers were actually bureaucrats and functionaries of the growing state and party apparatus, or were soon to be trained as technicians and administrators in the new Soviet schools and institutes. In the long run the new men were too formidable for the "literaries" supporting Trotsky. Organization and the technicians of organization had triumphed. But Stalin held one more trump card. For some time he had opposed Trotsky's concept of "World Revolution" with his own politically astute theory of "Socialism in One Country". The slogan "World Revolution" undoubtedly appealed to the young and ardent student admirers or to the impatient Red Professors who were anxious to carry the logic of Marxism to its conclusion, but to the practico it signified an idealistic tilting at windmills. After the hectic years of the Revolution, the Civil War and Intervention, he craved a breathing spell, a respite of security and stability which the magic symbol "Socialism in One Country" temptingly promised. Trotsky was outplayed by a master hand. Little by little he was forced to retreat. Year by year he was progressively relieved of his offices, and the end was expulsion from the Party, exile from the Soviet Union, and assassination in Mexico. Playing one intellectual leader against another Stalin succeeded in removing all from positions of power. His attack upon the intelligentsia was manifest in the decline of Soviet culture beginning about 1928. The brilliant experimentation of the early years disappeared. Creative activity was suffocated. Art and literature were sacrificed for the sake of conformity. The day of the party line in culture had arrived.

Signalling the fundamental change that had taken place within the regime was the nature of the all-Stalinist Political Bureau of 1931, so strikingly different from the Political Bureaus of the early twenties, headed by Lenin and dominated by the intellectuals.[1] Eight of the ten members in 1931 were Party functionaries, hand-picked subordinates of Stalin, of whom only three can with any certainty be iden-

[1] For details as to personnel, *How Russia is Ruled*, p. 267.

tified as of middle- or upper-class origin. Voroshilov and Kalinin, the remaining two, had never been in the Party bureaucracy and were of humble lineage. With an eye to enhancing their power and cementing the masses over whom they ruled, the new bureaucrats could now put into operation a cult of the irrational. Cults of leadership, of Soviet patriotism and of Great Russian superiority—all reminiscent of devices of the Tsarist regime—were sanctioned. Intellectuals who form the conscience of the body politic would trouble the regime no longer.

Stalin's attack upon the intellectuals in the Soviet Union had repercussions throughout the international Communist movement. Intellectuals began to leave the national communist parties in the middle twenties, when it became clear that the Communist International was little more than an instrument of Soviet foreign policy. The increasing tempo of the bureaucratization of the national communist parties, the growing demands for ideological conformity, and the cultivation of the idea of Soviet infallibility contributed to their anxieties. Supported by Stalin, working-class leaders such as Thorez in France and Thalmann in Germany wrested the control of the national communist parties from the intellectuals. Well-known intellectual leaders in the German Communist Party—Paul Levy, Max Hoelz, Heinz Neumann—eventually either committed suicide or died under dubious circumstances. In America Jay Lovestone and his colleagues, many of whom were graduates of the City College of New York, dominated the Communist Party upon the death of the intellectual leader, Walter Ruthenberg, only to be ousted in 1929 by Foster and Browder. New statutes adopted by the C.P.U.S.A. specified that the Central Executive Committee must consist of at least 51% workers.[1]

Information upon the situation in nineteen communist parties in 1934 revealed that of the 497 members of the

[1] Martin Jones, "Organisational Steps Towards Bolshevization of the American Communist Party", *International Press Correspondence*, Vol. 9 (May 24, 1929), p. 532.

central committees of these parties, 321 or 64% were
workers.[1] The history of the composition of the Central
Committee of the French Communist Party was typical. At
the Congress of Tours in 1920, four of the thirty-two members elected to the central committee were workers. After
the death of Lenin, working-class representation rapidly increased until by 1929 forty-eight or 70% of the sixty-nine
member central committee were workers.

An exception to this general pattern is the Communist
Party of Great Britain. Since its foundation in 1920 intellectuals have always had a very much smaller role in its
governance than they have had in any other section of international communism. In addition, history, size, and general
outlook have made the C.P.G.B. unique among the communist parties of the great industrial powers. Unlike Continental and American communism the British party did not
result from a major split in the ranks of the Social Democrats.
The nucleus of British Communism was the small British
Socialist Party, affiliated to the Labour Party, that was heir
to H. M. Hyndman's Social Democratic Federation. Joining
the British Socialist Party were a variety of radical elements:
the left wing of the Socialist Labour Party, a group of syn-
dicalists that had seceded from the Social Democratic
Federation in 1903 under the leadership of James Connolly;
the Workers Socialist Federation, later the British Communist Party, led by Sylvia Pankhurst; the South Wales
Socialist Society; the Communist Labour Party of Willie
Gallacher and Dave Ramsay; intellectuals from the National
Guilds League; dissenters from the Independent Labour
Party; and members of numerous small sects like the Socialist
Prohibition Fellowship. Although the C.P.G.B. was founded
in London, July 31 to August 1, 1920, the union of these
groups was not completed until the Third National Congress
of April 1921 when the Party rules were drafted.

British communism has to a great extent been shaped by

---

[1] Chernomordik, "The Question of Communist Cadres", *Communist
International*, Vol. XI (December 5, 1934), pp. 929–930.

its development in the shadow of what has become the largest
and most powerful Social Democratic Party in the world.
Much of the history of the C.P.G.B. and its differences from
communist parties elsewhere can perhaps be explained by
the gargantuan strength and effectiveness of the Labour
Party. By 1920 the Labour Party had over four million
members, and never in its subsequent history did the membership drop below two million. Winning 4·2 million votes
in the election of 1922, Labour went on to poll 8·3 million
votes in 1935. Numerically, the German Social Democratic
Party was stronger than the Labour Party at a much earlier
date. However, its postwar growth, not as great as that of
the Labour Party, was abruptly terminated by Hitler. The
existence of the Labour Party has undoubtedly retarded the
growth of the C.P.G.B., whose diminutive size probably has
been vital in determining other aspects of its character.

The C.P.G.B. has always been smaller than any communist party of a major industrial power. With scarcely
more than 2,500 members at the foundation, the size increased suddenly to 10,730 in 1926, the year of the General
Strike, to dwindle to 1,376 by 1930. The growth in the
thirties was much less dramatic than that of the French and
American parties, reaching only 15,570 in the year of
Munich. During the middle of the Second World War a peak
of over 55,000 was attained. Subsequently, there was a decline to about 33,000 in 1955, dropping after the Hungarian
uprising of 1956, to less than 25,000. The perennially small
membership has perhaps consisted of fewer representatives
of the middle classes than is true of other communist parties.
But there has been a similar high annual turnover rate of
members, at times well over 40%, that has facilitated oligarchic control by a hard core of true believers. If a conclusion about the membership can be drawn it is that in all
probability the British masses tend to be politically conservative. Those who are radically inclined can turn to
the Labour Party. As a consequence the C.P.G.B. has
been compelled to grope its way forward, cautiously and

empirically, carefully attempting to adjust its policy to the "objective economic situation".

British communists seem more moderate in their outlook, less engrossed with theoretical questions, and less hesitant to associate with non-communists than communists of other nations. The penchant for the middle road, for the compromise and tolerance so much a part of British society, has left its impress. The C.P.G.B. has never become a closed society with distinctive mores isolated from the rest of society. Hatred has not been as significant as it has elsewhere in shaping the relations of communist and non-communist. In trade unions there tends to be somewhat greater fraternization. No great stigma is attached to a Labour M.P. who associates with communists or writes for their publications. Among communists and non-communist intellectuals, the bonds of family, school, university, profession, and club to some extent bridge the gap resulting from ideological differences. If loyalty to Eton and Balliol means little to the communist, it may certainly temper the feelings of his former non-communist classmates towards him. Beatrice Webb described the tolerant state of affairs in the entry of her diary for September 4, 1920.[1] She mentions the visit of foreign socialist leaders who were invited over for a week by the Fabian Society. At the same time they had an unexpected "lightning" visit from the two Bolsheviks, Krassin and Kamenev. This free mixing of communists and Fabians perplexed the foreign socialists. They saw it

> . . . as an amazing example of an almost anarchic tolerance on the part of the Fabians of hostile schools of Socialist thought. It was strange enough, they explained, to see Guild Socialists and members of the new English Communist Party on terms of intimate comradeship with Fabians, but to invite the official representatives of Lenin, who had expressly denounced all Fabians as traitors, and

[1] Margaret Cole, ed., *Beatrice Webb's Diaries 1912–1924*, introduction by Lord Beveridge (London: Longmans, 1952), p. 190.

the Webbs as particularly pernicious ones, was really carrying the principle of tolerance too far!

It is generally agreed that the C.P.G.B. has been directed by leaders of higher than average ability. Rank and file members have apparently held them in greater esteem than has been the case in other communist parties. The continuity of leadership, even for a communist organization, is remarkable. A comparison of the lists of Party leaders for 1923 and 1945 would show a good proportion of names common to both: Pollitt, Dutt, Gallacher, Rust, Campbell, Hannington, and Horner. Delegates to the Sixth Congress of the C.P.G.B. gave Pollitt, Dutt, and Gallacher the greatest number of popular votes, 71, 71, and 65 respectively. By 1930 the Party was under their control. Today if their power is not what it was, they are still nominally leaders: Gallacher as President, Pollitt as Chairman, and Dutt as Vice-Chairman. Such a record of survival is unparalleled among any of the world's leading communists.

The partnership in power of Harry Pollitt and Rajani Palme Dutt is one of the fascinating episodes of British Labour history. Pollitt, an affable boiler-maker from Lancashire, was a great orator and skilful labour organizer. Dutt, honours graduate of Balliol, was the austere Eurasian theoretician, completely dedicated to the revolutionary cause. It was a wedding in the twenties of thought and action in the true Leninist style. The two radicals were responsible for the drafting and the implementation of the Party's *Report on Organisation* of 1922, in line with the Comintern's directives to Bolshevize the national parties by transforming them into highly centralized, bureaucratic instruments of revolution. Great resistance, especially among the intellectuals, met these demands for discipline and conformity, and an ever greater subservience to Moscow. Pollitt and Dutt were also vigorous champions, supported by a minority, of the 1928 change in the Comintern line which called for unceasing struggle instead of collaboration with the

Social Democrats, branded as "social-fascists". Moscow rewarded Pollitt with the General Secretaryship of the Party in August 1929. Before the end of the year the majority faction that had opposed him capitulated, losing its seats on the executive.

The long tenure of Pollitt and Dutt has been due to a combination of factors: their own talents; their early realization that organization was the key to party control, and their success in using it; their loyalty to the Kremlin and the blessing which it conferred upon them; their ability to command and to retain the respect of the ranks; and possibly the presence of only a few intellectuals at the centre to complicate matters. Furthermore, the Lilliputian dimensions of the C.P.G.B. meant that there were fewer competitors than would have been the case in a large mass party. In a way the metamorphosis of the C.P.G.B. has been a model of communist development, although ironically it has never become more than a negligible political force in the most highly industrialized and urbanized nation of Western Europe. A greater irony, however, is that Pollitt and Dutt should have based their rise to power on those very same Comintern principles of Bolshevization that Lenin realized were "almost exclusively Russian", and not applicable to differing situations and conditions. But Lenin was impotent to halt what he had started twenty years before.

The C.P.G.B. like the Labour Party has been fundamentally a working-class movement. The groups which coalesced in the C.P.G.B. were organizations of workers advocating the ideas of syndicalism and industrial unionism. With the exception of Sylvia Pankhurst, no intellectual had conspicuously participated in the arrangements leading to the Foundation Conference. J. T. Murphy, attending the Second Congress of the Comintern in July 1920, was struck by the fact that only one member of the British delegation of eight was an intellectual, Sylvia Pankhurst, and she had arrived when the Congress was all but over. This was a distinct contrast to the other delegations, including the Russian,

heavily weighted with intellectuals.[1] Few intellectuals were
elected to the early Executive Committees of the C.P.G.B.
Only three of the fourteen members of the Provisional Executive Committee could possibly qualify as intellectuals: C.
L'Estrange Malone, William Mellor, and Dora B. Montefiore. At no time during the decade were more than two or
three intellectuals on Executive Committees of an average
size of eighteen to twenty. The total came to seven: Malone,
Mellor, Montefiore, Walton Newbold, Dutt, Page Arnot, and
Andrew Rothstein. Three very shortly left the party
(Malone, Mellor, Walton Newbold); Dora Montefiore died;
and of the remaining three only Dutt remains a leader.

Since 1930, only six or seven intellectuals have been
elected to any single Executive Committee, usually of thirty
or more members. Dutt has been joined by two intellectuals, the party careerists, Emile Burns and James Klugmann. A handful of prominent men in their fields have been
on the Executive, no doubt as a gesture to the intellectuals
inside the party, and for the prestige that their names would
bring outside the party: Professor J. B. S. Haldane, formerly
Weldon Professor of Biometry in London University, and
world renowned geneticist; Professor George Thomson, a
classicist from Birmingham University; Arnold Kettle,
literary historian and critic of Leeds University; Ivor
Montagu, film director and producer; G. C. T. Giles, Head
Master of Acton County School for Boys, and President of
the National Union of Teachers; Allen Hutt, internationally
known typographer, a labour historian and journalist.

What is the explanation of this scarcity of intellectuals
among the leaders of the C.P.G.B., a scarcity which also
distinguishes it from the Continental communist parties?
To begin with, a cultural factor is involved: the intellectual
has never possessed the esteemed status in British society that
he has had elsewhere, in France and Italy for example.

---

[1] J. T. Murphy, *New Horizons* (London: John Lane, 1941), p. 139. The
British delegates were Murphy, Pankhurst, Gallacher, Willie MacLaine,
Tom Quelch, Jack Tanner, Dave Ramsay, Helen Crawfurd.

Second, the C.P.G.B. as part of the British labour movement, has reflected its most obvious characteristic, the overwhelming working-class composition of both its membership and leadership. Third, a large body of alienated, discontented intellectuals has never existed in Great Britain. For the most part intellectuals have been solidly middle class, forming a staunch pillar of the status quo. Fourth, the British colonies and commonwealth have no doubt provided a convenient outlet for the energies of the disgruntled activistic intellectual. Finally, because of the small size of the C.P.G.B. and its failure as a parliamentary party, young intellectuals interested in making a career out of left-wing politics have preferred to enter the large and powerful Labour Party. Moreover, at Oxford, responsible for the education of more Members of Parliament than any other university, the influence for the last thirty years of Professor G. D. H. Cole upon young men inclined to the left has been very great. A Socialist activist with little sympathy for British communism, and a popular teacher, Professor Cole had no comparable rival from the ranks of communism as mentor of the left-wing intellectual.

This absence of intellectuals from the leadership of the C.P.G.B. is perhaps just one manifestation of a basic anti-intellectualism that has marked the party as it has to some extent the whole British labour movement. George Orwell in 1937 bitterly condemned British Socialism for "bourgeois baiting", prophesying that if the trend continued the valuable and enthusiastic support of many members of the middle-classes would be lost.[1] The letter to *Plebs* by J. Lewis in February 1922 is fairly typical of the tendency:

I'm not in love with these intellectuals! As a matter of fact they are not a bit plebeian in spirit and would be regarded by an average crowd of workers as a lot of conceited asses, I'm afraid. . . . It's awfully difficult when you

[1] George Orwell, *The Road to Wigan Pier* (London: Gollancz, 1937), pp. 260–261. In reply, Harry Pollitt called Orwell "a disillusioned little middle-class boy. . . ." *Daily Worker*, March 17, 1937, p. 7.

move in a rather small advanced intellectual circle, to realise how tiny your world is and how little it influences the world of workers.[1]

To which the communist intellectual, Maurice Dobb, replied by reminding the readers of *Plebs* who belittled intellectuals and their theories not to forget

. . . that if Marx had not spent time on "highly speculative stuff" and "in doing the thinking" in the British Museum there would probably be no I.W.-C.E. [International Working-Class Education] movement today. Those who do the "thinking" are as much doing "spade work" as those who impart what has been already thrashed out.[2]

The working-class members of the C.P.G.B. have not hesitated to criticize the intellectuals. Pollitt, Gallacher, Murphy, and Bell all remark upon the unreliability and opportunism of the communist intellectuals in the twenties. Emphasis is placed upon the fact that communism is above all a proletarian movement and that the C.P.G.B. is a proletarian party. No less a person than Dutt was castigated for not adopting "the approach of a Marxist, but that of an intellectual, who has lost touch with realities", and as an individual who "knows only resolutions, theses, ballot results . . . newspaper cuttings, etc." [3] One of the few intellectuals of the nineteen-twenties who took advantage of the hostility of the proletarians, turning it to his own benefit, was William Mellor with his North Country accent and evangelical oratory. The working-class audience would roar hilariously when he shouted that it was untrue that the

---

[1] J. Lewis, "Is The Plebs on the Wrong Track?" *Plebs*, Vol. XIV (February 1922), p. 52.

[2] Maurice Dobb, letter to the Editor, *Plebs*, Vol. XIV (March 1922), p. 89.

[3] J. T. Murphy, "A Reply to R. P. Dutt," *Communist International*, New Series, No. 10 (July 1925), p. 100; E. W. Cant, *Workers' Life*, Nov. 29, 1929, p. 6.

only good communist was one whose "arse stuck out of the seat of his pants".

But this almost cathartic abuse of the intellectual did not cease with the passing of the twenties. Bob Darke writes that his Party cell in Hackney in 1931 was a "little society of café revolutionaries". He remarks that he witnessed the growth of the Hackney Communist Party "from a loose-gathering of two dozen intellectual wastrels into a storm-troop of men and women drawn from all branches of working-class life".[1] Nor has this attitude disappeared today. At the afternoon session of March 30, 1956, of the Twenty-Fourth National Congress of the C.P.G.B., Edward Jackson, whose bold attack upon the Executive Committee was not reported in the *Daily Worker*, referred to the danger of intellectuals "wrecking" the Party. Sectarianism, he charged, was not at the root of the Party's difficulties. The trouble was the infiltration of the Party by middle-class members, and the Executive Committee's fear of offending them. Resurrecting the old scapegoat, Harry Pollitt, at the closed session of the Congress on April 1, 1956, is reported to have blamed the intellectuals for the discontent in the Party following Khrushchev's exposure of Stalin.[2] Since Pollitt's speech, a new wave of anti-intellectualism seems to have swept the party as a result of the revolt of the intellectuals over Hungary.

British communism, therefore, from its earliest stage furnishes an extreme example of a tendency that has characterized the international communist movement since the domination of Stalin. Like all communist parties the C.P.G.B. was converted from a group of revolutionary idealists into a monolithic, bureaucratic machine. Organization became the supreme end, and the theory of Marxism–Leninism little more than a dogma: a comprehensive, rigid, and centrally controlled plan for thought and action. Oppor-

[1] C. H. (Bob) Darke, *The Communist Technique in Britain* (London: Collins, 1953), pp. 35–36. Also see pp. 12, 18–19, 28.

[2] Letter by A. R. L. in *Daily Worker*, April 25, 1956, p. 2.

tunity of leadership was seldom offered to the intellectual, and then only to the rare one who had proved his unswerving conformity to the party line and his devoted loyalty to Moscow. In view of these facts it is something of a paradox that such a dazzling array of intellectual virtuosi turned to communism in the nineteen-thirties. Under such conditions the reasons for this migration to the extreme left were as compelling as the subsequent association with the party was disillusioning.

PART I
HISTORY

B

. . . Marxism becomes an Old Curiosity Shop in which political amateurs and literary dilletanti can rummage for decorative oddments, just as they rummage in the Caledonian Market for old china, pewter plates, and bawdy prints.

T. A. Jackson, *Dialectics* (1936)

Many of the younger sons of governing families, following the best English tradition, have prepared for the leadership of the next revolution by joining either the Socialist or the Communist party. When England "goes Communist"—and it is hardly possible to believe that we can continue for another fifty years without some drastic change in our economic system—no doubt the party in power will call itself the "Conservative Cooperative party" and, as usual, half the Government will be Old Etonians.

Douglas Goldring, *Odd Man Out* (1935)

CHAPTER II

TO THE LEFT

A BRITISH RADICAL intelligentsia, comparable to the long-established continental intelligentsias, did not appear until the nineteen-thirties. In the main British intellectuals had always been Liberal or Conservative. Then between 1928 and 1933 a change occurred in their outlook. Just before the opening of the new decade, G. D. H. Cole sensed "a disquieting insecurity" among young intellectuals.[1] Their pursuit of pleasure ceased to be satisfying. A new seriousness came to the fore in the place of the former *joie de vivre*. Increasing attention was given to politics. Whereas sex and æsthetics had been the major topics of conversation, now everybody began to talk politics. As time passed the politics of the intellectual moved leftward to socialism and communism. What began as a political awakening became a great radicalization.

Radical politics flourish in a seed-bed of catastrophe. Great Britain during the thirties experienced a series of shattering domestic and international crises. Of most immediate impact was the severity of the Great Depression. From 1929 the unemployment of insured workers rapidly increased, reaching a peak of 2,955,000 in January 1933. Recovery was slow and uneven. Although by 1934 unemployment in Greater London, Birmingham and Coventry was below 10%, in the distressed areas, such as Jarrow and Merthyr, it was 60%. The poverty, the malnutrition, the dole, and the mass protestations by streams of Hunger Marchers converging upon London contributed to the leaden atmosphere.

Unemployment also directly affected the middle classes.

[1] G. D. H. Cole, *The Next Ten Years in British Social and Economic Policy* (London: Macmillan, 1929), p. 16.

In the Spring of 1934 out of a total "black-coat" force of
about two million, including the professional and clerical
occupations, between 300,000 and 400,000 were unemployed.
Some of the most promising university graduates turned to
teaching and tutoring for want of better opportunity. W. H.
Auden, Arthur Calder-Marshall, C. Day Lewis, Michael
Redgrave, Edward Upward, and Christopher Isherwood
are but a few. Positions in foreign colleges, universities, and
schools were taken by Rex Warner, Malcolm Muggeridge,
Julian Bell, William Empson, and William Plomer. The
situation was well expressed by Auden:

> *The only thing you never turned your hand to*
> *Was teaching English in a boarding school.*
> *To-day it's a profession that seems grand to*
> *Those whose alternatives an office stool;*
> *For budding authors it's become the rule.*
> *To many an unknown genius postmen bring*
> *Typed notices from Rabbitarse and String.*
>
> . . . .
>
> *More, it's a job, and jobs to-day, are rare:*
> *All the ideals in the world won't feed us*
> *Although they give our crimes a certain air.*
> *So barons of the press who know their readers*
> *Employ to write their more appalling leaders,*
> *Instead of Satan's horned and hideous minions*
> *Clever young men of liberal opinions.*[1]

Student publications, such as *Student Vanguard*, repeatedly
spoke of the menace of middle-class unemployment. International Communist organs warned that the enemployed
black-coats were filling the ranks of fascism, as proved to be
the case with the small British Union of Fascists led by Sir
Oswald Mosley. Alarmed by the general trend, the Seventh

[1] W. H. Auden, "Letter to Lord Byron", in W. H. Auden and Louis
MacNeice, *Letters from Iceland* (London: Faber and Faber, 1937), pp.
210–211.

World Congress of the Comintern meeting in August 1935 called for intensified work among the middle classes.

The miserable, drab lives of a people on the dole were not relieved by the presence of an imaginative and adventuresome government. Timid, vacillating, uninspired in its politics, although by no means completely incompetent in its handling of the economic situation, the British Government was the only conservative government of the time among the great industrial powers. To make matters worse, the Labour Party seemed to offer little alternative. The Labour Government of 1929–1931 had hardly risen to the occasion of the financial crisis, and was overwhelmingly defeated in the election of 1931. Left-wingers viewed the National Government of 1931 as a "sell-out" by Mac-Donald and his colleagues to the Conservatives, thereby seeming to confirm the "social-fascist" line of the communists. Mosley and Strachey resigned from the Labour Party to form an action group, The New Party. In 1932 Maxton, Brockway, and others led the I.L.P. out of the Labour Party, and Sir Stafford Cripps founded the Socialist League. Five years later these two groups signed a unity manifesto with the C.P.G.B., which had been unsuccessful in its attempts to gain affiliation to the Labour Party.

Always in the background of crisis at home was the worsening international situation. After the Wall Street crash of 1929 event piled upon event in the arena of human affairs, seeming to spell the end of civilization, if not the doom of mankind. The year 1930 opened with the sabre-rattling of Mussolini and the continued disastrous decline of the German economy. In the September election, the National Socialists gained ninety-five new seats in the Reichstag. Street fighting in Germany and the rise of Nazi barbarism were witnessed by young intellectuals like David Guest and Humphrey Slater, who returned to Britain convinced that communism was the only defence against fascism and war. Other intellectuals such as Auden, Isherwood, Spender, John Lehmann and Naomi Mitchison saw fascism at work in

Germany and Austria. Militarism was also gaining a foot-
hold in the Far East. Mukden was occupied by the Japanese,
who proceeded to conquer the whole of Manchuria. And
again the young intellectuals of Britain were on hand: Bell,
Empson, Plomer, Auden, and Isherwood.

If January 1933 marked the economic nadir in Britain,
for world diplomacy it opened an event-crammed year which
would propel mankind into the greatest war of history.
British journals struck a particularly pessimistic note from
the beginning of the year. The democratic nations seemed
to be floundering on with no purpose or direction to their
actions. Hitler on January 30 became Chancellor of Germany, and shortly afterwards the Reichstag was burned.
Japan withdrew from the League of Nations, launching an
attack upon China. Threatened with the collapse of its
banking system, the United States in the Spring abandoned
the Gold Standard, and depreciated the dollar. The collapse
of the deliberations held in the Summer ended the hope of
world economic collaboration. Arabs and Jews clashed in
Palestine in October. Withdrawing from the World Disarmament Conference, Hitler announced his decision to
leave the League of Nations. Corruption at its worst was revealed in the sordid Stavisky scandal in Paris, followed by
the fall of the Daladier Government in February 1934. The
rise to power of Pierre Laval, one-time member of the Communist Party and now an arch conservative, and an attempted fascist coup in Paris, brought little relief to despair-
ing hearts. Chancellor Dollfuss, after repressing the Social-
Democrats in Austria, was assassinated by the Nazis in July
1934. The year 1935 opened with Hitler's repudiation of the
disarmament provisions of the Treaty of Versailles and
closed with Mussolini's invasion of Ethiopia. Germany
occupied the Rhineland on March 7, 1936. A short time
later General Franco landed upon the Iberian Peninsula, the
gambit of a long and bloody civil war that became the
proving ground for the approaching world conflict. Austria,
Czechoslovakia, Munich—the men of democracy had utterly

failed to dam the flood of disaster. Their hesitancy and lack of foresight left the power of political democracy paralysed in a time of crisis.

Small wonder that politics became a byword among intellectuals. There was a growing belief that drastic political measures would be required to cure the human environment of its pernicious malady. The spectre of unemployment and economic chaos, and the very destruction of civilization itself, sensitized the intellectuals to communism. John Maynard Keynes sympathetically portrayed them to Kingsley Martin:

> There is no one in politics today worth sixpence outside the ranks of liberals except the post-war generation of intellectual Communists under thirty-five. Them, too, I like and respect. Perhaps in their feelings and instincts they are the nearest thing we now have to the typical nervous nonconformist English gentlemen who went to the Crusades, made the Reformation, fought the Great Rebellion, won us our civil and religious liberties and humanised the working classes last century.[1]

An early sign of something astir was a new literary "movement" signalled by the publication of W. H. Auden's *Poems* in 1930, and Hugh MacDiarmid's "First Hymn to Lenin" in 1931. In the following year came *New Signatures*, edited by Michael Roberts, with poems by Auden, Lehmann, Spender, Day Lewis, Plomer, Empson, and Bell. None of the poems were overtly revolutionary, but the esotericism of Eliot and Pound had vanished, while some exhibited a distinct social awareness. Roberts, in a second anthology, *New Country* (1933), called upon intellectuals to prepare the way for an English Lenin and to aid the workers in destroying the class system.[2] He concluded his introduction by admitting that

[1] "Democracy and Efficiency", J. M. Keynes interviewed by Kingsley Martin, *New Statesman and Nation*, Vol. XVII, New Series (January 28, 1939), p. 122.

[2] Michael Roberts, ed., *New Country: Prose and Poetry by the Authors of New Signatures* (London: Hogarth Press, 1933), pp. 10, 13–14, 20.

what followed was not "proletarian art". Its importance
lay in that "it shows how some of us are finding a way out of
the individualist predicament".

Marxism soon became the fashion not only in poetry and
literature but in other fields of endeavour. The Marxist conception of the function of science and the role of the scientist
in society gained wide currency, dominating the British
world of science within a decade. Marxists of all shades and
varieties appeared. The popularity of Marxism no doubt
facilitated the discovery of the working man by the intellectual. Many were sincere in their desire to establish a
cordial, understanding relationship with the proletariat. For
others the proletarian set a new fad. He was fawned upon,
and upheld as the chosen instrument of history. In speech,
manner, and dress, he was slavishly imitated. But whatever
the motives and the approach of the intellectual, the admiration for the proletarian was only too infrequently recipro-
cated.

The most striking feature of the thirties, setting it off from
the previous decade, was the widely growing regard for the
Soviet Union. At a time when western capitalism was beset
with unemployment, the Soviet Union, having embarked
upon its first five year plan, was maintaining full employment in a herculean effort to industrialize and urbanize a
feudal, agrarian land. For many intellectuals Soviet Russia
was the one hope of the future. Books and articles favourably
reporting every aspect of Soviet life were eagerly de-
voured by a hungry audience. Pilgrimages to this new land
of promise were made by British people from every walk of
life. One of the most publicized visits was that of George
Bernard Shaw and Lady Astor in 1931. Although some of
the ardent Russophiles remained contemptuous of British
Communism, for others the Soviet Union proved to be the
best selling-point for the home-grown product. Societies
were organized in Britain for the sponsoring of Soviet films
such as "Mother", "The End of St. Petersburg", "The
General Line", "Storm Over Asia", and "Earth". An

occasional British Russophile even cultivated his beard *à la* Lenin.

No longer was social disgrace the penalty for visiting Russia, as it had been in certain circles during the nineteen-twenties. Now, one was much more likely to be ostracized if he criticized the country of the Bolsheviks. Objective assessments were rare. Every allowance was made for the obvious lack of political democracy in the Soviet Union. The Soviet State, it was generally explained, had only recently been organized in a country lacking the democratic traditions of the west. Democracy, therefore, in the Soviet Union differed from western political democracy. Soviet democracy was economic in character, bringing to the citizenry greater equality and more freedom from economic insecurity than could be found under capitalism. The corollary to this argument was that economic democracy formed the basis of all true democracy. Hence the so-called political democracy in capitalist countries was really only a sham. A vociferous, active opposition had little or nothing to do with true democracy, for political dissent was merely the reflection of economic conflict. In Soviet society no such hostility existed. Consequently, the dictatorship of one party and even of one man was compatible with democracy because Communist dictatorship was in the interest of the majority. All this was being confidently stated in Great Britain at the very time, as we are informed by the present Soviet leaders, that Stalin was securing his dictatorship by means of an inquisition of terror and violence.

Four writers, although none was a member of the Communist Party, probably did more than anyone in England to popularize communism and the Soviet Union and to make them respectable. They were John Strachey, Sidney and Beatrice Webb, and Harold J. Laski. Strachey's contribution, in books such as the *The Coming Struggle for Power* (1934) and *The Theory and Practice of Socialism* (1936) is obvious. Obvious, because he was a fellow-traveller strictly adhering to the party line. A member of a well-known family,

educated at Eton and Oxford, and a former Labour M.P.,
Strachey was able to use his journalistic talent and his excellent grasp of Marxian and classical economics to considerable advantage in the service of communism. He knew
what he was about, and he said it fairly clearly. There was
little nonsense or naiveté in his advocacy. The goal was a
Soviet Britain, and the instrument of realization a revolutionary communist party patterned after the Bolshevik model.

The Webbs, prominent members of the Labour Party and
social scientists of international repute, did not "discover"
the Soviet Union until the thirties. Their story, in many ways
so typical of the time, bears recounting. Although opposing
allied intervention, they had never looked upon the Soviet
Union with any great warmth. Communism seemed little
better than Fascism to Beatrice Webb, who condemned the
1917 Revolution as "the greatest misfortune in the history
of the Labour movement".[1] A loss of faith in the virtue of
gradualism, resulting from the failure of Labour's Second
Government, and a friendship with the Russian Ambassador,
Sokolnikov, brought about a change of view.[2] When Sidney
Webb was freed from his duties as a member of the Cabinet
by Labour's defeat in the election of 1931, he and Beatrice
settled down to a meticulous study of the Soviet Union.
Beatrice's diary contains this entry for May 17, 1932: "In
spite of our old age, Sidney and I have had a delightful time
together since he left office; and studies and thoughts about
Russian Communism have added to the zest of our honey-
moon companionship." The last entries of the published
Diaries contain passages contrasting the public morality of
the Soviets with the corruption existing in America and in
Britain. On January 4, 1932, Beatrice wrote that the Soviet
Constitution "almost exactly corresponds . . . on the secular

[1] The Webbs' views are described in Margaret Cole, *Beatrice Webb*
(London: Longmans, 1945), pp. 164–177; and in Barbara Drake, "The
Webbs and Soviet Communism", in Margaret Cole, ed., *The Webbs and
Their Work* (London: Muller, 1949), pp. 221–232.

[2] Margaret Cole, ed., *Beatrice Webb's Diaries 1924–1932* (London:
Longmans, 1956), p. 265, entry for February 4, 1931.

side" to the Webbs' own *Constitution of a Socialist Commonwealth*, possessing, however, a spiritual power missing from
their own. The repository of this spiritual power was the
Communist Party, although she confessed that "we don't
quite like that soul". Moscow welcomed them ceremoni-
ously, for they had a wide reputation in Russia owing to
Lenin's translation of their *History of Trade Unionism*. The
outcome of the trip is concisely summarized by Barbara
Drake: "The Webbs fell in love with Soviet Russia. They
saw in it the emergence of a new civilization . . . the realization of Socialist dreams." [1]

All other political interests were put aside. Russian Communism became the central passion of their lives. They
uncritically accepted the Moscow Trials and the Nazi–
Soviet Pact, although the latter was a distinct shock.[2]
Sidney Webb returned to Russia in 1934, and the following
year their two-volume work *Soviet Communism: A New
Civilization?* was published. It created a stir in the intellectual world, becoming one of the most widely read and influential works in Britain. The book, a surprise to many who
saw it as a reversal of the Webbs' former position, probably
did more than any other to enhance the myth of the Soviet
Union. The second edition of *Soviet Communism* appeared in
1937, without a question mark after "A New Civilization",
testimony that the Webbs had discovered "A New Civilization". They found in Soviet Communism the apotheosis of
all their values: in the planning—the application of science
and reason to the reconstruction of society; in the "puritan-
ism" of the regime; and in the "moral" dynamism of the
Communist Party. Essentially Benthamite utilitarians, the
Webbs, with little sympathy either for the masses or for
equalitarianism, conceived of Gosplan as the first human
agency designed to put into practice the great pleasure–pain
calculus of the founder of Philosophic Radicalism.[3]

[1] Barbara Drake, *op. cit.*, p. 227.   [2] *Ibid.*, pp. 230–231.
[3] See preface by Beatrice Webb to Pat Sloan, *Russia Without Illusions*
(London: Muller, 1938), p. viii.

Another personality who stamped the Decade of the Left with his political views was Professor Harold J. Laski.[1] Upon his death, so Kingsley Martin recounts, an Oxford don wrote that the decade of the thirties might well be called the "Age of Laski". The development of his attitude towards Communism and the Soviet Union roughly paralleled that of the Webbs, but was much more complex. As early as 1923 Laski coupled communism with fascism, denouncing both. In his book *Communism* (1927) he underscored the similarities between communism and religion, criticizing the controls and discipline of organized communism, and the machiavellian "United Front From Below" line of the Comintern with its attack upon Democratic Socialism. Laski's attitude changed with the increasing threat of fascism and the growing disaster of the depression. Martin asserts that by the end of 1931 Laski expressed the opinion that he held until the outbreak of war. He quotes Laski: "Socialist measures, in a word, are not obtainable by constitutional means", and "if Socialists wish to secure a State built with the principles of their faith, they can only do so by revolutionary means".[2] According to Professor Deane, Laski's subsequent political beliefs are distinctly schizophrenic.[3] At the same time that he upheld legal and constitutional procedures, and damned the use of violence, he maintained that gradualism was impossible and that revolution was inevitable. He considered Soviet Russia the sole centre of creativeness in a rapidly disintegrating world, and failed to understand how Attlee and the Labour Party could place their faith in the decadent institutions of political democracy.

[1] Laski was such a voluminous writer, that for the purposes of this brief discussion the author has relied upon Herbert A. Deane, *The Political Ideas of Harold J. Laski* (New York: Columbia University Press, 1953); and Kingsley Martin, *Harold Laski (1893–1950): A Biographical Memoir* (London: Gollancz, 1953).

[2] As quoted in Martin, *op. cit.*, pp. 83–84. Also see Deane, *op. cit.*, pp. 201–203, who refers to Laski's article, "The Position and Prospects of Communism", *Foreign Affairs*, Vol. XI (October 1932), p. 100.

[3] Deane, *op. cit.*, pp. 206–218.

Deane contends that during the thirties Laski, the "Encyclo-
pedist" with a firm belief in reason, in gradual and legal
change, and with a hatred for myth, became an advocate of
revolution, who analysed values and beliefs in terms of
interest or ideology. He was increasingly sceptical of the
efficacy of thought and persuasion in the building and maintenance of society. All that was irrational in communism, its
religious character, the fervour and faith exhibited by its
adherents, became the object of his admiration. In a rather
interesting review of Deane's book, Martin defends Laski as
one who was neither "consistently hostile" to the U.S.S.R.
nor a fellow traveller.[1] But he fails to explain or justify
Laski's loss of confidence in democratic institutions and his
blindness to the iniquities of the Soviet system of politics.
Too involved in the struggle of his time, Laski was never able
to eye it dispassionately. He was, above all, a man of the
thirties, moved by a deep sense of moral indignation at the
injustices that he saw about him.

Many other intellectuals of the non-communist left besides Laski were not simply unreasoning apologists for
Soviet Communism. *The New Statesman and Nation* is a good
index of their opinion, for example, in regard to a contro-
versial issue such as the Moscow trials. However, first it is
necessary to point out that Britain did not give the attention
to the trials that they received in America. The British
Trotskyists who might have raised a hue and cry over the
trials, as in America, were very weak numerically, financially,
and organizationally. They were largely workers lacking the
highly articulate support of intellectuals comparable to the
American group composed of Jay Lovestone, Sidney Hook,
Max Eastman, James Burnham, Bertram Wolfe, and Max
Schachtman. Moreover, the Spanish Civil War, always
much more of a reality in Britain than in America, deflected
much of the interest from the 1936–1938 trials, completely
absorbing the energies and emotions of the intellectuals.

[1] Kingsley Martin, "Books in General: The New Obscurantism", *New
Statesman and Nation*, Vol. XLIX (May 28, 1955), p. 753.

Finally, the most influential and widely publicized reporting of the trials supported the official position of the Soviet Government. As far back as the Metro-Vickers trial of 1933, the able correspondent of the Liberal *News-Chronicle*, A. J. Cummings, had endorsed both the conduct of the trial and the verdict of the court. Later, in the period of the Spanish Civil War, a number of very skilful apologists, who had attended some of the trials, whole-heartedly upheld them in lectures, articles, and books. Two of them were the highly respected Socialist lawyers, D. N. Pritt and Dudley Collard, whose observations were especially weighty because of their record in the defence of civil liberties.[1] Another was the persuasive communist, Pat Sloan, a Clare College honours graduate in economics, who had lived and worked in the Soviet Union for several years, and was an active leader in the Friends of the Soviet Union.[2] The efforts of Pritt, Collard and Sloan, if not completely allaying the doubts and anxieties of many on the left, at least succeeded in having a neutralizing effect.

The *New Statesman and Nation* and many of its readers failed to succumb to the rationalization of these astute propagandists. Although affirming friendship with the Soviet Union, the *New Statesman* strived to preserve a critical independence. There can be no doubt about the scepticism and hostility of the *New Statesman's* comments upon the various trials.[3] In July 1937, "Critic" (Kingsley Martin) and Leonard Woolf vigorously defended the veteran Socialist H.N. Brailsford, highly critical of the trial of the Soviet

[1] See D. N. Pritt, *The Zinoviev Trial* (London: Gollancz, 1936); Dudley Collard, *Soviet Justice and The Trial of Radek and Others*, introduction by D. N. Pritt (London: Gollancz, 1937).

[2] See Pat Sloan, *Soviet Democracy* (London: Gollancz, 1937); and the same author's *Russia Without Illusions*, preface by Beatrice Webb (London: Muller, 1938).

[3] See the following references in the *New Statesman and Nation*, New Series: Vol. V (April 22, 1933), pp. 495–496; Vol. XII (August 29, 1936), pp. 273–274; Vol. XII (December 26, 1936), p. 1054; Vol. XIII (January 30, 1937), pp. 148–149; Vol. XV (March 5, 1938), pp. 359–360; Vol. XV (April 16, 1938), p. 648.

generals, against the verbal onslaught of the communist leader R. Palme Dutt.[1] For its stand in these matters the *New Statesman* incurred the wrath not only of Dutt, but also of other leading communists and communist sympathizers, including Pat Sloan, Ivor Montagu, Roy Pascal, Dudley Collard, Albert Inkpin, and M.H.D. (Maurice Herbert Dobb?).[2]

Nevertheless, the *New Statesman* did not hesitate to admit its friendship and admiration for the Soviet Union.[3] To all true Socialists, according to the *New Statesman*, the Russian Revolution should be the landmark of the century. In the perspective of history the significance of the vast economic programme of Soviet Communism would take precedence over the somewhat questionable actions of the O.G.P.U. and the bureaucracy. Political liberty would not be realized in the Soviet Union for a long time to come. However, many of the present actions of the Soviet State, which had an "overwhelming desire for peace", could be explained by its fear of capitalist encirclement. Kingsley Martin concluded that for the British Socialist the correct approach to the Soviet Union was

> ... to give general, but critical support to the one country in the world which has adopted a planned Socialist economy. But a legislative change may be misleading unless the actual administrative tendencies in the regime are constantly and critically watched. Russia is not made perfect or even good merely by the adoption of a Socialist constitution. Socialism gives the promise and possibility

[1] See *New Statesman and Nation*, Vol. XIV, New Series on the following dates: July 3, 1937, pp. 6–7; July 10, 1937, pp. 68–69; July 17, 1937, pp. 106–107; July 24, 1937, pp. 144–145; July 31, 1937; pp. 181–182.

[2] See *New Statesman and Nation*, New Series: Vol. XII (September 5, 1936), pp. 314–315; Vol. XIII (January 2, 1937), p. 11; Vol. XIII (February 6, 1937), pp. 198–199; Vol. XV (March 12, 1938), pp. 403–404; Vol. XV (April 23, 1938), p. 684.

[3] See the following articles in the *New Statesman and Nation*, New Series for the sentiments expressed in this paragraph: Vol. XII (September 5, 1936), p. 308; Vol. XIV (November 6, 1937), pp. 758–760; Vol. XV (January 22, 1938), pp. 126–128.

of greater happiness and greater economic sanity than is
possible under capitalism. But there can be no greater
disservice to the cause of Socialism than to assume that
an edict is the same thing as a fact and a critic the same
thing as an enemy. The Socialists' duty is to watch the
tendencies at work in the U.S.S.R. with the closest and
most critical attention and to be outspoken when they
appear to be directed away from the ideals that the
U.S.S.R. set out to realise.[1]

This policy of friendly criticism of the Soviet Union did not
commit the *New Statesman* to the support of Trotsky. Martin
never expressed a very high regard for Trotsky's stability
of character.[2] Nor was he impressed by the evidence given
in the first volume of the Dewey Commission Report, and
the second volume was evidently neither mentioned nor
reviewed in the *New Statesman*.[3]

One, therefore, must be wary in generalizing about the intellectual pro-Sovietism of the thirties. There was un-
deniably a widespread and often myopic veneration for the
Soviet Union, in some cases reaching the proportion of a
cult. But except for communists and fellow-travellers, the
admiration of the left was often tempered by criticism. In
addition, the thirties produced some acute analyses of Soviet
communism and "Soviet democracy", by intellectuals of all
political denominations: on the right, Harold Macmillan's
Reconstruction: A Plea For a National Policy (1933); in the
liberal centre, F. A. Voight's *Unto Caesar* (1939); on the left,
Walter Citrine's *I Search For Truth in Russia* (1936), and Evan
Durbin's *The Politics of Democratic Socialism* (1940).

[1] *New Statesman and Nation*, Vol. XIV, New Series (November 6, 1937),
p. 760.
[2] *New Statesman and Nation*, Vol. XIII, New Series (April 10, 1937), pp.
581–582; (May 22, 1937), p. 839.
[3] *New Statesman and Nation*, Vol. XIV, New Series (November 6, 1937),
p. 760. Issue was taken with Martin upon the merits of the first volume
in a letter from Charles Sumner, Secretary of the British Committee for
the Defence of Leon Trotsky: *New Statesman and Nation*, Vol. XIV, New
Series (November 13, 1937), pp. 790–791.

Changes in the intellectual life of a nation can often be perceived at an early date among university students. Prior to the nineteen-thirties British students had never exhibited the political fervour so characteristic on the continent. Consequently, it must have been with some satisfaction that Karl Radek was able to announce to the Congress of Soviet Writers in 1934 that "In the heart of bourgeois England, in Oxford, where the sons of the bourgeoisie receive their final polish, we observe the crystallization of a group which sees salvation only together with the proletariat".[1] The beginning of an unprecedented political ferment took place in 1931, when embryonic communist organizations were established at London and Cambridge Universities by students returning from Germany. The Cambridge communists worked within the University Socialist Club, from which the orthodox Socialists withdrew in 1934, only to return in 1936. At University College, London, the Gower Socialist Society, founded in the Autumn of 1931, met in a pub for over a year because university authorities refused to recognize it. A Marxist Society saw the light of day at the London School of Economics in 1931, and the radical Cosmopolitian Society replaced the old International Society. Oxford's notorious October Club, founded in January 1932, was banned in November of the following year, ostensibly for its criticism of the Officers' Training Corps.

Student radicalism took firm root during 1932. Several radical publications appeared. In Cambridge the *Outpost*, surviving for three issues, was sponsored by a variety of student societies which believed that the University needed a "journal of radical thought". A joint product of the movement at the different universities, the *Student Vanguard*, lasted for two years. Contingents of Hunger Marchers passing through Oxford and Cambridge on their way to London were met by militant students and dons, who placed themselves at the heads of the columns. Meeting these straggling

---

[1] *International Press Correspondence*, Vol. 14 (September 14, 1934), p. 1270.

processions of unemployed men was the first real contact that
many of the undergraduates, coming from affluent middle-
class families, had made with the proletariat. It proved to
be a profoundly moving experience for the more sensitive
ones. About this time the Oxford Union voted by a majority
of 67 that "in Socialism lies the only solution to the problems
facing this country". Shortly afterwards, on Thursday,
February 9, 1933, the Union resolved by 275 to 153 that it
would "in no circumstances fight for its King and Country".

The phenomenal radicalization of the students is indicated
to some extent by the rapid growth of the student societies.
The October Club had three hundred members at the end of
its first year. From two hundred members in 1933, the Cambridge Socialist Club increased to over six hundred in 1936.
By 1938 it had almost one thousand members in a university
of less than five thousand undergraduates. In 1933 the revolutionary student socialists under the leadership of the young
Cambridge communist, John Cornford, were strong enough
to found a Federation of Socialist Societies, consisting of ten
affiliated organizations in England and Scotland. Marx
House, Clerkenwell Green, a communist cultural centre
occupying the building in which Lenin had once edited
Iskra, was the scene of the second conference of the Federa-
tion in January 1934. Merging with the old University
Labour Federation four years later to form the Student
Labour Federation, it achieved in 1939 a membership of
3,500 in thirty-five affiliated sections with an ardent Marxist,
Brian Simon, as President. The record of attendance of
British students at international meetings is also informative.
Only five were present in August 1932 at the Amsterdam
"Anti-War Congress". Of the one hundred students from
twenty-two countries who met in Paris a year later to discuss
the fight against fascism and war, thirty were British. Max
Morris of University College, London, today a leading member of the Communist Party in the field of education, pre-
sided.

But British universities in the thirties were not solely incubators of communism and extreme socialism. Fascism and religion, particularly Buchmanism, were attracting sizeable student audiences. Many members of the political societies were not active participants. The radical movement was concentrated almost entirely in London, Oxford and Cambridge—where the children of the leisure-classes were educated. The majority of the left-wing activities were to be found among the students of the arts and certain of the sciences, particularly biology and physics. Very few of those studying for the professions of law, medicine, and engineering seemed to be inclined in this direction. Finally, only a small proportion of the radical activists were members of the Communist Party; perhaps no more than one thousand at any one time. Most of these probably drifted out of the Communist Party after a very short period. Student communism, in addition to being fashionable, served the useful purpose of arousing the political and social sensibilities of numerous alert and intelligent youths.

Spain was the beginning of politics for many a British intellectual. Fighting between the Government and the rebel forces of General Franco lasted from 1936 until the early part of 1939. The British left was a dedicated and vehement opposition to the Franco forces, indignantly denouncing the official "non-intervention" policy of the British Government. The Spanish Loyalist cause was advanced in Britain by a constant flow of articles, pamphlets, and books; by lectures, mass meetings, demonstrations, relief and aid organizations, etc. Besides those who actually fought in Spain, many Britishers in public life visited the front, giving their support to the Loyalists. Among them were leftist writers including Auden, Spender, Day Lewis, Strachey, and Cyril Connolly. Prominent leaders of the left were joined by people of note from the centre and right such as Eleanor Rathbone, the Independent M.P.; the Liberals, Richard Acland, Wilfred Roberts, and Sir Walter Layton; and the Conservatives, the Duchess of Atholl and Robert Boothby.

Although sympathy for the Loyalists was extensive it was

not unanimous. The Government pledged itself to a neutral course, as did many of its supporters, including *The Times*. Young Tory M.P.s like R. A. Butler and Lennox-Boyd openly supported Franco. Harold Macmillan, however, remained a confirmed anti-fascist. Men of letters who approved of Franco were the Catholic writers Douglas Jerrold and Arnold Lunn; the historian, Arthur Bryant; the painter, novelist, and critic extraordinary, Wyndham Lewis; and Evelyn Waugh. T. S. Eliot and Somerset Maugham deplored the Spanish struggle, but held themselves aloof from it.

On the British left, the reaction of the Haldanes was not unusual. Young sixteen-year-old Ronald Haldane, a son of Mrs. Haldane's previous marriage, volunteered in 1936 to fight in Spain. He was wounded and invalided home. This act plunged Professor J. B. S. Haldane and Mrs. Haldane into the fray. She joined the Communist Party, becoming Honorary Secretary of the Dependents Aid Committee, serving as a Comintern organizer and receptionist of recruits in Paris, and working among the British volunteers at the front. Professor Haldane visited Madrid during the Winter of 1936–1937 to advise the Spanish Government on questions of gas defence. Back again in the Spring of 1937 to tour the front, he volunteered to deputize for Frank Pitcairn (Claud Cockburn), *Daily Worker* correspondent and editor of *The Week*, whose passport had been withheld by British authorities. Haldane's comment was, "As a scientist whose business it is to discover and publish truth, I am proud to do what I can to take Pitcairn's place and see that Eden does not keep the truth from the people of Britain." [1] Returning in the Winter of 1937–1938, he donated blood in Barcelona, and hitch-hiked around the war-torn country, sleeping in stables packed with mules and people. In Britain the Haldanes spent their time on committees, raising funds, and lecturing.

Organizations of eager supporters of the Republican cause

[1] *Daily Worker*, April 5, 1937, p. 1; Barrister, "Passport to Spain", *New Statesman and Nation*, Vol. XIII, New Series (April 3, 1937), pp. 549–550.

mushroomed throughout the country: Friends of Spain, Spanish Medical Aid Committees, Committees of Spanish Relief, and The Commission of Inquiry into Alleged Breaches of the Non-Intervention Agreement in Spain. They were a further example of the selfless service of so many British people devoted to humane causes. Their contribution to the struggle against Franco in funds, supplies, and the mobilization of public opinion was invaluable. It is no reflection upon the undoubted good that they did and the sincerity of their members to say that behind many of them was the master hand of Willie Münzenberg, the Comintern's genius of propaganda. According to Arthur Koestler the actual policy-making body of The Commission of Inquiry into Alleged Breaches of the Non-Intervention Agreement in Spain was a "communist caucus" consisting of the two communist secretaries and others.[1] Münzenberg sent his personal assistant to see that the Commission functioned smoothly, and Koestler himself was asked to keep an eye on things. If Münzenberg was not behind all such organizations, at least the Communist Party exerted every effort to support them and to encourage their work. Philip Toynbee, son of the historian, and a Party member at Oxford during the Spanish conflict, relates that in the Winter term of 1936 his chief task as a leading communist student "was to proliferate Spanish Defence Committees throughout the university, as a moth lays its eggs in a clothes cupboard".[2]

The young poets of the left found fresh inspiration in the heroic stand of the Republicans. Their lines in honour of Spain are perhaps the highest expression of their passion for politics. One has only to recall Auden's "Spain"; "The Nabara" of Day Lewis; and the poems of MacNeice and Rickword. John Cornford and Charles Donnelly showed a promise that the fate of battle did not allow to be fulfilled.

[1] Arthur Koestler, *The Invisible Writing: An Autobiography* (London: Collins with Hamilton, 1954), p. 323.
[2] Philip Toynbee, *Friends Apart: A Memoir of Esmond Romilly and Jasper Ridley in the Thirties* (London: MacGibbon and Kee, 1954), p. 87.

Cornford concluded his "Full Moon at Tierz: Before the Storming of Huesca", with the following words, expressing the idealism of the young radical dedicated to what he believed to be the just cause:

> *But facts are stubborn things. Here, too, in Spain*
> *Our fight's not won till the workers of all the world*
> *Stand by our guard on Huesca's plain,*
> *Swear that our guard fought not in vain,*
> *Raise the red flag triumphantly*
> *For Communism and for liberty.*[1]

Somewhat less than 50,000 foreigners fought in Spain, including over 40,000 in the International Brigade, which never consisted, however, of more than 15,000 at any one time.[2] British volunteers in Spain totalled 2,762. Their casualties were exceptionally high: 1,762 wounded and 543 killed. About one-half of those killed were members of the Communist Party of Great Britain or the Young Communist League. It is difficult to estimate the number of British intellectuals who participated in the fighting, drove ambulances, or otherwise assisted at the front.[3] The most widely known communist intellectuals were John Cornford, son of Francis MacDonald Cornford, the Cambridge

[1] Stephen Spender and John Lehmann, eds., *Poems For Spain*, introduction by Stephen Spender (London: Hogarth Press, 1939), p. 29.

[2] For statistics see Thomas Henry Wintringham, *English Captain* (London: Faber and Faber, 1939), p. 237; *Daily Worker*, January 9, 1939, p. 1. The "Roll of Honour" of the British Battalion is found in William Rust, *Britons in Spain: The History of The British Battalion of the XVth International Brigade* (London: Lawrence and Wishart, 1939), pp. 189–199.

[3] A few of the intellectuals and students were: W. H. Auden, Sidney Avener, Ralph Bates, Julian Bell, Lorimer Birch, Clive Bronson, Felicia Browne, Noel Carritt, Christopher Caudwell, Lewis Clive, Claud Cockburn, John Cornford, Charles Donnelly, Malcolm Dunbar, Ralph Fox, David Guest, Richard Haldane, Sid Hamm, R. M. Hilliard, Sam Lesser, David Mackenzie, Leslie Maugham, Arthur Olorenshaw, George Orwell, Wogan Philipps, John Rickman, Esmond Romilly, Giles Romilly, Humphrey Slater, John Sommerfield, Christopher Thornycroft, Miles Tomalin, R. Traill, Peter Whittaker, T. H. Wintringham.

classicist, and Frances Cornford, the poet; David Guest, son of the future Labour peer, Lord Haden-Guest; Christopher Caudwell, a brilliant young Marxist critic and poet; and Ralph Fox, the novelist and critic. All four died on the battlefield. Perhaps the greatest tragedy of the non-communists in Spain was the death of the young poet Julian Bell, son of Clive and Vanessa Bell. Those who survived included Auden; the novelist, Ralph Bates; the journalist, Claud Cockburn; George Orwell; Wogan Philipps, the painter; and Esmond and Giles Romilly, nephews of Sir Winston Churchill. Spain was the first and last crusade of the British left-wing intellectual. Never again was such enthusiasm mobilized, nor did there exist such a firm conviction in the rightness of a cause. Disillusion had not yet sapped the idealism of the young.

New magazines and reviews of varying quality and length of life appeared in the thirties. One of the earliest, the longest lived, and the best, Geoffrey Grigson's *New Verse* (1933–1939), soon became a major outlet for the work of contemporary poets. Individualism rather than a particular political line was its credo: "a reasoned attitude of toryism is welcomed no less than a communist attitude". *Storm*, claiming to be the "Only Magazine of Revolutionary Fiction", shortly began publication. It announced itself as an organ of the "new peoples' culture", a "virile and progressive counterblast to the reams of counter-revolutionary dope that are contained in other organs of popular fiction". Among its contributors were Tom Wintringham, Rhys J. Williams, and Rayner Heppenstall. An early call for "shock-brigaders" to increase the circulation failed to prolong its life. Then there was the *Cambridge Left*, and the one-man organ of the Christian communism of J. Middleton Murry, *The Wanderer*, published from his home, the Old Rectory of Larling, near Norwich. The "New Britain Movement" publications under the successive titles of *New Atlantis*, *New Albion*, *New Britain*, and *New Europe* were the most handsomely designed journals of the thirties.

The Week, a cyclostyled news-letter edited by Claud Cockburn, was one of the most influential of the publications.
Cockburn, a former *Times* correspondent in America, who,
under the *nom de plume* of Frank Pitcairn, reported the
Spanish Civil War for the *Daily Worker*, started it with seven
subscriptions in the mid-Spring of 1933. His purpose was to
publish the "inside" news collated from the rumours and
gossip picked up at cocktail parties and the chancellories of
the world. Cockburn writes that by 1935 *The Week*

> . . . was one of the half-dozen most often quoted in the
> press of the entire world. It included among its subscribers
> the Foreign Ministers of eleven nations, all the Embassies
> and Legations in London, all diplomatic correspondents
> of the principal newspapers in three continents, the
> Foreign Correspondents of all the leading newspapers
> stationed in London, the leading banking and brokerage
> houses in London, Paris, Amsterdam and New York, a
> dozen members of the United States Senate, twenty or
> thirty members of the House of Representatives, about
> fifty members of the House of Commons and a hundred
> or so in the House of Lords, King Edward VIII, the
> secretaries of most of the leading trades unions, Charlie
> Chaplin and the Nizam of Hyderabad.
>
> Blum read it and Goebbels read it, and a mysterious
> warlord in China read it. Senator Borah quoted it re-
> peatedly in the American Senate and Herr von Ribben-
> trop, Hitler's Ambassador in London, on two separate
> occasions demanded its suppression on the ground that it
> was the source of all anti-Nazi evil.[1]

In 1934 *Viewpoint* appeared, changing its name after the
first number to *Left Review*, edited by two well-known communists, Montagu Slater and T. H. Wintringham, and
Amabel Williams-Ellis, the sister of John Strachey. Its
policy was stated to be the following:

[1] Claud Cockburn, *In Times of Trouble: An Autobiography* (London:
Hart-Davies, 1956), p. 226.

Viewpoint stands for militant communism and against individualism and metaphysics in the arts. It declares that the work of art is an organic individual creation and that it can only exist in its integrity in a classless society, in a completely communistic state; that art must become the production and the property of all.

The objectives were made more specific by Wintringham in June 1935: (1) as an organ of all left-wing writers; (2) as a means of expression for writers of working-class origin; (3) to assist in working out a Marxist line for criticism and literature; (4) as a medium of propaganda, especially against war and fascism. *Left Review*'s circulation of three thousand in 1935 was said to put it in second place among all the literary monthlies. But in 1936 a general deterioration set in, reducing it to little more than a cultural appendage of the C.P.G.B.

Plan was a non-party publication of the Federation of Progressive Societies and Individuals which was supported by C. E. M. Joad, Vera Brittain, Kingsley Martin, Harold Nicolson, Bertrand Russell, Rebecca West, and Leonard Woolf. The Federation and its journal advocated World Government, and regional and world planning based on production for use instead of for profit. Other planks in its platform were a universal system of education, and the abolition of all restrictions upon the development and full expression of the human personality. Despite the generally high calibre of its articles, *Plan* survived for only five years from 1934 to 1939.

From 1936 onwards there was a profusion of new publications. *Controversy*, becoming *Left* and finally *Forum*, lasted until 1950 under four editors: Dr. C. A. Smith, J. F. Horrabin, Jon Evans, and George Padmore. An independent journal, striving for a classless society and a socialist co-operative commonwealth, it offered an "open forum" to all shades of left-wing opinion and analysis. John Lehmann edited *New Writing* and its successors, *Folios of New Writing*,

Daylight, and *New Writing and Daylight*. His concern was to publish the prose and poetry of the new writers, except fascists and reactionaries. A most ingenious monthly was *Fact*, edited by Raymond Postgate and an editorial board that included G. D. H. Cole, George Lansbury, Arthur Calder-Marshall, Francis Meynell, and Stephen Spender. Each number consisted of one lengthy monograph of about one hundred pages selling for sixpence. Representative contributions were G. D. H. Cole, *Economic Prospects: 1938 and After;* Ernest Hemingway, *The Spanish Civil War;* and Marcel Prenant, *Biology and Man: Past and Future*. By 1939, 200,000 of these monthly booklets had been sold. Postgate, in an extremely interesting comment, likened the task that confronted contemporary intellectuals to that of the Encyclopedists: the dissemination of enlightenment and knowledge. *Fact* was to become a sort of latter day *Encyclopédie*. He wrote:

> The readers of the Encyclopédie became suddenly aware that the evils under their eyes were not isolated errors, but part of an imbecile system, and, at the same time, that there were all over France and most of Europe thousands of other persons who knew exactly what was wrong and could be their allies in changing it. This knowledge produced action: and it is due as much to the Encyclopedists as to anyone else that witch-hunting and barons' tyranny are now such forgotten monstrosities that we cannot well imagine what life under them was.[1]

To say that the Left Book Club was synonymous with the radical political ferment of the nineteen-thirties is an obvious exaggeration. But there can be little doubt about the importance of the Left Book Club either as a powerful voice and moulder of left-wing opinion or as a mass movement in its own right. It was Britain's nearest equivalent of a popular front. The architect of this movement was Victor Gollancz, the publisher. He was born in London in 1893, and was

---

[1] "Ourselves", *Fact*, No. 1 (April 1937), p. 7.

educated at St. Paul's and New College, Oxford: he came of
a Rabbinical family, but his father was a small business-man.
A Liberal from a very early age, he subsequently became a
Christian Socialist as he still is, and joined the Labour Party.
He founded his publishing house in 1928, and has made a
name as a sponsor of numerous humanitarian causes, the
latest being the abolition of capital punishment, and nuclear
disarmament.

The Left Book Club was launched in May 1936 with the
object of providing the knowledge for building a United
Front against fascism and war, and of preparing the way for
socialism. A Selection Committee consisting of Gollancz,
Harold Laski, and John Strachey chose the book of the month.
The authors ranged from a communist like R. Palme Dutt
to the Liberal Mr. E. D. Simon, now Lord Simon of Wythen-
shawe. Supporters of the Club included Socialists, Liberals,
Communists, many unattached "Progressives", and even
Conservatives. Among the most prominent were Sir Stafford
Cripps, Sir Richard Acland, Sir Norman Angell, Mr.
Wilfred Roberts, and Mr. Robert Boothby. A monthly
bulletin, the *Left Book News*, shortly becoming the *Left News*,
went to all members. It regularly contained an editorial by
Gollancz, general news of the Club, columns by Strachey
and Ivor Montagu, and a review of the Club selection either
by Laski or Strachey.

The Club expanded so rapidly that at the end of the first
month there were 12,000 members and twelve study circles.
A peak of nearly 60,000 members and 1,200 groups was
reached in April 1939. At that time it was calculated that
1,566,700 books had been circulated during the previous
years. Rallies, meetings, lectures, week-end and vacation
schools were arranged by the Club. The Rev. Dr. John
Lewis, a nonconformist clergyman with communist sym-
pathies, was appointed full-time organizer of the local discussion groups. Functional groups in the professional and
cultural spheres were formed for scientists, doctors, engineers,
lawyers, teachers, civil servants, poets, writers, artists,

musicians, and actors. A periodical, *Poetry and the People*, edited by L. J. Isserlis and Philip Martin, was published by the Poets Group, featuring poems and articles by Edgell Rickword, A. L. Morton, Jack Lindsay, Montagu Slater, Alan Bush—all communists.

Is it possible to say how influential the communists were in the Left Book Club? Gollancz has stated in the second volume of his autobiography that they were more influential than they ought to have been, though he doubts whether this could have been avoided without a danger of "hamstringing the movement—with such an objective! [namely, of preventing war]—or even of killing it." [1] Scarcely a year after the foundation of the Club, he felt it necessary to deny that it was a communist front. [2] Some years later, he lashed out at those who would turn the Club groups into "bastard C P locals". [3] So there seems to be little doubt that communism threatened the independence of the organization. Club policy, in the main, paralleled the official communist line, yet this was to be expected in the days of the Popular Front. At the outbreak of war the Club ceased to have an official policy. The split among the Selectors, with Gollancz and Laski following a pro-war anti-communist line, and Strachey adhering to an anti-war pro-communist line (until the invasion of the Low Countries in 1940) also occurred among the members, leading to many resignations in both camps. Sometimes the number of Club selections of books by communist authors is offered as evidence of communist dominance. On the average, however, less than fifty per cent of the selections for each year were written by communists. Of greater importance than the nature of the Club's policy, in any attempt to estimate the degree of communist penetration, is the percentage of communists who were members,

[1] Gollancz, *More for Timothy: Being the Second Instalment of an Autobiographical Letter to His Grandson* (London: Gollancz, 1953), pp. 356–357.

[2] Gollancz, "Editorial", *Left News*, No. 15 (July 1937), p. 420.

[3] Gollancz, "Keynes—and Other Things", *Left News*, No. 48 (April 1940), p. 1469.

said to have been about 6,000 out of 36,000 in April 1940, and the positions that some of them held in the Club organization. Strachey, a communist sympathizer, was a member of the Selection Committee. Dr. John Lewis, likewise a communist sympathizer, was in a position as organizer to exert great influence in the Club, though little evidence is available to show that he seized this opportunity. At least three of the key professional groups, the Scientists, the Poets, and the Writers, were dominated by communist intellectuals, and a high percentage of regular contributors to *Left News* were communists. All this, however, was to be expected, for it was the communists who set the pace everywhere in the Popular Front movement. From the communist standpoint the importance of the Left Book Club was rather in the personal relations that could be established between communists and non-communists. The Club went out of existence in 1945: the victory of the Labour Party, Gollancz explained, rendered its continuance unnecessary.

An outline of the activities and interests of the intellectuals of the thirties would be incomplete without some mention of another movement, "Mass-Observation". Two young Cambridge intellectuals, Charles Madge, a communist poet and reporter on the *Daily Mirror*, and Tom Harrisson, an anthropologist, founded it in January 1937. They believed that the truth about human behaviour could be revealed only if the methods of science were applied to the study of man. By employing a corps of voluntary and professional observers, panels of experts, public opinion sampling techniques, applause meters, etc., Madge and Harrisson hoped to discover the nature of the mass-life of the mass-man from the cradle to the grave. Voluntary work for Mass-Observation soon became fashionable. By 1940 there were 2,000 part-time observers: the man on the street with pad and pencil, the silent stranger in the corner of the pub—a new species had arisen, the Mass-Observer. A series of pamphlets and books, charting the behaviour of mass-man, was published. In 1940 a weekly intelligence service, *Us*, was organized. One of the first and most novel of the Mass-Observation experiments was Charles Madge's venture in Geoffrey Grigson's *New Verse*, for May 1937, the Mass-Observation poem "Oxford", a montage of the sensations of twelve undergraduates. The appeal of Mass-Observation cut across party and political affiliation. The increased social awareness of the intellectual and his growing anxiety over the predicament of mankind were reflected in its popularity. "Fact" became the one absolute value in a cosmos of fractured icons. Mass-man was the "real" man, although he was non-existent. The very involvement in observing, compiling, and synthesizing facts was an emotional therapeutic. Mass-Observation, like communism, was in a sense irrationalism clothed as science.

As the vogue of communism increased, questions were raised about the nature of its relationship to Christianity. A number of symposiums were devoted to the subject, notably *Christianity and the Social Revolution* (1935), and *Christianity and Communism* (1937). In his introduction to the former, Canon Raven, Regius Professor of Divinity in Cambridge University, voiced the Christian's concern with the troubles of the time by saying that even if no rapprochement between communism and Christianity was possible, it would be wise for socially conscious Christians to study communist thought and the communist criticisms of the Christian Church.[1] The latter volume, edited by H. Wilson Harris, was a collection of essays originally appearing in the *Spectator*. Dean Inge and Father D'Arcy subjected communism to merciless criticism; John Strachey defended it; while the others, such as Dr. Joseph Needham and Reinhold Niebuhr, attempted to demonstrate that communism and Christianity possessed a common denominator.

A striking example of the influence of communism was the number of Christians who professed to be "communists".

---

[1] John Lewis, Karl Polanyi, and Donald K. Kitchin, eds., *Christianity and The Social Revolution* (London: Gollancz, 1935), p. 26. Contributors included W. H. Auden, Conrad Noel, John Cornford, Dr. Joseph Needham, Julius Hecker, Rheinhold Niebuhr.

Their communism was seldom orthodox, and some were quite unsympathetic towards Soviet Communism. A pioneer of "Christian Communism" in Great Britain was the "Red Vicar" of Thaxted, Conrad Noel. The grandson of Lady Gainsborough and cousin of Noel Buxton, he studied at Corpus Christi College, Cambridge, and Chichester. He was the Vicar of Thaxted for thirty years until his death in 1942. Noel, neither an orthodox communist nor a conventional Christian, was an Anglo-Catholic, who stressed the æsthetic importance of the ritual of the High Church service. Gustav Holst, a resident of Thaxted, became musical director of the church, and Mrs. Noel revived the famous Morris dancing of the village. A small but influential movement developed within the Church of England as a result of Noel's efforts. His radicalism, however, was not confined to attempts at bringing beauty and colour into the Church. He preached the social gospel of Christ, calling him "a militant revolutionist". The Red Flag and the Sinn Fein banner were given positions of honour next to the Cross of St. George in Thaxted Church. Always a dissenter, he led a faction out of the Church Socialist League to found the League of the Kingdom of God, and the Catholic Crusade. Although he was one of the first to rejoice at the news of the Russian Revolution he proved his unorthodoxy by saying to Madame Litvinov that it was not Dialectical Materialism that had brought about the Revolution, but the mystical element in the Russian people.[1]

A fervent disciple of Noel is the internationally famous Cambridge bio-chemist, Dr. Joseph Needham, a member of the Labour Party who dedicated his book of essays, *Time, The Refreshing River* (1943), to "Conrad Noel Priest of Thaxted and Prophet of Christ's Kingdom on Earth". Dr Needham's Christian communism rests upon three essential articles of faith: (1) a devout belief in the social teachings of

[1] Sidney Dark, ed., *Conrad Noel: An Autobiography; With a Memoir of His Childhood By a Cousin and Tributes By Kingsley Martin, Harry Roberts, and Richard Church* (London: Dent, 1945), p. 108.

C

Christ; (2) a conviction that communism embodies these teachings; (3) a historicism that envisages the culmination of history in the establishment of a communist *regnum dei*.[1] Communism, for Needham, is the religion of the future. That it seeks to dispense with God does not preclude its fundamental religious nature. The essence of religion is the "sense of the holy", manifested in the ethical tenets that are cherished by communists, and that will become objectified in a world communist commonwealth. In this society of the future, "Love thy neighbour" will be taken literally. Complete human equality will be the rule. Leadership and social cohesion will rely not so much upon manipulation from without as upon an inner self-discipline—the rule of man, rather than the rule over man. Because the Christian Church has failed to put these ethical precepts into practice, Dr. Needham sees that "The phoenix of the Kingdom is rising from the ashes of the Churches failure". Social evolution, he believes, is continuous with biological evolution. Each higher stage in the development of human institutions represents a more advanced ethic. Communism is the highest social form, not only because historically it appears later than capitalism, but also because it embodies the supreme ethic of Jesus of Nazareth. The communist commonwealth will be the fruition of man's noblest achievements, the fulfilment of the longings of all Christians. It is their duty to do everything in their power to usher in this new holy order upon earth. Dr. John Lewis shared Dr. Needham's views on many of these points. His words summarized their commonly

[1] Dr. Needham's views on religion are found in the following works: Lewis *et al.*, *op. cit.*, pp. 163–179, 416–441; Joseph Needham, "Materialism, Science, and Religion:—Thoughts of a Young Scientist on the Testament of an Old One", *Fact*, No. 17 (August 15, 1938), pp. 80–97; and the same author's *Time: The Refreshing River* (*Essays and Addresses, 1932–1942*) (London: Allen and Unwin, 1943); and his *History Is On Our Side: A Contribution to Political Religion and Scientific Faith* (London: Allen and Unwin, 1946). Also see the friendly but acute criticism of a fellow biologist, G. E. Hutchison, *The Itinerant Ivory Tower: Scientific and Literary Essays* (New Haven: Yale University Press, 1953), pp. 119–129.

held beliefs, although perhaps in a more emotional strain than Dr. Needham customarily used:

> We cannot expect any recovery of the Jesus of History in those who are reconciled to the social order and its moral values, or who flinch from class and party strife.
>
> The apocalyptic crisis has descended upon our age, not prematurely as in the time of Jesus, but in the fullness of time. Opportunity as it confronts us is also the final sifting of chaff from wheat, the day of judgement.
>
> The Church may try, but it cannot succeed to-day in crucifying the Christ. The new Christ is an insurgent proletariat, the uprisen people of God, and the Church which fails to do Him reverence must be cast forth into the outer darkness.
>
> The Day of the Lord is at hand.[1]

John Middleton Murry, the illustrious critic and editor of the *Adelphi*, also espoused a form of Christian communism. However, he differed from Needham and Lewis in his belief that although communism in some form was inevitable for England, it would be the greatest folly to follow in the footsteps of Soviet Russia.[2] He was appalled at the horrors of Russian communism. The only communism for Britain would be an indigenous, national growth—a "human" communism. This communism, an amalgam of social Christianity and Marxism, was the enemy of all religions because it was the one religion, the only "living" religion of the contemporary world. To the objection that Communists did not believe in God, his answer was that in reality they did. For what, he asked, was the difference between believing in God and believing in man and his capacity to build a glorious future? Naturally, we should have qualms about the communist future, but,

---

[1] Lewis *et al.*, *op. cit.*, p. 102.
[2] See John Middleton Murry, *The Necessity of Communism* (London: Cape, 1932); and the same author's, *The Defence of Democracy* (London: Cape, 1939).

Was the coming Reign of God, which Jesus foresaw, a thing of terror or a thing of joy? . . . It was both, as Communism, its earthly paradigm, is both. That the individual man should make the thing of terror a thing of joy, by anticipating the revolution in his own heart and mind, was the whole gospel of Jesus. It is the whole gospel of Marx. . . . The Communist Manifesto of Marx is the summons to the modern world to repent.[1]

From the early thirties Murry had a platform for his views in the quarterly, *Adelphi*. He founded a communist settlement at Langham, near Colchester, which he intended to be the nucleus of a communist university. His dreams of a discipleship that would disseminate the new gospel of communism never materialized.

Professor John Macmurray of London University was as forthright as Murry in attacking the Soviet system.[2] The transformation of the ideas of Marx into a rigid orthodoxy was equally repulsive. Throughout the history of Christianity, he maintained, the idea of a communist society, one in which property was held in common under the governing principles of "brotherhood, Equality, and freedom", had emerged on frequent occasions. Such a society was central to the teachings of Jesus, and was often clearly described in the New Testament. Communism is simply the offspring of Christianity. Christianity "implies communism" and communism "presupposes Christianity". Today, however, orthodox Christianity opposes the conception of the actualization of the brotherhood of man, while, ironically enough, its greatest champion is communism. Christianity and communism are in a state of "dialectical opposition". Each has defects that the other can remedy. The one has withdrawn from the real world, the other from the spiritual world.

[1] Murry, *The Necessity of Communism*, p. 117.
[2] John Macmurray, *The Philosophy of Communism* (London: Faber and Faber, 1933); John Macmurray, *Creative Society: A Study of The Relation of Christianity to Communism* (London: Student Christian Movement Press, 1935).

Hence the antagonism that exists between them is not a cause for despair. It is merely a prelude to a higher synthesis, a sign that "the Kingdom of Heaven is at hand". Christianity, before it can transform communism, must first revolutionize itself. By doing this "it will find that the transformation of communism is nothing but the transformation of Christianity into its own proper form." [1] In the classless society, eventuating from the new synthesis, man would at last become a free and rational being—a human being.

The dimensions of the communist movement during the thirties were not great. Only a fraction of the total number of British students turned to communism. Even the most vocal organ of the left, the *New Statesman and Nation*, on occasion criticized the Soviet Union. Moreover, many intellectuals who called themselves communists could never pass muster as party liners. Marxism was indeed an Old Curiosity Shop in which many persons rummaged. Beliefs other than communism won throngs of adherents in the thirties. The British Union of Fascists under Sir Oswald Mosley, two years after it was founded in 1932, boasted 20,000 members. The C.P.G.B. only exceeded this figure during and after the Second World War. The Social Credit ideas of Major Douglas and the New Britain Movement were not lacking in support. Pacifism was a growing and important movement. Catholicism, Buchmanism, and Mass-Observation had their devotees. Socialism was still by far the most popular political creed of the left. At this time Gaitskell, Durbin, Jay, and Crossman were young intellectuals in the Labour Party.

Political radicalism was not popular with the masses. The intellectuals of the left were politically somewhat isolated from the nation as a whole. Labour suffered a resounding defeat in the 1931 General Election, although considerable strength was regained in 1935. The Communist Party held only one seat in the House of Commons, won in 1935 by Willie Gallacher. In spite of the depression and the gloomy outlook in world affairs, the country tended to be to the right

[1] Macmurray, *Creative Society*, p. 149.

of the intellectuals, as was its government. Further illustration that the left-wing intellectuals were out of touch with the masses was provided by the reaction to the 1935 Jubilee in honour of the twenty-fifth year of the reign of King George V. From all reports, the response of the masses was extremely enthusiastic. The pageantry of the affair was a welcome respite in the drabness of their lives. Intellectuals of the left, however, protested against this expense in a time of crisis. Communism, therefore, had little opportunity of becoming a broadly based movement, in spite of its hold on some of the intellectuals.

But even among the intellectuals there was no mad rush to jump upon the communist band-wagon. *New Verse* of October 1934 reported the results of a questionnaire sent to forty British and American poets.[1] To the question "Do you take your stand with any political or politico-economic party or creed?", over one-half of the twenty answers received were in the negative. Only four mentioned communism; they were Dylan Thomas, Norman Cameron, Gavin Ewart, and Hugh MacDiarmid. Another poll was taken by *Left Review* after the commencement of the Spanish Civil War.[2] British writers and poets were asked about their commitment in the Spanish Civil War: "Are you for, or against, the legal Government and the People of Republican Spain? Are you for or against, Franco and Fascism?" Approximately twelve per cent of the 148 authors who responded were either neutral or pro-Franco.[3] The breakdown of the answers of the *New Statesman* staff writers is instructive.[4] There was no

---

[1] *New Verse*, No. 11 (October 1934), pp. 3–22.

[2] "Authors Take Sides" (London: *Left Review*, 1937).

[3] The neutralists were Ruby M. Ayres, Vera Brittain, Rhys J. Davies, Norman Douglas, T. S. Eliot, Vyvyan Holland, Charles Morgan, Sean O'Faolain, Ezra Pound, W. J. Turner, Derek Verschoyle, Alec Waugh, H. G. Wells, Vita Sackville West, Malachi Whitaker. The supporters of Franco were Edmund Blunden, Arthur Machen, Geoffrey Moss, Eleanor Smith, Evelyn Waugh. As might be anticipated, George Bernard Shaw's answer was "unclassified".

[4] See Critic, "A London Diary", *New Statesman and Nation*, Vol. XIV, New Series (December 25, 1937), p. 1094.

uniform anti-Franco extremism even in this voice of the left.
W. J. Turner and Vita Sackville West were neutralists.
David Garnett and Raymond Mortimer expressed a liberal
anti-fascist sentiment. The answers of Brian Howard, Cyril
Connolly and V. S. Pritchett were more to the left.

A list of the influential non-communist intellectuals (or
even of the non-leftists) would be very long. William Empson, a contemporary of Auden, satirized him and his left-
wing friends:

> *Waiting for the end, boys, waiting for the end.*
> *What is there to be or do?*
> *What's become of me or you?*
> *Are we kind or are we true?*
> *Sitting two and two, boys, waiting for the end.*
>
> . . . .
>
> *Shall we make a tale, boys, that things are sure to mend,*
> *Playing bluff and hale, boys, waiting for the end?*
> *It will be born stale, boys, stinking to offend,*
> *Dying ere it fail, boys, waiting for the end.*
>
> . . . .
>
> *What was said by Marx, boys, what did he perpend?*
> *No good being sparks, boys, waiting for the end.*
> *Treason of the clerks, boys, curtains that descend,*
> *Lights becoming darks, boys, waiting for the end.*
>
> . . . .
>
> *Waiting for the end, boys, waiting for the end.*
> *Not a chance of blend, boys, things have got to tend.*
> *Think of those who vend, boys, think of how we wend,*
> *Waiting for the end, boys, waiting for the end.*[1]

A young Oxford don, D. W. Brogan, lampooned the intellectuals of the left:

Marxism, by which Stalinism is here meant, is now
fashionable. It appeals strongly to what Miss Rose
Macaulay has called "the not so very-intelligentsia", to

[1] William Empson, "Just a Smack at Auden", *Collected Poems* (London:
Chatto and Windus, 1955), pp. 62–63.

bourgeois who find the world very threatening and still
cling to the illusion that comes so easily to their class, that
there *must* be a way out; but the worker still remains deaf.
The Communist Party and its sympathizers are a Mexican
army of generals, colonels and even lieutenants, but
workers and soldiers are scarce.[1]

John Maynard Keynes had no love for the British Com-
munist Party and found little of economic interest in Russia.[2]
A consistent and penetrating critic of Soviet Communism
was Bertrand Russell. His book, *The Practice and Theory of
Bolshevism*, first published in 1920, was reissued in 1948 without substantial change. And there were many others, I. A.
Richards and F. R. Leavis at Cambridge, Eric Gill, Herbert
Read, Desmond MacCarthy, Laura Riding, Harry Kemp.
Rayner Heppenstall has recently written that his life in the
thirties was "marginal". Although he was associated off
and on with Murry and the *Adelphi*, politics held little interest
for him. He decries the usual stereotype of the thirties, citing
his own experience, and concluding,

> . . . it does seem to the point that one could be some kind
> of writer and of "young intellectual" all through the
> thirties and yet remain so far outside what is now regarded
> as the mainstream. It did not, at the time, even seem the
> mainstream. Auden, Spender and Day Lewis did not,
> from any point at which I found myself, in the least ap-
> pear to dominate the age.[3]

The Soviet Union was not the only external focus of
interest for those dissatisfied in Britain. A considerable
number of Liberals and Independents—the left-centre of
British politics—eyed the New Deal experiment in the United

---

[1] D. W. Brogan, "The Mirage of Moscow", *Fortnightly Review*, Vol.
CXXXV. New Series (May 1934), p. 524.

[2] R. F. Harrod, *The Life of John Maynard Keynes* (London: Macmillan,
1951), pp. 365, fn. 1; 450–451.

[3] Rayner Heppenstall, "Decade Talk", *New Statesman and Nation*, Vol.
LI (April 14, 1956), p. 377.

States with great interest.[1] British trade-union leaders of the more empirical kind preferred the direction that America was taking to that of the Soviet Union. Keynes, from the beginning, had been a leading supporter of Roosevelt and the New Deal. In July 1934 the Next Five Years Group, consisting of Liberals like Norman Angell, Gilbert Murray, and Lord Allen of Hurtwood (Clifford Allen), issued a declaration, "On Liberty and Democratic Leadership", which praised Franklin Roosevelt. H. G. Wells was also excited by the New Deal. Towards the end of the decade even such left-wing stalwarts as Laski, Jennie Lee, and John Strachey began to view the American experiment with favour. Strachey in particular had been impressed by the application of Keynesian economics in America. This interest was to be a factor in his ultimate rejection of communism.

In bare outline these were some of the features of the nineteen-thirties. Against a background of domestic and international crisis, the intellectuals emerged from their previous political doldrums. Communism and the Soviet Union became potent sources of attraction. Was communism during the thirties a grave threat to British intellectual life? Was George Orwell justified in his charge that "For about three years, in fact, the central stream of English literature was more or less directly under Communist control"?[2] Were the nineteen-thirties, to use a hackneyed expression, a "red decade"? Upon the basis of all evidence, the answer is a conclusive no. That many young and promising intellectuals were attracted to communism is unquestionable, but the depth and longevity of their belief were limited. Few adhered to party orthodoxy, if they belonged to the party at all. For most it was a momentary flirtation or an act of defiance and desperation. This is not to say that Communism might not have constituted a danger, that it did not influence

[1] See Henry Pelling, *America and The British Left: From Bright to Bevan* (London: Black, 1956), pp. 133–145.
[2] George Orwell, *Inside The Whale, and Other Essays* (London: Gollancz, 1940), p. 163.

creative work in the thirties, or that it did not have a lasting impact upon British intellectual life. It is, however, a warning against the easy generalization, and the inclination to exaggerate a socio-political tendency. Others besides Orwell are masters of the art.

CHAPTER III

MILD MANNERED DESPERADOES

A PERIOD AND a movement have been described. What
of the people themselves? Who were the "mild mannered
desperadoes", as Beatrice Webb once called the British intellectuals who turned to communism?[1] What do we know
of their families, their education, and their occupations? A
brief catalogue of this information yields some interesting
facts, particularly when the intellectuals of the thirties are
compared to those of the twenties.

The intellectuals who were attracted to communism in
the nineteen-twenties formed a very small group.[2] Many
of them, if they were not already distinguished, were
later to become so.[3] Their families were mainly middle-

[1] Margaret Cole, ed., *Beatrice Webb's Diaries 1924–1932* (London:
Longmans, 1956), p. 14, entry for March 6, 1924.

[2] Some, like Philips Price, were never members of the Party. The subse-
quent analysis utilizes biographical data for the following intellectuals,
who were either party members or sympathizers during the nineteen-
twenties: R. Page Arnot, Emile Burns, Maurice Dobb, Clemens Palme
Dutt, Rajani Palme Dutt, W. N. Ewer, Ralph Fox, Walter Holmes, J. F.
Horrabin, Cecil L'Estrange Malone, William Mellor, Francis Meynell,
Dora Montefiore, J. T. Walton Newbold, Sylvia Pankhurst, Raymond
Postgate, M. Philips Price, Andrew Rothstein, Shapurji Saklatvala, Philip
Sprat, Dona Torr, Freda Utley, Ellen Wilkinson, T. H. Wintringham.
These are some of the most prominent intellectuals. Some in the
twenties such as A. L. Morton, Allen Hutt, G. C. T. Giles, and Montagu
Slater did not become widely known until the thirties, and will be
treated with the intellectuals of that period. A few in the list above,
Burns, R. P. Dutt, and others, still loyal communists today, receive
further attention elsewhere.

[3] In politics: the widely publicized war-time aeronaut and postwar
Liberal M.P., Labour M.P. from 1928 to 1931, and Parliamentary
Private Secretary to the Minister of Pensions in 1931 (Malone); a member of the Macmillan Committee on Finance and Industry under the
second Labour Government (Walton Newbold); a leading member of
the Labour Party and first Minister of Education in the Attlee Government (Wilkinson); a Labour M.P. of long service and Parliamentary

class.[1] Although they received the conventional public
school education, it was usually not the most expensive or
the most fashionable kind.[2] About two-thirds went up to
Oxford and Cambridge.[3] At Oxford, R. P. Dutt, T. H.
Wintringham, and Andrew Rothstein were Balliol men.[4]

Charity Commissioner from 1945 to 1950 (Philips Price); a founder of
the Communist Party of India (Sprat).

In journalism and publishing: the future Editor of the *Daily Herald* and
a founder and first Editor of *Tribune* (Mellor); the Diplomatic Correspondent of the *Daily Herald* (Ewer); a well-known journalist, publisher's
agent, civil servant, and connoisseur of food and wine (Postgate); a
brilliant cartographer and illustrator of educational books (Horrabin);
a book designer and typographer, founder of the Nonesuch Press, who
was knighted (Meynell); the official historian of the National Union of
Mineworkers (Arnot); the Vice-Chairman of the C.P.G.B. and Editor of
the *Labour Monthly* (R. P. Dutt).

[1] Emile Burns was the son of James Burns, Treasurer of St. Christo-
pher-Nevis, and the grandson of Patrick Burns, Auditor-General of the
Leeward Islands. His brother, Sir Alan Cuthbert Burns, since 1947 has
been the permanent United Kingdom Representative on the Trustee-
ship Council of the United Nations. M. Philips Price was born into an
old Liberal, land-owning Gloucestershire family related to the Trevelyans
and the Huxleys. Francis Meynell's mother was the poet, Alice Meynell.
The father of Raymond Postgate was Professor of Latin in Cambridge
and his maternal uncle was T. E. Allen, the Oxford Homeric scholar.
The father of the Dutts was an Indian physician with a Cambridge practice who married a Swedish lady. Shapurji Saklatvala was a member of
the extremely wealthy and powerful Tata family of Bombay. Theodore
Rothstein, father of Andrew, was a Bolshevik living in England, who
headed the first Soviet delegation to the United Kingdom, and became
the first Soviet Minister to Persia. William Herbert Utley, father of
Freda, was a colleague of George Bernard Shaw on the old Liberal *Star*.
Dona Torr was the daughter of W. E. Torr, Canon of Chester Cathedral.

[2] None attended Eton, Winchester, or Rugby. The sole Harrovian
was Philips Price. Some of the other schools were Perse (Postgate, R. P.
Dutt); Charterhouse (Dobb); Gresham's (Wintringham); Buxton
(Walton Newbold); Owens (Rothstein).

[3] Institutions attended by the others were: London School of Economics (Utley); University of Manchester (Wilkinson, Walton Newbold); Glasgow University (Arnot); Trinity College, Dublin (Meynell);
Royal Naval College, Dartmouth (Malone); Sheffield School of Art
(Horrabin); Royal College of Art (Pankhurst).

[4] Fox was a contemporary at Magdalen of John Strachey and Montagu
Slater; Postgate was a graduate of St. Johns; and Mellor, a theological
student at Exeter.

Trinity College, Cambridge, claimed Philips Price, W. N. Ewer, and Emile Burns.[1]

Two generalizations can be made about the activities of these young radicals. First, they were neither poets nor scientists. Only one, Maurice Dobb, chose an academic life. Many became left-wing journalists. At the time of the foundation of the C.P.G.B. the staff of the *Daily Herald* included Mellor, Meynell, Postgate, Philips Price, Ewer, Walter Holmes, and Dona Torr. Second, before they became interested in communism most of the intellectuals had been active politically, usually in the Labour movement. Some had been conscientious objectors during the war: R. P. Dutt, Postgate, Mellor, and Ewer. Guild Socialism was probably the most influential doctrine among them. The idea of "workers control" stemming from French Syndicalism, and to a lesser degree from the industrial unionism of the I.W.W. in America, developed in Great Britain from about 1910 onwards. Largely through the efforts of A. R. Orage and his remarkable journal, *New Age*, Guild Socialism became an organized political movement, enthusiastically supported by many young intellectuals.

Some of the most active young Guild Socialists were officers or members of the staff of the Fabian Research Department, established in the Autumn of 1912 by Sidney and Beatrice Webb. Shaw was Chairman until the end of the war, and G. D. H. Cole Honorary Secretary from 1916 to 1924. The Department soon became a focal point for a little band of Guild Socialists; Page Arnot, the paid Secretary; R. P. Dutt, the International Secretary, Mellor, Ewer, Meynell, Wilkinson, Postgate, Horrabin, Rowland Kenny, Maurice Reckitt, Eva Reckitt, Ivor Brown, George Lansbury, and Clifford Allen. By 1918 the Department had been completely captured by the Guild Socialists and severed formal connection with the Fabians.

A number of these young idealists of the Labour Research

[1] Also at Cambridge were C. P. Dutt (Queens); and Dobb (Pembroke).

Department, as it was now known, gradually became interested in communism. Rejecting Fabianism, and impatient with the Labour Party, they committed themselves
to Guild Socialism's aim of an equalitarian workers' state.
Their most cherished dreams seemed to be answered when
the Russian Revolution erupted at the end of the Great
War. Britain, they concluded, would soon follow with a
revolutionary communist organization. The course of the
great experiment in Russia was eagerly followed. Philips
Price, then Moscow correspondent of the *Manchester Guardian*,
began his study of Marxism. Sylvia Pankhurst organized
the People's Russian Information Bureau, and spoke
throughout the country against intervention. Colonel
Malone was one of the first visitors to the workers' republic,
returning a confirmed communist protagonist. Ralph Fox,
a member of a Quaker relief mission, discovered his hope of a
new world. Outside Russia there was no greater sympathy
for the Leninist adventure than in Britain. Among British
left-wing intellectuals the enthusiasm for the first great revolution since 1789—truly totalitarian in its economic,
social, and political implications—knew no bounds. No
secret police, purges, or concentration camps yet existed in
Russia to temper their exuberance. Stalin was not even a
name, and the newly formed Communist International was
hardly more than a world forum of passionate revolutionaries.

A small group at the Labour Research Department, with
Dutt in the foreground, caught up in the pro-Russian and
pro-communist torrent, began to prepare themselves for the
revolution and the seizure of power in Britain. Gathering
periodically in Belgravia, this " little knot of mild mannered
desperadoes" discussed reports prepared by members of the
group, and made plans for the British revolution and the new
society. In 1920 they took the first important step on the road
of action by merging with the industrial unionists of the
British Socialist Party and the Socialist Labour Party to form
the Communist Party of Great Britain. Guild Socialist delegates to the Foundation Conference included Mellor, Page

Arnot, Walter Holmes, and Ellen Wilkinson. The Labour Research Department became the prize of the communist fraction. G. D. H. Cole was provoked into resigning in the Spring of 1924. A year later, Tom Bell, the head of Agit-Prop of the C.P.G.B., could say:

> In Great Britain we already have a kind of Information Department, the "Labour Research Department", which collects statistics, conducts investigations into wages, movements, etc. This Department is not a Party concern, but is under the control of the Party.[1]

It is against this background that the intellectuals of the nineteen-thirties who were attracted by communist ideas should be examined.[2] Among them were many literati and

---

[1] *International Press Correspondence*, Vol. 5 (May 6, 1925), p. 538.

[2] The following list of non-scientists and scientists is not solely one of Communist Party members but includes some of those who at one time or another during the thirties and forties expressed a sympathy for communist ideas. For many the fascination of these ideas was only temporary. A few such as Briffault, Childe, Johnson, Pritt, Haldane, and Levy belong to an older generation.

Among the non-scientists were the following: W. H. Auden, Derek Blaikie, Robert Briffault, Alec Brown, Guy Burgess, Alan Bush, Arthur Calder-Marshall, Christopher Caudwell, V. Gordon Childe, Claud Cockburn, John Cornford, Kitty Cornforth, Maurice Cornforth, Benjamin Farrington, Ralph Fox, G. C. T. Giles, Richard Goodman, C. M. Grieve, David Guest, Charlotte Haldane, Denis Healey, David Hedley, Margot Heinemann, Christopher Hill, Rodney Hilton, Paul Hogarth, Eric Hobsbawm, Allen Hutt, Christopher Isherwood, Hewlett Johnson, Arnold Kettle, V. G. Kiernan, F. D. Klingender, James Klugmann, Bernard Knox, John Langdon-Davies, Beatrix Lehmann, Cecil Day Lewis, John D. Lewis, Jack Lindsay, G. C. Maclaurin, Donald Maclean, Louis MacNeice, Charles Madge, Ivor Montagu, A. L. Morton, Roy Pascal, Fred Pateman, Wogan Philipps, John Platts-Mills, D. N. Pritt, Edgell Rickword, Giles Romilly, Francis Scarfe, Humphrey Slater, Montagu Slater, Pat Sloan, R. Swingler, George Tate, George Thomson, Philip Toynbee, Edward Upward, Rex Warner, T. H. Wintringham.

The scientists included Lorimer Birch, P. M. S. Blackett, J. D. Bernal, E. H. S. Burhop, J. G. Crowther, Cedric Dover, J. B. S. Haldane, F. LeGros Clark, Hyman Levy, S. Lilley, Alan Nunn May, Dorothy M. Needham, Joseph Needham, N. W. Pirie, C. F. Powell, Martin Ruhemann, David Shoenberg, R. L. M. Synge, C. H. Waddington, Nora Wooster, W. A. Wooster.

scientists who had shown little political interest prior to their radicalization. Something of the virtuosity of the literati is indicated if we recall that Day Lewis and Auden were to hold the Chair of Poetry in Oxford University; that John Lehmann was to found and edit the reviews, *New Writing* and *London Magazine*; that Louis MacNeice, the poet, and Rex Warner, the novelist, were to serve as Directors of the British Institute of Athens; and that Philip Toynbee was to become a literary critic of the *Observer*.[1] The scientists included Professor J. B. S. Haldane, the distinguished geneticist and popularizer of science; Dr. Joseph Needham, the renowned Cambridge bio-chemist; and Professor J. D. Bernal, a pioneer in the X-Ray analysis of matter. Impresssive honours and numerous awards including three Nobel prizes were to be won by the scientists.[2]

Many of the radicals of the thirties seem to have been the first intellectuals of new bourgeois families, generally more prosperous than the families of the intellectuals of the twenties. The occupations of their fathers were largely professional, as the following incomplete catalogue suggests, with business a poorly represented vocation.[3]

Prominent Liberal Families	Journalism	Medicine
Haldane	Caudwell	Auden
Lehmann	Lehmann	Guest
Maclean	Spender	Needham
Montagu	Strachey	
Spender		*Academic*
Strachey	*Church*	Cornford
Toynbee	Day Lewis	Haldane
	Langdon-Davies	Toynbee
Business	MacNeice	
Calder-Marshall	Warner	*Armed Services*
C. Haldane		Burgess
		Isherwood
		Madge

[1] Day Lewis and Toynbee were Party members.

[2] Blackett, Powell, and Synge are Nobel Prizemen. Blackett and Bernal have received Royal Medals; and Haldane, the Darwin Medal. Only Haldane was ever a member of the Communist Party.

[3] This is not a list of Communist Party members.

Something of the disintegration of Liberalism as a dynamic faith in modern industrial society may be reflected by the fact that at least seven were from prominent Liberal families.

The family trees of some of the intellectuals are of interest. Giles Romilly and Philip Toynbee, distant cousins, belong to the famous Villiers line. Romilly is a nephew of Lady Churchill. Toynbee is a son of historian Arnold Toynbee and grandson of Gilbert Murray, the classicist. Claud Cockburn is a descendent of Lord Cockburn, the eminent Scottish Chief Justice. The great grandfather of John Lehmann was Robert Chambers, founder and publisher of *Chamber's Encyclopædia*.

The ancestry of Dr. Joseph Needham, one of the least known and most intriguing, can be traced to a few hardy medical men of the seventeenth and eighteenth centuries.[1] Marchamont Needham, author of *The Case of the Kingdom Stated* (1647), collaborated with John Milton in editing the newspaper of Parliament. At the time of the Restoration he retired from public life and returned to the practice of medicine. Dr. Joseph Needham, a Fellow of the Royal Society, published his *Medulla Medicinae* in 1665. The Cambridge physician, Walter Needham, dedicated his *De Formato Foetu* (1667) to Robert Boyle. A noted "man-midwife" of the eighteenth century was Joseph Needham, of Devizes. John Turberville Needham (1713–81) wrote several books defending the principle of spontaneous generation. One was an attack upon Voltaire who had accused him of being a Jesuit.

Several of the intellectuals belong to what Nöel Annan calls the " intellectual aristocracy " of England.[2] From the second half of the nineteenth century non-conformist families like the Macaulays, the Peases, the Wedgwoods, the Darwins, and the Stephens have played a pre-eminent role in

[1] Dr. Needham has never been a member of the Communist Party.
[2] Nöel Annan, "The Intellectual Aristocracy", in J. H. Plumb, ed., *Studies in Social History: A Tribute to G. M. Trevelyan* (London: Longmans, 1955), pp. 243–287.

the intellectual life of Great Britain. Members of the Clapham Sect, Quakers, Unitarians, and Philosophic Radicals, they entered the new professions of a rapidly industrializing Britain. They left their mark upon the civil service, the universities, the church, and the publishing world. The families have all intermarried, and have grown in numbers as well as in distinction. They have spanned the gap between intelligence and action by entering politics and furnishing both sides of the House of Commons with some of its most accomplished members. The genius of modern British culture is in no small part their genius.

Four members of the "intellectual aristocracy", all distantly related, with whom we are concerned are: J. B. S. Haldane, John Strachey, John Cornford, and R. L. M. Synge.[1] The lineage of the Haldanes goes back to Bishop Burnet. Professor Haldane's father was J. S. Haldane, a famous advocate of the vitalist theory in biology. One uncle, Lord Haldane, was the Hegelian philosopher, reorganizer of the British Army, and Labour Lord Chancellor. Another was Lord Eldon, the Conservative Lord Chancellor. Haldane's sister is the novelist Naomi Mitchison who is married to G. R. Mitchison, wealthy barrister, Labour M.P., and spokesman on housing. The Stracheys are descended from an Elizabethan Essex family. John's father was John St. Loe Strachey, Editor of the *Spectator*. A cousin was Lytton Strachey of the Bloomsbury Circle. The mother of John Cornford, Frances, the poet, was a Darwin. R. L. M. Synge, kinsman of John Millington Synge, the Irish playwright, is related by marriage to the Stephens.

Wogan Philipps and Ivor Goldsmid Samuel Montagu are the only intellectuals who are sons of peers. Wogan Philips is the eldest son and heir of Laurence Richard Philipps, the first Baron Milford of Llanstephen. Baron Milford, the sixth son of the late Reverend Sir James E. Philipps, is a "soft drink" magnate, possessing a large interest in Schweppes and

---

[1] John Strachey and R. L. M. Synge were never members of the Communist Party.

Kia-Ora Ltd. Wogan's wife is Tamara Rust, a Russian, widow of the late William Rust, who was the Editor of the *Daily Worker* and a member of the Political Committee of the Communist Party of Great Britain. There is, then, a high probability that the House of Lords will have its first communist member within the course of a few years. The father of Ivor Montagu was the second Baron Swaythling. The first Baron, the son of Louis Samuel of Liverpool, assumed the name of Montagu by Royal Licence and founded the London banking firm of Samuel Montagu and Company in 1853. A Liberal Member of Parliament from 1885 to 1900, he became Baronet in 1894, and Baron in 1907. Ivor's elder brother, the third Baron Swaythling, is married to Jean Knox, former Director of the Auxiliary Territorial Service. Another brother, Ewen Edward Samuel Montagu, a barrister, is Recorder of Southampton and Judge Advocate of the Fleet.[1]

The intellectuals were scattered among the best public schools.[2] Honours must go to Eton for having educated the greatest number of future radicals. No less than seven were there: Haldane, Giles, Strachey, Philipps, Lehmann, Burgess, and Hedley. The Old Etonians seem to have been the most stalwart of communists. Haldane and Giles have been members of the Executive Committee of the C.P.G.B., and Strachey was the most articulate communist ideologue during the thirties. Today, Giles and Philipps are still active Party members, while Burgess created an international incident by disappearing behind the Iron Curtain. Although

[1] Ewen Montagu's recent remark in court that the Merchant Navy employed "half the scum of England" was fully reported in the *Daily Worker*, January 30, 1957, p. 3, and accompanied by the resentful comments of seamen. No reference was made to the Montagu family relationship.

[2] These intellectuals were not necessarily members of the Communist Party. Some of the schools and the students are as follows: Gresham's (Wintringham, Auden, Maclean); Oundle (J. Needham, Guest); St. Paul's (Calder-Marshall, Klugmann); Marlborough (MacNeice); Rugby (Toynbee); Stowe (Cornford); University College School (Spender, M. Cornforth); Winchester (Madge, Synge); Clifton (Waddington).

there are few detailed accounts of the public school experiences of the intellectuals, overt revolt against established authority and middle-class values seems to have been rare during this period of their lives.

A majority of the intellectuals attended Oxford and Cambridge Universities. Few were educated in London, and fewer still in the provinces. An analysis of the distribution of the intellectuals between Oxford and Cambridge must take into consideration their different age-groups.[1]

BIRTH	OXFORD	CAMBRIDGE
1. Before 1900	Childe, Haldane, Langdon-Davies, Pritt, Rickword.	
2. 1900–1910	Auden, Calder-Marshall, Cockburn, Fox, Day Lewis, MacNeice, M. Slater, Spender, Strachey, Warner.	Brown, Giles, Hutt, J. Lehmann, Montagu, Morton, Pascal, Philipps, Sloan, Thomson, Upward.
		Scientists Bernal, Blackett, D. Needham, Pirie, Powell, Waddington, N. Wooster, W. A. Wooster.
3. 1910–1920	Blaikie, Goodman, Healey, Hill, Hilton, Platts-Mills, Tate, Toynbee.	Burgess, Cornford, K. Cornforth, M. Cornforth, Guest, Heinemann, Hobsbawn, Kettle, Kiernan, Klugmann, Knox, Maclaurin, Maclean, Madge, Pateman.
		Scientists Birch, Burhop, Lilley, May, Shoenberg, Synge.

Those born before 1900 were educated at Oxford. The non-scientists of the second group, born between 1900 and 1910, seem to be divided rather evenly between Oxford and

[1] Again it should be emphasized that this is not a list of Communist Party members.

Cambridge. The scientists, however, give the lead to Cambridge. Those belonging to the third group, born between 1910 and 1920, went up to Oxford and Cambridge in the late twenties or during the thirties. A striking fact about this group—including non-scientists—is its concentration at Cambridge. When the intellectuals of the thirties are considered as a whole, without separating them into age groups, it appears that about twice as many were at Cambridge as at Oxford. If the scientists are excluded, Cambridge still holds a slight lead.

A large number of the intellectuals were centred, during the thirties, at Trinity College, Cambridge. Even on the basis of incomplete biographical data this is the inescapable fact that emerges from an examination of the collegiate distribution of the intellectuals within the two universities.[1] The young intellectuals at Trinity College in the thirties formed the nucleus of the Cambridge student communist organization. David Guest, whose father is the present Labour peer, Lord Haden-Guest, after going up to Trinity from Oundle in 1929 spent a year at the University of Göttingen studying mathematical philosophy under Hilbert. Upon his return to Trinity in 1931, convinced by what he had seen of the Nazis that communism was the only hope for mankind, he helped to organize the University Branch of the C.P.G.B. and became its Secretary. His friend, Maurice Cornforth, another philosophy student of Trinity,

---

[1] The *major* collegiate concentrations by decade follow. Intellectuals of the twenties have been included and are starred. Names do not indicate Communist Party membership.

OXFORD: *Balliol* 1900–1920 (R. P. Dutt*, Rothstein*); 1920–1930 (Wintringham*); 1930–1940 (Healey, Hill, Hilton, Platts-Mills); *Magdalen* 1920–1930 (Fox, M. Slater, Strachey).

CAMBRIDGE: *Kings* 1920–1930 (Giles, Montagu, Thomson); 1930–1940 (Hobsbawm); *Magdalene* 1920–1930 (Blackett, Madge, Philipps); *Pembroke* 1920–1930 (Dobb*, Pascal); 1930–1940 (Kettle); *Trinity* 1900–1920 (Burns*, Ewer*, Philips Price*); 1920–1930 (Lehmann); 1930–1940 (Burgess, Burhop, Cornford, Cornforth, Guest, Kiernan, Klugmann, Shoenberg, Synge); *Trinity Hall* 1930–1940 (Maclean, May, Pateman).

became the Secretary of the Cambridge City Branch which was formed shortly afterwards.[1] Circumstances prevented Charles Madge, student poet of Magdalene College, from succeeding Guest as Secretary of the Student Branch, so John Cornford, another Trinity man, took the post. Guest unsuccessfully attempted to establish a section of the National Unemployed Workers Movement in the town of Cambridge, and he and his comrades, including James Klugmann and Guy Burgess, were instrumental in organizing the unprecedented waiters' strike at Trinity. Today three of the leading ideological leaders of the C.P.G.B. are Old Trinitarians: Emile Burns of the older generation, James Klugmann, and Maurice Cornforth. Family ties existed even here, for Cornforth married Klugmann's sister, Kitty, a communist of Girton College. Had not Cornforth and Guest been killed in Spain, Trinity's contribution to the C.P.G.B. leadership undoubtedly would have been greater. It is not surprising that Trinity became the focal point of student communism in Cambridge and in the whole of Britain. Trinity was the largest Cambridge College, noted for its scientific and historical studies. An important factor was the presence of the communist don, Maurice Dobb, who as a Fellow of the College was in a position to be adviser, tutor, father-confessor, and friend to the young radicals.

An adequate explanation, however, of this phenomenon at Trinity cannot neglect the scientists, and this involves the larger question of the radicalization of the scientists in the University. Here the institutional factors that may have facilitated the dissemination and contributed to the popularity of communist ideas must be stressed, rather than the appeal of the ideas themselves. Physicists and biochemists were the scientists most influenced by communism. Both sciences were being revolutionized at Cambridge. Blackett, Shoenberg, Nunn May, and Burhop were continuing the work of Rutherford on the atom. Bernal and others were

---

[1] Both Guest and Cornforth had studied under Ludwig Wittgenstein, but were repulsed by his ultimate scepticism.

pioneering with Sir William Bragg in the field of crystallography. The frontiers of biochemistry were being pushed
back by Haldane, the Needhams, Waddington, and Pirie
under the guidance of Sir Frederick Gowland Hopkins.
Scientific innovators of this sort are individuals of great intellectual brilliance, often egocentrics who adopt uncon-
ventional attitudes in their interpersonal relations, and who
are attracted by non-conformist social philosophies. Haldane,
Bernal, and Joseph Needham were typical.[1]

In addition the directors of the new developments in the
two sciences were politically tolerant liberals. The atmosphere of their laboratories and lecture rooms was not hostile
to any radical political ferment among the students and
young researchers. In Physics, Lord Rutherford and Sir
William Bragg were of this kind. Dr. Alex Wood, a very
popular teacher of physics, was a crusading socialist and
pacifist, in whose memory the present Cambridge City
Labour Hall is named. Also there was the excellent example
of ability and character set by Kapitza, the Soviet physicist
working under Rutherford.

In Biochemistry, Sir Frederick Gowland Hopkins, the
much loved and respected director of the Sir William Dunn
Institute of Biochemistry, had once been a friend and neighbour of Ramsay MacDonald. Sir Charles Sherrington wrote
of Hopkins, "I fancy that after biochemistry his greatest interest lay in socialism; his views were quite to the left." [2]
Haldane was a lieutenant of Hopkins for ten years, and the
Needhams, sincere believers in the social gospel of Christ,
were also senior members of the Laboratory. The Laboratory
was a remarkable melting pot of eager and adventuresome
scientists and students from all over the world. The *esprit de*

[1] Of the scientists mentioned in this paragraph evidence available to
the author indicates that only Professor Haldane was ever a member of
the Communist Party.

[2] *Lancet*, 1947 (1) p. 728, as quoted in Joseph Needham and Ernest
Baldwin, eds., *Hopkins and Biochemistry 1861–1947: Papers Concerning Sir
Frederick Gowland Hopkins, O.M., F.R.S., with a Selection of his Addresses and
a Bibliography of his Publications* (Cambridge: Heffer, 1949), p. 99.

corps was exceptionally high, for they were young pioneers working and living together on a hitherto unsettled and un-explored frontier. The environment was relaxed, convivial, and tolerant—intellectually stimulating. A comic journal *Brighter Biochemistry* was produced annually by the staff from 1923 to 1931. All contributed to it, including Hopkins himself. A mounting concern with the outside world was expressed by the fact that in 1931 "as clouds began to gather on the horizon with the course of events in Central Europe, there was a general decline in gaiety, and the journal *Brighter Biochemistry* was discontinued." [1] What better place could there be for the free exchange of ideas, for serious conversations about the state of the world, the social implications of science, and the politics of the left?

One further point should be noted. Biochemistry and physics were on common ground in the field of crystallography. The controversy in biology between the vitalists and the mechanists was of fundamental concern not only to biochemists like Needham, but also to physicists and crystallographers like Bernal. The Theoretical Biology Club of Cambridge provided a forum for the discussion of these problems by those who were interested. The Needhams, Waddington, Bernal, and other associates of long standing thus had another "fixed" opportunity for discussion, where political and social as well as scientific views could be exchanged. The Cambridge Heretics, a society founded in 1904 to encourage the scientific-rationalist point of view, performed a similar function among the students. In the nineteen-thirties communists and communist sympathizers formed a powerful bloc within this organization.

When the intellectuals went down from their universities for the last time, they faced the problem of employment in a society in which jobs for young bourgeois graduates were at a premium. Many of the scientists stayed on to pursue research in their universities. A few of the arts graduates like Hill and Thomson found their niche in the academic world.

[1] Needham and Baldwin, *op. cit.*, p. 321.

A great many of the poets and writers, in the absence of a ready patronage, became journalists.[1] Others turned to teaching, tutoring, and giving English lessons at home and abroad.[2]

Perhaps one of the most unusual careers of any of the intellectuals was that of Christopher Caudwell, the pen name of Christopher St. John Sprigg. Leaving school for a job on the *Yorkshire Post*, he soon went to London, where he edited the journal, *British Malaya*. With his brother he founded an aeronautical publishing house. He designed "an infinitely variable gear", details of which were published in *Automobile Engineer*. But this was only the beginning of his many and varied accomplishments. Before he reached the age of thirty—he was killed in March 1937 in Spain—he had written eight detective novels and one serious novel, *This is My Hand*, and many poems and short stories. His technical bent found expression in five books on aviation. Finally, he produced four major works, three of criticism, and one of science. At the end of 1935 he joined the Communist Party, and less than a year later went to Spain. He did not mix with other Party intellectuals or engage in Party intellectual work, preferring the company of "proletarian" communists, and sharing with them the menial chores and routine activities of Party life.

Here then is a brief natural history of the intellectuals. The differences between those of the twenties and thirties are fairly apparent. There were so many more in the thirties, young, inexperienced literati and scientists with little previous interest in politics. The contrast to the politically conscious Guild Socialists of the twenties, some of whom had been jailed for their political and social convictions, could not be greater. Politics had become a passion before their discovery of communism. The intellectuals of the thirties generally came from more affluent families than those of the

---

[1] Among them were Cockburn, Madge, Montagu, Rickword, H. Slater, M. Slater, Spender, Strachey, Toynbee.

[2] This was true of Calder-Marshall, Day Lewis, Giles, Guest, Sloan.

twenties. Leading sheltered lives, they had seen and felt
little in the way of hardship. They were sent to the best public schools, Eton figuring prominently among them. A
majority went up to Cambridge where they were concentrated at Trinity College. Upon graduation they earned
their livelihood as academicians, journalists, and school
teachers.

The fact that only a handful of the intellectuals of either
decade was of the "intellectual aristocracy" further sub-
stantiates Nöel Annan's view that "the pro-consular tradi-
dition and the English habit of working through established
institutions and modifying them to meet social needs only
when such needs are proven are traits strongly exhibited by
the intelligentsia of this country." [1]

Without an intellectual aristocracy so closely tied to the
middle classes, the revolution of the intellectuals of Great
Britain might have been of vast, even catastrophic dimensions. No doubt the traditional family relationships cush-
ioned the impact of communism and restrained many of
the nation's intellectuals from supporting the communist
crusade. On the other hand, the great toleration of British
society for the political "eccentricities" of many of its young
intellectuals may have resulted from their belonging to respected middle-class families so often bound together not
only by ties of blood and marriage, but also by those of
school, university, and club. Moreover, the "tea-party"
communism of many of the intellectuals can be traced in
part to these factors. "Mild mannered desperadoes" is indeed an apposite description of these young radical virtuosi.

[1] Annan, *op. cit.*, p. 285.

L'inquiétude, c'est réaction organique, la colique des décadences. Ceux que réfléchissent et que d'efforcent de regarder un peu plus loin que l'immediat, sont inquiets. On cherche les voies, on cherch du neuf. On sent bien qu'un changement se prépare. Mais ne le comprend pas qui vent.

Henri Barbusse, *Manifeste aux intellectuels* (1927)

All of a sudden I felt that all the things around me were toys to handle and control, that I had the power in a tiny, easy world.

C. P. Snow, *The Search* (1934)

CHAPTER IV

ESCAPE FROM THE WASTELAND

THE SOCIAL, ECONOMIC, and political conditions of the nineteen-thirties sensitized many intellectuals to the new ideas of communism. But the conditions were not themselves the causes of the great radicalization. The struggle for the sympathy and allegiance of the intellectual took place in the world of ideas. Ultimately, this is what distinguished the attraction of the intellectuals to communism from a similar movement among the masses. A central question to be asked, therefore, is what happened to the ideas of the intellectuals in contact with the ideas of communism?

Any attempt to analyse the appeal of communism in terms of ideas is confronted with the problem of the efficacy of psychological and economic explanations. Some who have been influenced by psycho-analytical procedures tend to reduce political behaviour to the data of early childhood experience, just as the Marxist, in theory at any rate, writes politics as a kind of shorthand for economics. Each in his own way considers politics a façade of reality. The effort of the Freudian and the Marxist to reduce one existential category to a more fundamental existence called " reality " is an intellectual habit as old as the Milesians, and sometimes just as fallacious as it is old. Reductionism of this kind often does less to explain than to explain away. More is revealed about the one who employs such a method than about the object of its application. The danger of the Freudian and Marxist approaches to politics is that politics with all its unique features and problems disappears. Political theory is transformed by their skill into ideology, a rationalization of childhood maladjustment or economic interest. Ideas are no longer evaluated on their own merits, but on the basis of their origins or their consequences. They become tools of manipulation in the hands of the therapist, the propagandist, and the public relations expert. These ideologists study ideas not for what they express in themselves but as indicators of conformance to, or divergence from, certain norms. All of this is not to say that psychological and economic factors are of no importance whatsoever.

Arthur Koestler, as a former communist and a student of psychology, may be turned to with profit at this point. In the novel *Arrival and Departure* (1943), he advanced the notion that has just been criticized, namely that the determinate of individual politics is the formation of the personality in childhood. Eleven years afterwards in the first volume of his autobiography Koestler explained the almost mass "conversion" of the young European intellectuals to communism in the thirties as "a sincere and spontaneous expression of an optimism born of despair, an abortive revolution of the spirit, a misfired Renaissance, a false dawn of history".[1] European intellectuals had gravitated to communism for similar reasons, despite differences of childhood experiences. He warned against confusing the psychological and political levels in the explanation of the conversion to communism. Childhood experience may create a susceptibility to communism, but does not affect the validity or invalidity of communist ideas. Koestler's conclusion is that communism is not simply neuroticism, although neuroticism may create a predisposition for communism. Therefore, it follows that not all communist intellectuals or even a majority are necessarily neurotic.

In the light of these remarks, it is important to consider the interpretation of the appeal of communism to the British intellectuals of the nineteen-thirties by the novelist Virginia Woolf, who, besides being an artist of great sensitivity, lived through the period and knew many of the actors involved.[2]

[1] Koestler, *The Invisible Writing: An Autobiography* (London: Collins with Hamish Hamilton, 1954), p. 241.
[2] Virginia Woolf, "The Leaning Tower", *Folios of New Writing* (Autumn 1940), pp. 11–33. This was a paper read at a meeting of the

Mrs. Woolf begins by discussing some of the dominant writers of the late nineteenth and early twentieth centuries: Chesterton, Belloc, Maugham, Walpole, Forster, Lytton Strachey, Aldous Huxley, Middleton Murry *et al.* They possessed the penultimate in security and leisure. No sudden cataclysmic changes challenged their self-assurance that life would continue as they had always known it. Sociologically, they conformed to the same pattern: middle class, expensive educations, travel, etc. Mrs. Woolf describes the intellectual of this group

> . . . upon a tower raised above the rest of us; a tower built first on his parents' station, then on his parents' gold. It is a tower of the utmost importance; it decides his angle of vision; it affects his power of communication.[1]

Prior to 1914 such literary aristocrats were not overly conscious of their tower. Although they showed the greatest sympathy for the lower classes and assisted them to share in the cultural and intellectual riches of life, they had no wish to climb down among them.

From about 1925 until the beginning of the Second World War a new group of writers emerged: Auden, Day Lewis, Spender, Isherwood, and MacNeice. Like their predecessors they were tower-dwellers, but there was a difference in the tower, and what was seen from it. All that the new writers saw was change and revolution. Their works were written in the shadow of war. The tower had a tendency to lean, and to lean to the left, and when this happened those on the tower were acutely aware of their exalted position. They suddenly became conscious of their middle-class families and upbringing. This realization resulted in discomfort and self-pity that turned into anger at the tower—at the

---

Workers' Educational Association, Brighton, May 1940. An anticipation of her argument is found in the writing of her nephew Julian Bell. See Quentin Bell, ed., *Julian Bell: Essays, Poems and Letters*, foreword by J. M. Keynes (London: Hogarth Press, 1938), pp. 314–316.

[1] Woolf, *op. cit.*, p. 19.

D

society that had elevated them. But they faced a dilemma. How could they legitimately condemn the society by which they had so greatly profited? The solution was the discovery of a scapegoat that symbolized society, for example, the capitalist. All the time the tower was leaning farther to the left, for politics was becoming the chief interest of the new tower-dwellers. Their education prevented them from descending, as they could not be expected to sacrifice their talent for labour in the streets, the factories, or the fields. Their feeling of being trapped on a leaning tower was reflected in the confusion, bitterness, and violence of their work:

> During all the most impressionable years of their lives they were stung into consciousness—into self consciousness, into class consciousness, into the consciousness of things changing, of things falling, of death perhaps about to come. There was no tranquillity in which they could recollect. The inner mind was paralysed, because the surface mind was always hard at work.[1]

Although no great work was produced by them in the thirties, they were at least frank. Having failed to analyse society, they began to analyse themselves and talk about their own predicament. Hence in the nineteen-thirties more autobiographies were written by people under thirty than ever before.

What is wrong with this analysis? Mrs. Woolf seems to have fallen victim of her own metaphor. The symbolism of the leaning tower, leaning of course to the left, refers to the growing political consciousness of the intellectuals. Are we supposed to infer that the political awakening occurred as a result of the feelings of guilt, or that they arose once society had been surveyed from a left political position? Evidently the latter was intended, for it is only after the tower begins to lean that the tower-dwellers realize the nature of their elevation above society. Therefore if Mrs. Woolf is interpreted

[1] Woolf, *op. cit.*, p. 28.

correctly, the sudden political radicalization is the prime mover of the whole process, arousing the guilt feelings that in turn give way to anger against society, a hunt for a scapegoat, and a refuge in communism.

But what started the tower leaning? Why did the intellectuals turn to the left in the first place? If the cause of the initial impetus can be discovered, then the matter of guilt and self pity is no longer vital, although it may tend to accelerate the movement to the left. Mrs. Woolf's only answer, which seems to be no answer, was that the intellectuals turned to communism because of the depression, the threat of war, etc. Nothing is said about the chain of ideas that led from the one to the other. What do we know of the values and ideas of the intellectuals, while the tower was still erect and before they were aware of their predicament? What did Marxism offer that they lacked before? What was the nature of the contest of ideas that took place in the minds of the intellectuals from 1925 onwards? These are fundamental problems that must be examined.

The Victorian era ended in the bloody debacle that took the lives of some of the finest of the young men of Great Britain. Many Victorian ideals of morality and traditional values of liberalism began to be questioned. Intellectuals found an outlet for their disillusion in individualism and æstheticism. Among the young, words such as conscience, discipline, duty, honour, patriotism, and virtue no longer represented what was once venerated. The institutions of marriage, family, and religion also began to be taken less seriously. Professor Joad characterized the intellectual activity of the decade as "analysis leading to the disintegration of what was analysed." [1] Never before had so many works on psycho-analysis been published, nor had the followers of Freud been so numerous. The full implications of Whitehead and Russell's *Principia Mathematica* (1913) were only beginning to be realized. Ludwig Wittgenstein, the Austrian

---

[1] C. E. M. Joad, "The End of an Epoch.—I", *New Statesman and Nation*, Vol. VIII, New Series (December 1, 1934), p. 785.

protégé of Russell, published his *Tractatus Logico-Philosophicus*
in 1922, and began to teach at Cambridge. Under these influences and those of the neo-Machians in Vienna, philosophy was gradually becoming more concerned with linguistic
problems than with enquiries about the nature and purpose
of man and his world. A Marxist scientist of the thirties
reacted to the period by saying that many of the intellectuals
had entered a private dreamland of art and science.[1] Edgell
Rickword, who edited a literary paper, the *Calendar*, from
1925 to 1927, later wrote that certainty no longer existed,
except the certainty that one line of behaviour was no better
than another.[2] The only absolute truth, Rickword tells us,
was that no statement could be truer than another. There
was no morally preferable action, for it was thought that no
action could be entirely disinterested. Since human experience could not be completely comprehended by reason,
irrationality became the key to understanding.

Life for many in the twenties no longer seemed to be pur-
poseful. Pleasure for pleasure's sake was an increasingly accepted canon of all activity. Closely allied to this trend was
the cult of beauty for its own sake popularized by the Bloomsbury Circle of the Woolfs, the Bells, J. M. Keynes, Lytton
Strachey, E. M. Forster, and Duncan Grant. The Bloomsbury æsthetes were perhaps less typical of the intellectuals of
the nineteen-twenties than is often maintained. But the following words of G. E. Moore, summarizing their philosophy,
indicate that they were not too far removed from the main-
stream:

> By far the most valuable things, which we know or can
> imagine, are certain states of consciousness, which may be
> roughly described as the pleasures of human intercourse
> and the enjoyment of beautiful objects . . . it is only for

[1] J. D. Bernal, "The End of Political Delusion", *Cambridge Left*,
Vol. I (Summer, 1933), p. 11.
[2] Edgell Rickword, "Culture, Progress, and English Tradition", in C.
Day Lewis, ed., *The Mind in Chains: Socialism and The Cultural Revolution*
(London: Muller, 1937), p. 250.

the sake of these things—in order that as much of them as possible may at sometime exist—that anyone can be justified in performing any public or private duty; . . . they are the *raison d'etre* of virtue; it is they . . . that form the rational ultimate end of human action and the sole criterion of social progress. . . .[1]

The leading works were rebellious and experimental: the "debunking" of Lytton Strachey, whose *Eminent Victorians* (1918), opened the age, and Aldous Huxley; the revolt against realism of James Joyce and Virginia Woolf; the blood and sex mysticism of D. H. Lawrence. T. S. Eliot, who struck out on his own from the "Georgians" with *Prufrock* (1917) and *Poems* (1920), published *The Waste Land* (1922) most appropriately in the same year that the last volume of Georgian poetry appeared. *The Waste Land*, in addition to being a consummate work of art, is also an invaluable social document, telling us more about the spirit of the times than volumes of history and criticism.

Eliot's masterpiece is the distillation of the disquiet, the pessimism, the utter despair of man isolated in the wasteland of a mechanical civilization:

> *What are the roots that clutch, what branches grow*
> *Out of this stony rubbish? Son of man,*
> *You cannot say, or guess, for you know only*
> *A heap of broken images, where the sun beats,*
> *And the dead tree gives no shelter, the cricket no relief,*
> *And the dry stone no sound of water.*[2]

Western man is part of a gigantic machine, which like a treadmill is directionless. The esotericism of *The Waste Land*, with its complex symbolism and literary allusion, and the erudition of elaborate footnotes, is in harmony with the

[1] G. E. Moore, as quoted, no source given, in J. K. Johnstone, *The Bloomsbury Group: A Study of E. M. Forster, Lytton Strachey, Virginia Woolf, and their Circle* (London: Secker and Warburg, 1954), p. 41.
[2] T. S. Eliot, "The Waste Land", *Poems: 1909–1925* (London: Faber and Gwyer, 1925), p. 66.

spirit of the twenties. This is the development of a new
mandarinism, a withdrawal in revulsion from all social and
political responsibility—creating and writing for the initi-
ates of the closed circle.

The disgust with the futility of modern life as expressed by
The Waste Land, the alienation from society, and the utter disbelief, profoundly influenced young poets of the thirties like
Auden, Spender, Day Lewis, and John Cornford. Julian
Bell, perceptive son of Clive and Vanessa Bell, friend of Guy
Burgess and John Lehmann, saw the radicalization of the
young Cambridge intellectuals as "an attempt of a second
'post-war generation' to escape from the Waste Land".[1] The
attempt to escape from the loneliness of their isolation, from
the shipwreck of western values, and the desire for a refuge-
—these have all been suggested by R. H. S. Crossman as
being at the roots of the conversion to communism in the
thirties.[2]

It was the wasteland of capitalist Britain in the depression,
the drying up of the economy and the distress of the population, that brought the first lines of anguish from the poets.
Auden portrayed the blot of the Midlands:

Smokeless chimneys, damaged bridges, rotting wharves and choked
*   canals,*
Tramlines buckled, smashed trucks lying on their side across the rails;
Power-stations locked, deserted, since they drew the boiler fires:
Pylons fallen or subsiding, trailing dead high-tension wires. . . .[3]

The spectre of unemployment is at the centre of the wasteland of Stephen Spender:

> *They lounge at corners of the street*
> *And greet friends with a shrug of shoulder*

[1] Julian Bell, Letter to the *New Statesman and Nation*, Vol. VI, New
Series (Dec. 9, 1933), p. 731.
[2] R. H. S. Crossman, ed., *The God That Failed* (rev. ed.; New York:
Bantam Books, 1954), pp. 4–7.
[3] W. H. Auden, *Poems* (2nd ed., London: Faber and Faber, 1933), No.
XXII, p. 73.

And turn their empty pockets out,
The cynical gestures of the poor.

Now they've no work, like better men
Who sit at desks and take much pay
They sleep long nights and rise at ten
To watch the hours that drain away.

I'm jealous of the weeping hours
They stare through with such hungry eyes
I'm hounded by these images
I'm haunted by their emptiness.[1]

Day Lewis voiced his disgust at the cultural degeneration of
England,

Where the offal of action, the rinsings of thought
From a stunted peer for a penny can be bought.[2]

To understand how the wasteland of the mandarins of the
twenties could become the bourgeois decay of the communist intellectuals of the thirties, it is necessary to glance at one
of the most significant features of the intellectuals' perspective of the twenties: the lack of interest in politics. The
political sophisticates of the thirties were the political illiter-
ates of the twenties. Cyril Connolly remarked that in the
Oxford of his youth

... politics consisted of an occasional walking tour in
Albania. ... We would no sooner have attended a political meeting than we would have gone to church and we
were greatly impressed, in a ninetyish way, by money and
titles and the necessity of coming into closer contact with
them.[3]

[1] Stephen Spender, *Poems* (London: Faber and Faber, 1933) No. XVI,
p. 29.
[2] C. Day Lewis, "Poems from the Magnetic Mountain", No. 16, in
Michael Roberts, ed., *New Country: Prose and Poetry by the Authors of New
Signatures* (London: Hogarth Press, 1933), p. 224.
[3] Cyril Connolly, "A London Diary", *New Statesman and Nation*, Vol.
XIII, New Series (January 16, 1937), p. 73.

The outlook was much the same at Cambridge, as Christopher Isherwood testified:

> It seems odd now to think of the two of us [Isherwood and Upward] so excited, so passionately self-absorbed, in that little fog-bound room, thirteen years ago—declaiming poetry, jumping on the table, shouting "J'en appelle!" appealing to Wilfred or the Watcher in Spanish, keeping a journal of our imaginary lives called *The Diary of Two Shapes*, leaving on each others' breakfast-trays a series of indecent stories about Laily and the dons, in which we, the narrators, figured as "Mr. Hynd" and "Mr. Stern"—odd, when one remembers that this was the winter of Hitler's Munich Putsch, of Mussolini's final campaign against the democrats, of the first English Labour Government, of Lenin's death. Hitler's name was, I suppose, then hardly known to a dozen people in Cambridge. Mussolini was enjoying a certain popularity: rugger and rowing men, at this epoch, frequently named their terriers "Musso". The Labour Government and all its works were, for ourselves, comprehended in the withering word "politics" and therefore automatically dismissed as boring and vile. As for Lenin, he was a vaguely exotic figure, labelled along with Trotsky, in our hazy minds as an "anarchist", and therefore worthy of mild benevolence. I think that, if we had seen his photograph, with the short stabbing beard and the Mongolian eyes, we might even have patronizingly pronounced him "rats".[1]

Poetry was the central topic of conversation at Cambridge, according to Julian Bell, who upheld Isherwood's observation that politics was seldom considered or discussed.[2] John Lehmann turned to politics only after he had gone down from Cambridge, largely owing to the influence of Leonard Woolf,

[1] Christopher Isherwood, *Lions and Shadows: An Education in the Twenties* (2nd ed., London: Methuen, 1953), pp. 73–74.
[2] Bell, *loc. cit.*

and the fall of the Labour Government in 1931.[1] Christopher Caudwell was so engrossed in his writing and in aeronautics that he showed no awareness of politics until he was twenty-seven, when he spent a summer in Cornwall saturating himself in the communist classics.[2] W. H. Auden is reported to have detested politics at Oxford. His attention was later directed to politics through his interest in psychology, but he made no serious study of it as he did of religion.[3]

The disinterest in politics was not confined to the literati. Joseph Needham, the biochemist, recalled that he first heard of Bolshevism in the summer of 1918.[4] As an undergraduate at Gonville and Caius College, he was primarily interested in theology and philosophy, refusing to join the Union Society because he did not care to be involved in political debates. In *The Coming Struggle for Power* (1932), John Strachey discussed at some length the political apathy of the scientists, mentioning that J. B. S. Haldane had often viewed politics as nonsense and science as the only reality.[5] Haldane contended in 1927 that the scientific mind was best employed outside politics.[6] As late as 1932 he refused to accept either the American or the Soviet ideals, believing that both would lead to the "mechanization of life and standardization of man". He confessed that he had no love for machinery, owning neither motor car nor wireless.[7] The case of the American

---

[1] John Lehmann, *The Whispering Gallery: Autobiography I* (London: Longmans, 1955), pp. 177–178.

[2] Stanley Edgar Hyman, *The Armed Vision: A Study in the Methods of Literary Criticism* (New York: Knopf, 1952), p. 168.

[3] Stephen Spender, "Oxford to Communism", *New Verse*, "Auden Double Number", Nos. 26–27 (October–November 1937), pp. 9–10; "The Dog Beneath the Gown", *New Statesman and Nation*, Vol. LI (June 9, 1956), p. 656; "Profile of a Poet: W. H. Auden", *Observer*, December 9, 1956, p. 5.

[4] Needham, *Time: The Refreshing River* (London: Allen and Unwin, 1943), pp. 11–12.

[5] John Strachey, *The Coming Struggle for Power* (London: Gollancz, 1932), p. 185.

[6] J. B. S. Haldane, *Possible Worlds and Other Essays* (London: Chatto and Windus, 1927), p. 187.

[7] J. B. S. Haldane, *The Inequality of Man and Other Essays* (London: Chatto and Windus, 1932), p. 227.

physicist, J. Robert Oppenheimer, is somewhat similar.[1] Prior to his political awakening in the period of the Spanish Civil War, his isolation from domestic and world events was such that he was unaware of the Wall Street crash until some years after its occurrence. He had read neither newspapers nor popular magazines such as *Time* or *Harper's*, nor possessed a radio or telephone, nor voted in an election.

Consequently, the intellectuals of the thirties who were educated in the twenties came to politics suddenly with little previous political interest or experience. This political indifference was joined to a restless state of mind induced by what they saw as a wasteland from which no escape seemed possible. All this—the disillusion, scepticism, uneasiness, and political indifference—signifies nihilism. And when during the domestic and international crises of the thirties the world seemed on the verge of collapse, these nihilists discovered communism. Through it, they believed, lay the hope of escape, not by the way of thought—for had not thought proved impotent?—but by action, by transforming the wasteland of fact and idea into a verdant paradise.

W. H. Auden recently characterized the present age as one of frivolity rather than cruelty, offering the Nazi persecution of the Jews as an example.[2] This was no repetition of the inquisition, for the Nazis did not seriously believe that the Jews were subversive. It was simply a case of doing something, of doing anything. Killing and torturing Jews, bestial as it was, satisfied this craving to act. In a far less malignant fashion, the desire to act was widespread among the British intellectuals of the thirties. Action became a value in itself. Even the late John Maynard Keynes could upon occasion justify his position by this criterion. In the discussions of the Economic Advisory Council, formed in 1930 to assist the Labour Government, finding one of his proposals rejected he proceeded to recommend the opposite,

[1] John Mason Brown, *Through These Men: Some Aspects of Our Passing History* (London: Hamish Hamilton, 1956), p. 285.
[2] W. H. Auden, ed., *Kierkegaard* (London: Cassell, 1955), p. 16.

with the explanation: "The impossible thing is to do nothing. If you won't do what I think is right at least you should do the opposite." [1] Miss Storm Jameson, novelist and socialist, accused the British Labour Party of inaction:

> What matters in all this is that past experience, as well as all we know about human nature, warns us that socialism, like any other faith, loses its power with us in measure as it ceases to be a faith and becomes an establishment. Communism, like Fascism, lives because it gives the people something hard to do. Go out and get your head broken at Olympia. Stand for hours in the rain selling the *Daily Worker*. The command "Go" is a force releasing and re-creating energy. The prohibition "Don't go" creates nothing except apathy and the feeling of discouragement and emptiness. If our leaders said to us, "Go and demonstrate for Socialism", that would be something. They don't. They say "Sit at home, draw the curtains, keep calm; don't get excited, enthusiasm is unnecessary unless we happen to want it for some gesture allowed for in the plan of action we keep filed for use some time". The *Daily Herald* is waved before our eyes, inducing hypnotic sleep. *The Clarion* is withdrawn and an abomination like unto any other capitalist-press picture substituted. [2]

The attraction of the "Go" of communism is well summarized by Louis MacNeice in his article replying to Mrs. Woolf's "leaning tower" thesis. He declared that Marx exerted such a powerful influence upon the writers of the thirties, not on account of his economics or his theory of history, but because he had stressed the importance of changing bourgeois society. [3] The magic of communism in the thirties

---

[1] This account was given by Professor G. D. H. Cole, also a member of the Economic Advisory Council, at a celebration of the twenty-fifth anniversary of the New Fabian Research Bureau. See report in *Manchester Guardian*, July 10, 1956, p. 14.

[2] Storm Jameson, "To a Labour Party Official", *Left Review*, No. 2 (November 1934), pp. 32–33.

[3] Louis MacNeice, "The Tower that Once", *Folios of New Writing* (Spring, 1941), p. 39.

is to be found in Marx's eleventh "Thesis on Feuerbach":
"The philosophers have only *interpreted* the world, in various
ways; the point, however, is to change it."

The mandarins of the twenties had already contemplated
the world. The result was a cul-de-sac of disbelief. It was
now the business of the intellectuals of the thirties to act.
Their poetry reveals an overwhelming concern with action.
Auden demanded:

> *Shut up talking, charming in the best suits to be had in town,*
> *Lecturing on navigation while the ship is going down.*
>
> *If we really want to live, we'd better start at once to try;*
> *If we don't, it doesn't matter, but we'd better start to die.*[1]

In what was perhaps his most popular poem of the decade,
"Spain 1937", he announced that this was the age of action
and struggle, not of contemplation. Moreover, if men did
not act while the time was ripe, history would neither help
nor pardon them. Day Lewis professed:

> *Revolution, revolution*
> *Is the one correct solution—*
> *We've found it and we know it's bound to win.*
> *Whatever's biting you, here's a something will put life in you. . . .*[2]

The "Hymn" of Rex Warner concluded:

> *Now you can join us, and all together sing All*
> *Power not tomorrow but now in this hour, all*
> *Power to lovers of life, to workers, to the hammer, the sickle,*
> *the blood.*
>
> *Come then companions. This is the spring of blood, heart's*
> *heyday, movement of masses, beginning of good.*[3]

Charles Madge offered the following advice to the intellectuals:

[1] Auden, *Poems* (1933), No. XXII, p. 76.
[2] C. Day Lewis, "A Time to Dance", *A Time to Dance and Other Poems*
(London: Hogarth Press, 1935), p. 62.
[3] R. E. Warner, "Hymn" in Michael Roberts, *op. cit.*, p. 256.

But we have left school now; we turn the pages
Of a larger atlas; telegrams come in
From China, and the world is mapped on our brains
Rainbow from cell to cell. Look up and see
The new planet come to anchor. Turn the pages,
Go through with us the difficult early stages.
You watch, you cheer. But how much better in
The team itself. Half-time's late to begin.
If this sharp sense of life is in your brains,
Help us to bear these bitter growing pains
Theory and practice once in contact, see
The sparks fly. Comrades, yours fraternally. . . .[1]

One of the most interesting examples of this emphasis upon action is not found in the poetry or the novels of the intellectuals, but in a theory of art and science advanced by the amazing young poet and journalist, Christopher Caudwell.[2] He was deeply influenced by the Marxist instrumentalist theory of knowledge. According to this conception knowledge arises from man, the subject of sensation acting upon the object of sensation. All theory, therefore, is generated out of man's struggle with nature and society. Proceeding from these premises, Caudwell argues that science and art are guides to action. Science, it is true, provides an understanding of the world of outer reality. But before reality can be comprehended, it must be acted upon, opened up, manipulated by men acting in close association. Art is the understanding of inner reality, the inner universe of feeling and desire. The artist reveals this universe by "effectively experimenting with selected pieces of external reality".[3]

Neither science nor art, the one whose goal is truth, the other directed towards the production of beauty, result from

[1] Charles Madge, "Letter to the Intelligentsia", in Roberts, *op. cit.*, p. 233.
[2] See Christopher Caudwell, *Illusion and Reality: A Study of the Sources of Poetry* (London: Macmillan, 1937), pp. x–xi, 171–175, 293–301; and the same author's *Further Studies in a Dying Culture*, edited with preface by Edgell Rickword (London: The Bodley Head, 1949), pp. 94–98.
[3] Caudwell, *Illusion and Reality*, p. 293.

passive contemplation. They are the ends of a social process, of men acting in concert upon the external world. In each instance, only an abstract of the real world, a fragment, is handled. The difference between the two is that science is interested in relating its extract to the whole of the real world, whereas art aims at linking its "fragment" to the inner world of feeling. Hence, science and art are complementary. Together they can symbolize a complete universe, an organic whole. This symbolization depends upon the continual *conflict* between man and nature, between inner feeling and external reality. At any given time, science and art represent the accumulation of the past, one of truth, the other of beauty. This accumulation must serve to guide our further experimentation; hence the meaning of the statement that science and art are guides to action. The revolutionary creed of Marxism is the one systematic world outlook that gives proper emphasis to the idea of action. It is the master theory of activism, adherence to which entails an activistic conception of science and art. What better illustration of the obsession of the intellectuals of the thirties with the idea of action than in these views of Caudwell! Action becomes the criterion of politics as well as the standard of truth and beauty. This is no more than the logical conclusion of the nihilistic assumption.

The question arises as to the difference between fascism and communism from the standpoint of the appeal to the intellectual. Since fascism is activism, *par excellence*, and since the desire for action was such a potent force motivating the intellectuals, why did they not turn to the right instead of the left? Some of the poems written by members of the left seemed to differ little from the romantic pronouncements of the idealists on the right. This is true of Auden's *The Orators* (1932).[1] His exultation of violent political change was to be expected. Its surprise is the almost mystical worship of power and force, the adulation of an elite of the heroes of the

---

[1] W. H. Auden, *The Orators: An English Study* (London: Faber and Faber (1932), pp. 32, 94–95, 100–101.

air. An eroticism of masculine virility permeates the whole. There is a disquieting and irrational contempt for thought, and an emphasis upon work as an outlet for desire and anxiety. The masses are treated in a rather condescending and even disdainful manner. A sympathy for the underdog and a concern for the agonies of the world are notably absent.

The embryo of fascist romanticism in the work of Auden is striking, but should not have been completely unanticipated. Nihilism and activism are a common denominator of both communism and fascism. Fascism, however, promises nothing but more nihilism and greater activism until the world is consumed by hell fire. A fascist orgy of hatred and cruelty is not the most attractive enticement to those brought up in liberal democratic surroundings. Communism, at least, appears to offer something to men who can be moved by an appeal to the reasonable and to the humanitarian. As Professor Michael Polanyi has indicated, the great appeal of communism is its congruence with the two cardinal compulsions of the modern age, the scientific and the moral.[1] Communism claims to be the scientific harbinger of social justice on a universal scale. It pledges, in harmony with certain of the traditions of western civilization, a glorious future of human brotherhood to be secured by the scientific mastery of history and the rational control of society. The British intellectuals found in communism a ready-made instrument of action to be wielded in their nihilistic attack upon bourgeois values. The positive elements of communism constitute the other force of its attraction. The pure negativism of fascism was not for the heirs of liberalism. Escape from the wasteland was to be secured not only by involvement in deed, but also by a dream of the future:

> We shall build tomorrow
> A new clean town
> With no more sorrow
> Where lovely people walk up and down

[1] Michael Polanyi, *Personal Knowledge: Towards a Post-Critical Philosophy* (London: Routledge and Kegan Paul, 1958), pp. 226–248.

We shall all be strong
We shall all be young
No more tearful days, fearful days
Or unhappy affairs
We shall all pull our weight
In the ship of state
Come out into the sun.[1]

A vision of the future would be of little comfort if there was
not some assurance of its eventuality. Communism did exactly this by claiming to have discovered the laws of history
upon which was erected the Marxist science of society. To
the nihilist in search of an escape from the wasteland, communism extended the "scientific" system of Marxism. It
was a system of great human ingenuity, indeed of architec-
tonic grandeur, apparently logical, coherent, and reasonable.
The hesitating empiricist, bewildered by the flux of events,
no doubt turned in great relief to such a rationalistic system,
that so plausibly accounted for a great number of hitherto
inexplicable and unrelated phenomena.[2] Christopher Isherwood has related how Edward Upward's long and arduous
search for the certitude of a formula to reality ended in
communism.[3] By means of Marxism, Christopher Caudwell
was able to break down the barriers of what had been the
closed compartments of life, and to relate them all to the
general movement of society.[4] Fortified by their confidence

[1] W. H. Auden, *The Dance of Death* (London: Faber and Faber, 1933),
pp. 9–10. Also see C. Day Lewis, "Letter to a Young Revolutionary",
in Michael Roberts, *op. cit.*, p. 27. Stephen Spender has described Edward Upward's fixation with the future, blinding him to the realities of
the present, in Crossman, *op. cit.*, p. 238.

[2] See Dimitri Mirsky, *The Intelligentsia of Great Britain*, translated by
Alec Brown (London: Gollancz, 1935), p. 214 "What became important
in their eyes was not the materialistic dialectical method, but the re-
sultant fact that Marxism provides a well-built system of criteria. System,
system, system—that is what British intellectuals run crying after as soon
as they lose faith in aforementioned Nanny empiricism."

[3] Isherwood, *op. cit.*, p. 274.

[4] See preface by Edgell Rickword in Caudwell, *Further Studies in a
Dying Culture*, p. 9.

in the Marxist science, the intellectuals were able to face
the future more resolutely:

> Oh comrades, step beautifully from the solid wall
> advance to rebuild and sleep with friend on hill
> advance to rebel and remember what you have
> no ghost ever had, immured in his hall.[1]

The career of Mr. John Strachey is rather illuminating as
far as the general thesis of this chapter is concerned. Strachey
was an obvious deviant from the general pattern of the intellectuals who came of age in the nineteen-twenties. Never a
poet, he entered politics almost as soon as he went down from
Magdalen College, Oxford, joining the Labour Party in
1924 and contesting the Aston Manor Division in Birmingham. From that year he has always been deeply involved in
the politics of the left, both as observer and commentator,
and as a highly successful practitioner. Here then is the exceptional case of the experienced political activist who associated himself with communism in the nineteen-thirties. Yet
upon closer examination his commitment to communism
stemmed from roots not dissimilar to those of the intellectuals
just discussed.

Fortunately, Mr. Strachey wrote an article for the *Left Review* that sheds some light on the reasons for his conversion
to communism.[2] He begins with the rather startling statement:

> I have a stock answer to dear old ladies who ask me, "And
> why, Mr. Strachey, did you become a communist?"
> "From chagrin, madam," I reply, "from chagrin at not
> getting into the Eton Cricket Eleven."

Cautioning the reader that this remark must not be taken too
literally, Strachey explained that it was nevertheless true, if

---

[1] Spender, *Poems* (1933), No. XXII, p. 36.
[2] John Strachey, "The Education of a Communist", *Left Review*, No. 3
(December 1934), pp. 63–69. It should be pointed out that Mr.
Strachey, although calling himself a communist, and a regular and
featured contributor to the *Daily Worker*, was never a member of the
Communist Party of Great Britain.

getting into the Cricket Eleven symbolized one's adjustment to the environment as a whole. This, he added, did not mean that adherence to communism could be fully explained in terms of political neuroses; there was much more to it than that. The young men of the twenties emerged from the un-real but enchanting lives that they were leading at Oxford and Cambridge into a world of which they were in complete ignorance. The traditional moral and religious values were swept away by the tidal wave of the Great War:

> That whole unparalleled structure of repressions and taboos which the theorists and theologians of the Anglo-Saxon bourgeoisie had managed to build up had been smashed by the war, and for good or ill would not be re-paired.[1]

No longer was it possible for the intelligent and enquiring youth to pay homage to the ideological props of the British ruling class. A growing cynicism in regard to the Established Church, a demand for sexual freedom, and an interest in birth control were the earliest symptoms of youthful bewilder-ment and revolt.

Social iconoclasm was the first step of a few towards poli-tical radicalism. Strachey, among them, referred to his "political flounderings" between 1924 and 1931.[2] The fall of the Second Labour Government was crucial for his politi-cal development:

> It was necessary for me to see with my own eyes and at close range the mingled impotence and treachery of social democracy in action; to put my fingers upon the stigmata of the poltroonery of Henderson, Lansbury, and Green-wood, and my hand into the gaping spear wound of the turpitude of MacDonald, Thomas, and Snowden, in order to know that this corpse would never rise again. Not until this indisputable evidence had been thrust upon me was I

[1] John Strachey, "The Education of a Communist", *Left Review*, No. 3 (December 1934), p. 65.   [2] *Ibid.*, p. 67.

willing to admit that the British Social Democracy was not the friend, but the deadliest enemy, of the interests of the British workers.[1]

Before the election of 1931, Strachey with Allan Young, W. J. Brown, and Aneurin Bevan issued the pamphlet, *A National Policy: An Account of the Emergency Programme Advanced by Sir Oswald Mosley, M.P.*, calling for action to meet the economic crisis by steamlining the parliamentary system.[2] Shortly after its appearance Mosley resigned from the Labour Party to form the New Party with Strachey, Dr. Forgan, W. J. Brown, Lady Cynthia Mosley, Allan Young, and W. E. D. Allen of the Conservative Party. The New Party venture was, Strachey confessed, his last attempt to "avoid" communism.[3] But Strachey knew that his attempt was in vain when Mosley, facing a large crowd of hostile workers upon the steps of Ashton Town Hall, said to him, "That is the crowd that has prevented anyone doing anything in England since the war".[4] British fascism was born; Strachey resigned from the New Party, and allied himself with the communist cause. Britain, he thought at the time, had little chance; it was either communism and the "eternal cause of human culture, of science and of civilisation itself" or the "mental and moral suicide" of fascism.[5]

The theme that communism would stop the rot and save what was best in western civilization, incorporating it in a

[1] John Strachey, "The Education of a Communist", *Left Review*, No. 3 (December 1934), p. 68.

[2] Allan Young, John Strachey, W. J. Brown, Aneurin Bevan, *A National Policy: An Account of the Emergency Programme Advanced by Sir Oswald Mosley, M.P.* (London: Macmillan, 1931). Strachey, long an admirer of the unorthodox Mosley, dedicated his book *Revolution by Reason* (1925): "To O. M. who may some day do the things of which we dream". In it Strachey rejects the "inevitability of gradualness".

[3] Strachey, "The Education of a Communist", *Left Review*, p. 68.

[4] John Strachey, *The Menace of Fascism* (London: Gollancz, 1933), p. 161.

[5] Strachey, "The Education of a Communist", p. 69. Also see his first signed article in the *Daily Worker*, "Fascism in Britain—Mosley Not the Only Way", June 30, 1932, p. 6.

new way of life, appeared continuously in Strachey's subsequent writing. Dmitri Mirsky, generally complimentary of
Strachey, criticized him for this emphasis. He maintained
that it was an expression of Strachey's bourgeois origin and
upbringing. In his effort to persuade intellectuals to choose
communism and thereby save civilization, Strachey had reduced communism vis-à-vis fascism to the "lesser evil".[1]
There is considerable insight in Mirsky's criticism, for
Strachey had himself chosen communism only as a last expedient, as a "lesser evil". Although he had been a contemporary of Ralph Fox and Montagu Slater at Magdalen College, he had not joined the little band of "mild mannered
desperadoes". It was only after eight years of wandering in
the political wilderness, of uncertainty, inconsistency,
"doubts, hesitations, and errors", that he became a communist.

Strachey's early political life was a quest for an effective
instrument of action. He believed that he had ended this
search in the discovery of the communist party. The communist parties were the "organized movement to change the
world".[2] They were not conventional political parties,
apparatuses for winning votes, or debating societies, but
"New Model" parties, disciplined and centralized tools of
revolution, demanding great sacrifice from their members.
Society, said Strachey, was in a state of war. With such
weapons as the New Model parties at their disposal, the
workers and the bourgeoisie of good faith should not hesitate
to employ violence against the capitalist enemy. The alternative to such violence, whose goal was a new civilization,
would be the violence entailed in the collapse of civilization. The violence of fascism would usher in a Dark Age of
barbarianism and strife. Violence as employed by the
communists was justified, for it would be violence to
end all violence forever. But violent action by itself was not

[1] Mirsky, op. cit., p. 234.
[2] John Strachey, The Nature of the Capitalist Crisis (London: Gollancz,
1935), p. 16.

enough. It must be guided by the Marxist theory of society
that

> ... makes it possible to arrive at substantially certain,
> verifiable conclusions in sociological and political affairs.
> Thus the era of uncertainty, of guess-work, when one
> opinion was as good as another in such matters, since none
> could be verified, is over, and an epoch of genuine investi-
> gation, in which facts and deductions can be tested and
> established, has opened.[1]

So even the transition of Mr. Strachey from Oxford to the
Daily Worker follows the others; an attempt to escape from
the nihilism of the wasteland by means of the activism and
the hope of communism. Detailed evidence is lacking about
many of the intellectuals of a younger generation who discovered communism while still in the universities. The
pattern seems to be much the same, although considerably
telescoped in regard to time. Possessing a precedent for their
behaviour in the experience of the intellectuals who had
gone down in the twenties, and living in an environment in
which political radicalism had become fashionable, their
movement to communism was evidently a shorter and easier
one. Naturally there would be no long period of political
indifference, but the other characteristics of nihilism seem
to have been present.

The nihilism of the British intellectuals—their disillusion,
scepticism, and political indifference, ending in a sudden outbreak of political militancy—was not unique to the actors,
the place, or the time. Something similar had been occurring
in Europe since the latter half of the nineteenth century.[2]
The student Bazarov in Turgenev's *Fathers and Sons* (1862)
was the prototype of the nihilist. Also of interest is Raskol-
nikov of Dostoevski's *Crime and Punishment* (1865). The

---

[1] John Strachey, *What Are We To Do?* (London: Gollancz, 1938), p.
258.

[2] See the brief, but excellent analysis in Michael Polanyi, *The Logic
of Liberty; Reflections and Rejoinders* (London: Routledge and Kegan Paul,
1951), pp. 103–106; Michael Polanyi, *Personal Knowledge*, pp. 235–236.

Russian nihilistic intellectuals went to the countryside in the eighteen-seventies, cherishing the dream of founding, with the aid of the peasants, an agrarian socialist commonwealth. Nihilism was characteristic of a large segment of the Russian intellectuals until the 1917 Revolution.[1] In Germany, following the defeat in the Great War, a horde of uprooted, nihilistic intellectuals joined the Communist and Nazi movements. These were the "armed bohemians" of Konrad Heiden, the bitter, disinherited students, technicians, and members of the professional classes, who were nurtured on Stirner, Nietzsche, and George.[2] The extremist mass movements had an uncanny allurement for the non-political, those who were habitually indifferent to politics, the non-joiners and non-participants.[3] The nihilist found in communism and fascism creeds that mercilessly criticized and proposed to destroy the established order that he so hated, and that glorified violent action. Such revolutionary movements were a tempting and exciting refuge from their wasteland. Regardless of where they led or of what they accomplished, life in these movements satisfied the urge to belong and the need to act. The very dynamic of the movement was enough. No better symbol of the "armed bohemian" exists than the figure of Bertolt Brecht, whose writing even after he became a communist was haunted by his nihilism, by his passionate will to destroy.

The supreme nihilist is the secret conspirator who is ready to undermine and smash the edifice of government and society by means of spying and espionage. By embarking upon such a course he also destroys within himself those values which are the last vestiges of the civilization he so

[1] A British student of Russia recognized a similarity between the outlook of the Russian intellectuals just prior to the Revolution, and that of the British intellectuals in the twenties and early thirties; see R. D. Charques, *Contemporary Literature and Social Revolution* (London: Secker, 1933), p. 182.

[2] Konrad Heiden, *Der Fuehrer: Hitler's Rise to Power*, translated by Ralph Manheim (London: Gollancz, 1944), pp. 17, f.n. 1; 30–32.

[3] Hannah Arendt, *The Burden of Our Time* (London: Secker and Warburg, 1951), pp. 305, 310–311.

abhors: honesty, honour, duty, patriotism, and loyalty. To a certain type of advanced nihilistic intellectual, this becomes an almost mystic act of purification, the hair shirt of his new faith. Furthermore, by so doing he ceases to be a mere spinner of words and ideas. He is now a maker of history in the true sense, a secret artificer of events. More than this, he exists as a hidden force of destiny, the one reality in a world of Platonic appearances.

The pattern common to British and continental nihilism and its relation to communism is unmistakable. British nihilism has been more limited in regard to time and extent, and of a less intense and virulent nature than the continental version. This is probably true for the same reasons that British communism itself is a milder form than exists elsewhere. It is not a coincidence that Stephen Spender in 1935 published *The Destructive Element*.[1] The title, Spender tells us, came from Conrad, "In the destructive element immerse. That is the way", as quoted by I. A. Richards in his essay, "Science and Poetry" and applied by him to T. S. Eliot. Spender extends it to Henry James, Yeats, and D. H. Lawrence. What Spender fails to say, although he offers the evidence for saying it, is that the generation of writers to which he belonged, influenced by these high-priests of the "destructive element"—nihilism, had sought to escape from their dilemma by plunging into a new cult of destruction. Virginia Woolf has called attention to the destructiveness and emptiness of the work of these writers. Like Brecht they vigorously condemned bourgeois society, and were eager to assist in its destruction, but they could offer only the vaguest suggestions of what to put in its place.

---

[1] Stephen Spender, *The Destructive Element: A Study of Modern Writers and Beliefs* (London: Cape, 1935). For our purposes it does not matter that Spender in the thirties thought of destructiveness as social, the apprehension of political doom. He has recently admitted that he read into the writers of the twenties a "political cause", whereas they were actually concerned with a "moral situation". See Stephen Spender, *The Creative Element: A Study of Vision, Despair and Orthodoxy Among Some Modern Writers* (London: Hamish Hamilton, 1953), p. 10.

Instead of the oasis of escape from the wasteland which the British intellectuals believed they had discovered in communism, they found only a mirage concealing a desert of hatred, intolerance, deceit, and conformity. Richer by the experience and by the understanding that there was perhaps no easy escape, they retreated whence they came. Looking back upon the decade, Auden wrote:

> *Tonight a scrambling decade ends,*
> *And strangers, enemies and friends*
> *Stand once more puzzled underneath*
> *The signpost on the barren heath*
> *Where the rough mountain track divides*
> *To silent valleys on all sides,*
> *Endeavouring to decipher what*
> *Is written on it but cannot,*
> *Nor guess in what direction lies*
> *The overhanging precipice.*[1]

[1] W. H. Auden, *New Year Letter* (London: Faber and Faber, 1941), p. 28.

CHAPTER V

UTOPIANS OF SCIENCE

THE NIHILISTIC TENDENCIES of many scientists were evident in the "social relations of science movement" that seemed almost to dominate the British scientific world between 1932 and 1945. Rooted in the scientific-rationalist tradition as well as in communist theory, the movement captured the imaginations of scientists of varied social and political outlook: liberals, socialists, Marxists, communists, and "scientific humanists". With the exception, perhaps, of the Soviet Union, there was nowhere else a comparable movement among scientists, at least one so vigorous and influential.

The theory of science at the core of the movement owes a great deal to the rationalistic system of Historical Materialism. According to communist doctrine science is an important element of the superstructure of society, dependent for its development upon the economic structure of society. Like religion, philosophy, law, literature, and art, science is an ideology serving the material interests of the ruling classes. Hence no realistic distinction can exist between "pure" and "applied" science, as scientists under capitalism are so fond of making, for all science is ultimately an instrument of the ruling elite. It follows that the idea of the pursuit of knowledge for its own sake can only be wishful thinking. Communist ideologues continue by pointing out that in the Soviet Union two antagonistic classes, a ruling minority and an oppressed majority, no longer remain as in capitalist society. The Soviet people are divided into two friendly classes, the workers and the peasants, who are "self-governing". Science, therefore, which must always benefit the governing classes, exists in the Soviet Union for the advantage of the masses and not of the few. Only in a communist society can this occur, because all political arrangements reflect the will of the people.

A major influence upon this theory of science is apparently the activism of communism, the primacy given to practice in its relationship to theory. When the precept of Marx's eleventh "Thesis on Feuerbach" is transposed to the world of science, the consequences would seem to be obvious. Emphasis is accordingly placed upon the *application* of science, the practical results issuing from "pure" research. Practice is the standard for judging scientific achievement. The initiation, organization, and support of scientific endeavour is subject to its bearing upon the world of practice. Scientific research that does not have practical implications is pure fantasy rather than pure science. A "pure understanding" of nature, divorced from the realm of practice, is a self-contradictory concept. The understanding of nature is contingent upon human action directed to changing it, upon man's practical effort to master it. This is equally true of society. Scientific truth, as postulated by communism, is pragmatic, and therefore relative.

The Communist conception of science as propounded by some of the leading exponents of the social relations of science movement can best be summarized by contrasting it with the "liberal" idea of science.[1] In opposition to the

[1] For the "liberal" conception see the following: John R. Baker, "Counterblast to Bernalism", *New Statesman and Nation*, Vol. XVIII, New Series (July 29, 1939), pp. 174–175; John R. Baker, *Science and the Planned State* (London: Allen and Unwin 1945); John R. Baker, *The Scientific Life* (London: Allen and Unwin, 1942); John R. Baker and A. G. Tansley, "The Course of the Controversy on Freedom in Science", *Nature*, Vol. 158 (October 26, 1946), pp. 574–576; Herbert Dingle, "Science and Professor Bernal", *Science Progress*, Vol. XXXVII (April 1949), pp. 232–243; Michael Polanyi, *The Contempt of Freedom: The Russian Experiment and After* (London: Watt, 1940); Michael Polanyi, *The Logic of Liberty: Reflections and Rejoiners* (London: Routledge and Kegan Paul, 1951); Michael Polanyi, *Pure and Applied Science and Their Appropriate Forms of Organization*, Occasional Pamphlet No. 14 (Society for Freedom in Science: Dec. 1953); Michael Polanyi, *Rights and Duties of Science*, Occasional Pamphlet No. 2 (Society for Freedom in Science: June 1945); A. D. Ritchie, *Science and Politics*, Riddell Memorial Lecture, Nineteenth Series (London: Oxford University Press, 1947), pp. 9–13.

—the method of Dialectical Materialism—into all scientific disciplines. Thus the new type of intellectual culture, which dominates the mental activity of millions of workers, is becoming the greatest force of the present day.

Unquestionably the star of the papers was Bukharin's "Theory and Practice from the Standpoint of Dialectical Materialism", one of the most sophisticated treatments of this aspect of Marxism. Bukharin devoted a great deal of space to explaining the unity of theory and practice and the primacy of practice, laying the ground for the point that practice has been the source of all science. Science has existed for the purpose of extending and deepening practice in man's struggle with nature, and hence far from being self-sufficient it is intimately related to man's social life. Professor Hessen's "The Social and Economic Roots of Newton's 'Principia'" was of interest to many, because it applied the thesis elaborated by Bukharin to the study of the history of science. He attempted to demonstrate that Newton's conception of nature was a theoretical reflection of developments in navigation resulting from the social and economic forces leading men to discover new oceanic trade routes, etc. Other reports dealt with the relation of science to technology in the Soviet Union, and the organization and planning of Soviet science. The reaction of western scientists to this, their first over-all view of the progress of Soviet science and its role in the communist state, was generally favourable. They were impressed not so much by Dialectical Materialism as by the way in which the Soviet Government seemed to recognize the full worth of science, harnessing it in a rational fashion to the needs of society. Here, many felt, was an example meriting emulation.

The disillusion of the scientists with the chaotic state of political and social affairs, and their efforts to formulate a more appropriate role for science and the scientist in society, appeared with increased frequency after 1931. Sir Richard Gregory and his distinguished journal, *Nature*, were important factors in developing and spreading the ideas of the movement. A leading article in *Nature* of September 26, 1931, evidently written by Gregory, deplored the fact that governmental administrators had failed to appreciate the possibilities of science, permitting scientists little or no part in framing national policy. Less than a year later he stated that:

> Science not only creates new means of existence and new sources of employment by the discovery of new principles and substances, but also places extended use of power at the disposal of everyone. . . . Modern technical achievement and scientific thought foreshadow a new economic structure for society in which they should be used to exercise decisive influence upon the major policies of the State as well as upon their administration.[1]

A most outspoken editorial in *Nature* of July 28, 1934, proclaimed that a sharp distinction between pure and applied science was no longer tenable. Science, like any other human activity, must be planned if it is to produce optimum results in society. Any form of the planning of science would lead to a greater participation of the scientist in the activities of society. The editorial concluded by suggesting that science was capable of saving mankind if scientists were given a part in the management of society.

An early expression of social concern by an eminent British scientist was the Presidential Address of Sir Frederick Gowland Hopkins to the British Association for the Advancement of Science in 1933. He urged the formation of a "Solomon's House", composed of Britain's wise men. Nonpartisan in outlook, it would synthesize knowledge, appraise its progress and its impact upon society. Another President of the British Association, the renowned geographer, Sir Josiah Stamp, devoted his Address in 1936 to the social im-

---

[1] R. A. Gregory in *Progress and the Scientific Worker* (July–August 1932) as quoted in W. H. G. Armytage, *Sir Richard Gregory* (London: Macmillan, 1957), p. 117.

plications of science. A series of broadcasts upon "Science in the Changing World" was given on the B.B.C. during 1933. The following year Ritchie Calder, the Scientific Correspondent of Labour's *Daily Herald*, advocated the replacement of the House of Lords by a "Senate of Scientists".[1] Professor J. B. S. Haldane wrote to *Nature*, January 13, 1934, that a refusal to apply scientific method to the conduct of human affairs would precipitate the failure of the political and economic system, and with it the destruction of science itself. Seven years earlier he had written that politicians knew "ten times" as much about mass psychology as the psychologists, and that science in its present infancy could best be employed outside the political sphere.[2] If he thought otherwise, he himself would become a politician. Haldane's subsequent change of mind signified a general trend among the scientists of this period. Hyman Levy was willing to go a step farther than Haldane did in 1934. Reasoning that social experimentation would require a change in the status quo, he contended that the scientist must attach himself to a political movement that would strive for social change.[3] Only in this way would it be possible, Levy alleged, to possess government based on science, with society as the laboratory, and mankind the human material for experimentation. In the foreword to *The Frustration of Science* (1935), a collection of essays by Sir Daniel Hall, Bernal, Blackett, Professor V. H. Mottram, and others, Professor Frederick Soddy of Oxford advanced the opinion that

> The solution is for the public to acknowledge its real master [science], and, for its own safety, insist on being ruled not by the reflection of a reflection, but direct by

[1] Ritchie Calder, *The Birth of the Future*, foreword by Sir Frederick Gowland Hopkins (London: Barker, 1934), pp. 271 ff.

[2] J. B. S. Haldane, *Possible Worlds and Other Essays* (London: Chatto and Windus, 1927), pp. 183–189.

[3] Hyman Levy, *Science in an Irrational Society*, Conway Memorial Lecture, April 25, 1934; introduction by J. B. S. Haldane (London: Watts, 1934), pp. 60–61; Hyman Levy, *Thinking* (London: Newnes, n.d.), p. 207.

those who are concerned with the creation of its wealth rather than its debts.

The celebrated biologist, Julian Huxley, was also critical of democratic politics. Edward Conzé has recorded that Huxley's retort to the suggestion that he should stand for Parliament was that his life had been guided by a passion for truth and not for its "obscuration".[1] In *If I Were Dictator* Huxley pleaded for the intelligent control of socio-economic phenomena by the application of scientific method.[2] His ideal of an "organic" community would be composed of a hierarchy of corporations controlled by boards, representing ownership, management, and employees. Elections in the Huxleyan utopia would become superfluous, replaced by the most up-to-date scientific devices of public-opinion polling and sampling. Two public broadcasting corporations, one of the "Right" and the other of the "Left", in cultural matters as well as public affairs, would be substituted for the present party system. A Central Planning Council and a Science Council would replace Parliament, which Huxley claimed was nothing more than a "Talking-shop", over-worked and lacking expertise. Throughout the thirties Huxley espoused "some sort of scientific control of society in place of the unscientific game of politics and the mere play of impersonal economic forces. . . ."[3] Dr. Joseph Needham's Herbert Spencer Lecture of 1937 was an interesting attempt to apply science to an analysis of social development.[4] The whole universe since the beginning of time was envisioned as a "cosmic process" or system generating increasingly higher organizational wholes: physical, biological, and social. The

[1] Edward Conzé, *The Scientific Method of Thinking: An Introduction to Dialectical Materialism* (London: Chapman and Hall, 1935), p. 53.

[2] Julian Huxley, *If I Were Dictator* (London: Methuen, 1934), pp. 16, 19, 30 ff., 50–53. This is one of a series of volumes of the same title written by Lord Raglan, Lord Dunsany, St. John Ervine *et al.*

[3] Julian Huxley, foreword to Charles Madge and Tom Harrisson, *Mass Observation*, Mass Observation Series No. One (London: Muller, 1937), p. 6.

[4] Joseph Needham, *Integrative Levels: A Revaluation of the Ideas of Progress*, the Herbert Spencer Lecture (Oxford: Clarendon Press, 1937).

evolution of these organisms has been characterized by an increase in each of the following: the number of parts, their complexity of structure and relations; the "centralization" and "efficiency" of control over them; and the independence of the external environment. Needham's extension of this conception to society is exceedingly interesting. He began by maintaining that there existed a continuity between the inorganic, biological, and social orders. In so doing he was reviving the idea of progress on a long time scale. Although generally praising the Social Darwinism of Spencer, he firmly rejected the belief that capitalistic individualism was the crowning achievement of social evolution. Our civilization would be superseded by the still higher form of collectivism. This transition would be of the most revolutionary nature, comparable to the transformation of "lifeless protein to the living cell". In addition it was "inevitable", a necessary unfolding of the "cosmic process". For several reasons collectivistic society was a higher dialectical level than the capitalistic form from which it developed. The classlessness of the collective organism featured a complexity of structure and relationships far in advance of its class-stratified predecessor. Similarly, the common ownership of production and the conscious control of society and nature represented a "progressive" leap, like the biological superiority of the human brain to the twenty or thirty ganglia of the annelid.

By 1938 the various ideas which had been expressed in the course of the previous few years were so influential that *Nature* thought it necessary to issue a twenty-page supplement recording the opinions of leading British scientists upon the proposal for establishing a Society for the Study of Social Relations of Science.[1] The forty contributors included Haldane, Chalmers Mitchell, Huxley, Needham, Sir John Russell, Sir Henry Tizard, Bernal, Blackett, Lindemann (the late Lord Cherwell), Levy, Bragg, Hopkins, Wells, Laski, Morris Ginsberg, and A. V. Hill. For the most part the

[1] *Nature*, Vol. 141 (April 23, 1938), pp. 723–744. The background and history of this scheme are described in Armytage, *op. cit.*, pp. 158–169.

E

contributors supported such an organization, referring to the
great progress of science, and the dismal lag of social and
economic organization. Only four of the forty offered objec-
tions or warnings: Wells, Ginsberg, Blackett, and Professor
John L. Myres. Ginsberg felt that the techniques and
theories of the natural sciences could not be efficaciously
applied to social problems. Professor Myres considered that
scientists should not control "practical applications" of
science because they involved value judgments, and moral
and political choices having little to do with science. Nothing
came of the Society, but in the August of 1938, at the meeting
of the British Association, a Division for the Social and International Relations of Science was established under the
chairmanship of Sir Richard Gregory. The movement had
at last been formally recognized by the peers of British
science.

As the decade progressed the scientists' complaints about
conventional democratic politics became more numerous.
The biometrician, Lancelot Hogben, author of two best-
selling works, *Mathematics for the Million* (1936) and *Science for
the Citizen* (1938), declared that in this age of engineers man's
fate must not rest in the hands of "pamphleteers", "clever
talkers", "debaters", and "quoters".[1] Sir Peter Chalmers
Mitchell, the noted zoologist, was living in retirement in
Malaga when Franco's forces captured the city. He was
allowed to return to England, while his house guest, Arthur
Koestler, a member of the German Communist Party, was
imprisoned. Koestler's experience was related in *Spanish
Testament* (1938), dedicated to Chalmers Mitchell. In his
autobiography Chalmers Mitchell confessed that he had
passed to the extreme left not because of some sort of "post-
war neurasthenia", but because of his loss of hope.[2] Neither
politics nor religion, he thought, had proved of any aid to

[1] Lancelot Hogben, *Science for the Citizen* as quoted in Robert Graves
and Alan Hodges, *The Long Week-End: A Social History of Great Britain,
1918–1939* (London: Faber and Faber, 1940), p. 394.

[2] Peter Chalmers Mitchell, *My Fill of Days* (London: Faber and Faber,
1937), pp. 410–412, 416 ff.

man in his hour of need. All that was left was one of two
choices: the "ruthless tyranny" of fascism or the inspiring
ideal of communism.

The "political obscurantism" of the times was denounced
by F. LeGros Clark, a well-known nutritionist, who asked
how the transformation from a "C3" to an "A1" community
could be realized. Science was the answer:

> Science has no politics; it stretches out to pervade and
> at last control with its mild influence every sphere of
> human life, politics among the rest. Then science is, if you
> like it, supremely political after all.[1]

If scientists remained aloof from politics because they had
found it "to be a disreputable game" then, according to
Clark "they had better try to transform it into a pastime with
clean, scientific rules". Scientists should make every effort to
"inspire public and politicians alike with a taste for the
scientific decencies". Writing to *Nature* in January 1941,
Robert H. F. Finlay decried party government, calling for
scientific government whose aim would be "efficiency and
economy". Perhaps the most outspoken attack was that of
the agricultural chemist, Hugh Nicol, who blamed the
irrational operation of society upon the politician with his
abysmal ignorance of rudimentary scientific concepts

> . . . such as limiting values and the elementary theory of
> errors. It appears that his notions of equilibria are re-
> presented by arithmetical averages in a static two-phase
> system, and that he can conceive of no interactions more
> complex than those of a game of chess—in which one piece
> is moved at a time. The chances are even that subjective
> decisions will be wrong; nor is any test of their validity
> possible.[2]

---

[1] F. LeGros Clark, ed., *National Fitness: A Brief Essay on Contemporary Britain*, foreword by Major-General Sir Robert McCarrison (London: Macmillan, 1938), p. 5.

[2] Hugh Nicol, letter to *Nature*, Vol. 147 (June 28, 1941), p. 808.

The high point of the onslaught upon democratic politics was achieved by the Cambridge embryologist, C. H. Waddington, in *The Scientific Attitude* (1941). His principal thesis was that human affairs could be set right if we adopt a "scientific attitude", defined as "the matter of fact as against the romantic, the objective as against the subjective, the empirical, the unprejudiced, the *ad hoc* as against the *a priori*".[1] Modern culture—art, literature and philosophy— has completely failed to show a way to a new outlook and way of life, to a "promised land". Although, Waddington admitted, science had not been overly successful in this respect, it offered more hope than any other branch of human knowledge and culture: "What poets or artists or philosophers are there to match against the great scientists whose work has become of importance since the last war . . .?"[2] Science, insisted Waddington, was the sole intellectual movement to wage war steadfastly against fascism. Religion, democracy, and capitalism would be able to offer science little competition as a new basis for life after the war. They are, he implied, finished as vital forces in the modern world. In addition to accomplishing the material renovation of western civilization, science would provide the foundation of a moral renaissance by establishing a naturalistic system of ethics.[3] Democratic politics is soon disposed of by Waddington as a "pulsing pusillanimous rigmarole".[4] Elsewhere he compared the purity of the world of science to the corruption of the world of politics:

> Scientists have long been used to inhabiting a world in which the final word is left to the test of experience, but such a test is inevitably incompatible with a world ordered in accordance with official status and personal prestige.[5]

[1] C. H. Waddington, *The Scientific Attitude* (Harmondsworth, Middlesex: Penguin Books, 1941), p. 54.

[2] *Ibid.*, pp. 64–65.   [3] *Ibid.*, p. 26.

[4] *Ibid.*, p. 123.   This picturesque phrase seems to have been omitted from the second edition of the work published in 1948.

[5] C. H. Waddington, " Science and Government ", *Political Quarterly*, Vol. XIII (January–March 1942), p. 4.

Marxism, however, differed from democratic politics in that many of its basic ideas were almost identical with those underlying science.[1] It has made mistakes, Waddington conceded, particularly in its oversimplified psychology and in certain of its predictions in the field of social action. Nevertheless, these errors should not be sufficient reason to require the separation of Marxism and science.[2] By closely allying itself with science, communism would stand to gain more rigorous and accurate methods for social control, experiment, and prediction. On the other hand communism would greatly benefit science because it recognized the true value of science and was eager to put the results of scientific work into practice for the good of mankind. Moreover, communism offered science an ideal of a humane and equalitarian world state, and a vast laboratory for controlled social experiment.

Waddington was never quite willing to commit himself openly, as Bernal was, to the dictum that "science is communism". But there is this implication in portions of *The Scientific Attitude*. This is even clearer from what he added to the second edition about the "Operational Research" teams of scientists employed upon special projects by the British Government during the war.[3] Bernal believed that scientific activity epitomized the collective life. In scientific activity the individual was subordinated to a common purpose. Close and intimate collaboration, and the free exchange of ideas, advice, and criticism were absolutely essential.[4] The small work group such as is found in a modern scientific laboratory or an Operational Research team, rather than the ballot or the political party, is the *sine qua non* of true democracy.[5]

[1] Waddington, *The Scientific Attitude*, p. 81.
[2] *Ibid.*, p. 84.
[3] C. H. Waddington, *The Scientific Attitude* (Second and Revised ed.; West Drayton, Middlesex: Penguin Books, 1948), pp. 118 ff.
[4] J. D. Bernal, *The Social Function of Science* (London: Routledge, 1939), pp. 415–416.
[5] J. D. Bernal, *The Freedom of Necessity* (London: Routledge and Kegan Paul, 1949), p. 11.

The most thorough theoretical exposition of the movement, J. D. Bernal's *The Social Function of Science*, was published in 1939, to be followed two years later by another influential volume, J. G. Crowther's *The Social Relations of Science*. The newly formed Social Relations Division of the British Association convened a conference on "Science and World Order" in September 1941 at which the Soviet Ambassador Maisky announced that "there is no place in the U.S.S.R. for pure science".[1] The Association of Scientific Workers, a long-time crusader for the movement, sponsored a mass meeting in January 1943 on the Planning of Science, attended by many scientific notables. If this meeting marked the climax of the movement, the gathering of the British Association's Social Relations Division in December 1945 could be called the beginning of the end. The enthusiasm for the idea of planned science and for the precepts that sustained it was on the ebb.

The decline of the movement was largely due to the growth of a small but extremely articulate and hard-hitting opposition among the scientists. In 1939 their protests began to appear: first with Dr. John D. Baker's vigorous "Counter-blast to Bernalism" in the *New Statesman and Nation* of July 29, and second with Professor Polanyi's cogent "Rights and Duties of Science" in *The Manchester School of Social and Economic Studies* of October. Next, a running battle between A. V. Hill, Polanyi, and Baker on one side, and Bernal and Haldane on the other, took place in the correspondence columns of the *New Statesman* at the beginning of 1940.[2] The contention was over the restrictions upon the freedom of science in the U.S.S.R. In the same year Professor Polanyi published *The Contempt of Freedom*, an acute analysis of the theory and practice of the planning of science in the Soviet Union, and there appeared the first pertinent criticism of the movement

[1] As quoted in *Nature*, Vol. 148 October 25, 1941, p. 497.

[2] See the following references in the *New Statesman and Nation*, Vol. XIX, New Series: January 27, 1940, pp. 105–106; February 3, 1940, pp. 137–138; February 10, 1940, p. 174; February 17, 1940, p. 206; February 24, 1940, pp. 242–243; March 2, 1940, p. 276.

in *Nature*, September 21, 1940, by E. F. Caldin of Queen's College, Oxford:

> That science is pursued in the first place for its truth; that it cannot dogmatize about questions which touch on philosophy; that economics is not independent of ethics; that human nature demands culture, family life, and spiritual values before material comfort—all these considerations are too often ignored.

It was in 1940 that the Society for Freedom in Science was founded mainly through the efforts of Dr. Baker, Professor Polanyi, and Professor A. G. Tansley to combat what they believed to be the increasing menace to the freedom of science represented by the movement and its aim of a planned science. *Nature* refused to publish a statement of the objectives of the Society.[1] But by the personal work of its members, by lectures, publications, conferences, and after the war by a series of "Occasional Pamphlets", the Society largely succeeded in discrediting the movement. Not until the end of 1946 would *Nature* publish the views of the Society.[2] However, since the beginning of 1941, when *Nature* published a letter from Professor Polanyi, its leading articles had become increasingly moderate.[3] This letter was an eloquent defence of the liberal view of science:

> For the last ten years we have been presented by an influential school of thought with phrases about the desirability of a social control of science, accompanied by attacks on the alleged snobbishness and irresponsibility of

[1] *The Society for Freedom in Science: Its Origin, Objects and Constitution* (3rd ed.; Oxford: Committee of The Society for Freedom in Science, 1953), p. 9. There is no mention of the Society or of the controversy in Armytage's biography of Sir Richard Gregory.

[2] John R. Baker and A. G. Tansley, "The Course of the Controversy on Freedom in Science", *Nature*, Vol. 158 (October 26, 1946), pp. 574–576.

[3] For example: "Science, Politics and Government", *Nature*, Vol. 147 (March 8, 1941), pp. 275–276; "Science in Modern Life", *Nature*, Vol. 147 (May 10, 1941), pp. 551–553.

scientific detachment. The "social control of science" has proved a meaningless phrase. Science exists only to that extent to which the search for truth is not socially controlled. And therein lies the purpose of scientific detachment. It is of the same character as the independence of the witness, of the jury, of the judge; of the political speaker and the voter; of the writer and the teacher and their public; it forms part of the liberties for which every man with an idea of truth and every man with a pride in the dignity of his soul has fought since the beginning of society.[1]

The extraordinary aspect of the movement was the absence of dissent to its central ideas among scientists educated and living in the paradigm of a liberal environment. Few seemed to be aware of the implications of their beliefs, although many would have hesitated to subscribe to the extreme views of communist sympathizers like Levy, Haldane, Bernal, and Crowther. The generalities which they did accept with a singular lack of scientific perspicacity satisfied a certain vital need. The movement's theoretical perspective was marked by its severe criticism of western society, democratic government and politics, and the pluralistic mode of life.[2] It appealed to those scientists who, like their contemporaries among the literati, viewed themselves as hopelessly isolated in a wasteland. The activistic elements of the communist theory of science attracted the nihilistic scientist. Moreover,

---

[1] *Nature*, Vol. 147 (January 25, 1941), p. 119. This letter was a reply to the leading article "Cultural Significance of Scientific Method", *Nature*, Vol. 146 (December 28, 1940), p. 817.

[2] Professor P. M. S. Blackett was never as contemptuous of politicians as were some of his colleagues. The troubles of capitalist democracy, he maintained, could not be blamed upon the stupidity of the politicians. They were far from being stupid people. Only a change in the basic economic system that would allow the introduction of complete socialist planning would cure society of its present ills. See P. M. S. Blackett, "The Frustration of Science", in *The Frustration of Science*, foreword by Frederick Soddy (London: Allen and Unwin, 1935), pp. 133-134, 139.

the nihilism and activism of the movement were rendered more palatable by the stated end of benefiting mankind, of establishing an equalitarian and humanitarian world society in which science would play a crucial role. The social relations of science movement, therefore, had, like communism, and appeal because of the nihilistic malaise of the intellectuals. It was this that had turned many of the literati to communism, and it was this that caused scientists to seek refuge in the movement.

Another reason for the attraction of the scientists to the movement may be some of its "institutional" characteristics. The fact that the communist principles of the movement were not blatantly advertised, committing its adherents to the whole of the communist faith, would appeal to those whose nihilistic affliction was relatively mild or who normally would hesitate to become associated with a political creed as radical as communism. Any degree of commitment was possible, for it was a loosely integrated intellectual movement, never formally organized or institutionalized. Those who accepted only a few of the postulates of the movement, and they were probably in the great majority, could without qualm close their minds to the beliefs of the doctrinaires and the fanatics. These in turn possessed sufficient political wisdom to welcome every variety of supporter, no matter the number or the kind of reservations. As a result the movement was able to expand rapidly, and for the same reasons its collapse came suddenly. The movement got off to a good start because a few British scientists had a first-hand opportunity of witnessing the performance of the Soviet delegation at the London Congress in 1931. Then, there were the services of some very able and articulate publicists like Huxley, Hogben, Haldane, Bernal, and Levy. In addition, the support of Sir Richard Gregory with his all-powerful journal, *Nature*, was no small factor in the continuing influence of the movement. From the very beginning the movement possessed a very small but highly effective organizational weapon in the Association of Scientific Workers, the

prototype of such organizations throughout the world. Since
1935 Hopkins, Huxley, Bernal, Blackett, and Gregory have
all been officers of the Association. It sponsored a nation-
wide distribution of Bernal's *The Social Functions of Science*, and
convoked meetings and conferences for the purpose of dis-
seminating the ideas of the movement.

A third explanation of the radicalization of the scientists is
the insatiable impulse of some to control nature and society.
In its most exaggerated form this seems to have been the
prime motivation of Professor John Desmond Bernal, outstanding physicist, Stalin Prize winner, and recently elected
honorary member of the Soviet Academy of Science. His
frightening ideas were delineated in a book published
thirty years ago, *The World, the Flesh and the Devil: An Enquiry into the Future of the Three Enemies of the Rational Soul*
(1929). Like Huxley's *Brave New World* or Orwell's *1984*,
Bernal's volume is a vision of the future, differing from them,
however, in that he enthusiastically believed in the world that
he envisioned. He has attempted to consider the future in
terms of man's scientific control in three spheres: the
physical (the "world"), the biological (the "flesh"), and the
psychological (the "devil"). We need not be detained by
Bernal's description of the future conquest of the physical
world, interesting though it is, with all the paraphernalia of
science-fiction. For our purposes the contest with the "flesh"
is much more pertinent.

"Organic" man or man as we know him is definitely
limited in his development, Bernal explains; hence if human
evolution is not to be shortly ended the physical nature of
man will have to be radically altered. The man of the future
will be in the shape of a cylinder, "rather a short" one, a
"crustacean" with an external casing of one of the fibrous
materials. Inside, the brain, very carefully supported in
order to withstand shock, will be immersed in a constantly
circulating liquid of uniform temperature, similar to a
cerebral spinal fluid. Describing in great detail each arti-
ficial organ of this mechanical man, Bernal then discusses the

possibility of "complex minds", the linking together of several brains. With such an arrangement

> . . . the individual brain will feel itself part of the whole in a way that completely transcends the devotion of the most fanatical adherent of a religious sect.
> . . . It would be a state of ecstasy in the literal sense. . . . Whatever the intensity of our feeling, however much we may strive to reach beyond ourselves or into another's mind, we are always barred by the limitations of our individuality. Here at least those barriers would be down: feeling would truly communicate itself, memories would be held in common, and yet in all this, identity and continuity of individual development would not be lost. It is possible, even probable, that the different individuals of a compound mind would not all have similar functions or even be of the same rank of importance. Division of labour would soon set in: to some might be delegated the task of ensuring the proper functioning of the others, some might specialize in sense reception and so on. Thus would grow up a hierarchy of minds that would be more truly a complex than a compound mind.[1]

More "plastic" and "variable" and yet more "permanent" and "controllable" than organic man, the new species would ultimately become the standard type, with only a few of the old allowed to exist as curiosities. The climax of human evolution might be the disappearance of

> . . . consciousness itself . . . in a humanity that has become completely etherealized, losing the close-knit organism, becoming masses of atoms in space communicating by radiation and ultimately perhaps resolving itself entirely into light.[2]

[1] J. D. Bernal, *The World, the Flesh and the Devil: An Enquiry into the Future of the Three Enemies of the Rational Soul* (London: Kegan Paul, Trench and Trubner; 1929), pp. 53–54.
[2] *Ibid.*, p. 57.

Bernal admits that this is as far as modern science can fore-
see, and whether it would be a beginning or an end he does
not know. So much for the "flesh".

The "devil", Bernal points out, is a considerably more
difficult subject for scientific control. An end must first be
made to the inner confusions and desires of man. The power
of the id must be brought into complete harmony with the
realities of the external world. The solution to the problem
does not lie in reshaping the world in the image held by the
super-ego, but rather in bringing the super-ego in line with
reality. This would be accomplished by all the scientific
refinements of persuasion and manipulation, or, as O'Brien
bluntly puts it in Orwell's hell of the future, "tearing human
minds to pieces and putting them together in new shapes of
your own choosing". The establishment of a single all-
embracing metaphysic would end once and for all the
chaotic state of the present world of thought.

Directing these revolutionary conquests of the world, the
flesh and the devil would be the elite of scientific experts.
The dawn of their scientific rule would not occur, however,
until mankind had passed from a capitalist to a communist stage of history. Successful proletarian revolution
would become the means for the eventual domination of
science. After a time, the scientific bodies of the new world
soviet state would begin to conduct experiments independent
of the control of any civilian authority, and quite beyond the
comprehension of all who were not scientists. At that
moment the actual locus of sovereignty in the state would
pass from the civil to the scientific organizations of the world
polity, and the scientists would in reality constitute the government. Science at last would become the absolute director
of human destiny.[1] The supreme canon of all action and

[1] Ten years later Bernal rejected the idea of the rule of the "scientific-
king" for two reasons: (1) the problem of transferring control; (2) the
unfitness of present-day scientists to exercise such supreme control.
Hence, the rejection is not so much on the grounds of principle as of ex-
pediency. See J. D. Bernal, *The Social Functions of Science*, p. 398.

thought, of good and evil would be "scientific progress". An elite of scientific guardians, consisting of about ten per cent of the global population, by becoming mechanized would outstrip and separate itself from the rest of humanity. Temporarily, at least, this "di-morphism" would be incomplete because of the necessity of recruiting new members from the masses. Ultimately, however, the elite would constitute a self-contained and self-perpetuating caste, holding absolute power and checked only by the norm of "scientific progress" as defined by itself.

Two important functions would be performed by these guardians of science: the maintenance of the world as "an efficient food and comfort machine", and the pursuit of scientific knowledge. Psychology and physiology would be used to canalize the energies and ambitions of the masses into "harmless" occupations, and to devise manipulative techniques for rendering them utterly tractable "under the appearance of perfect freedom". An opium of the people seems to be justified by Bernal on the grounds that it would be in the services of science and not of superstition. This description of the world of the future is concluded with the suggestion that there might not be room on the earth for two such incompatible species as the "primitive" mass man and the new scientific hero:

. . . the old mechanism of extinction will come into play. The better organized beings will be obliged in self-defence to reduce the numbers of the others, until they are no longer inconvenienced by them. If, as we may well suppose, the colonization of space will have taken place or be taking place while these changes are occurring, it may offer a very convenient solution. Mankind—the old mankind—would be left in undisputed possession of the earth, to be regarded by the inhabitants with a curious reverence. The world might, in fact, be transformed into a human zoo, a zoo so intelligently managed that its inhabitants are not aware that they are there merely for the purposes of observation and experiment.[1]

The motive underlying Bernal's invention of this new republic of science is his desire for a perfectly "rational" scientific order. Human welfare, for Bernal the ultimate end of science, has been equated with progress, and progress in turn with an ever-increasing and more refined control. Time and time again Bernal warns the reader against a static scientific culture. The essence of progress, and therefore by definition of scientific control, is its dynamism. We must go on and on in a veritable frenzy of "improving", "refining", and "controlling". Societal good depends upon the degree to which mastery over all physical, biological, and psychological phenomena has been achieved. Marxism and communism are not ends in themselves, but the best available means of achieving the transfer of power to the scientist. Dictatorship by the scientist is the apotheosis of control, complete and totalitarian. Scientific control becomes the supreme value at the cost of the subjection of ninety per cent of mankind. Society is no longer even a laboratory, but a "human zoo".

Never have we been given a better glimpse of the disastrous consequences of the Baconian axiom, that knowledge is power, carried to its logical conclusion: power for the sake of power, unmollified by any moral or immoral values. There is no resting place for Bernal as there was for Aldous Huxley's Mustapha Mond of *Brave New World*, who saw the necessity in his scientific utopia of subordinating the eternal quest for truth to considerations of *raison d'état*:

I'm interested in truth, I like science. But truth's a menace, science is a public danger. As dangerous as it's been beneficent. It has given us the stablest equilibrium in history. . . . But we can't allow science to undo its own

[1] Bernal, *The World, the Flesh and The Devil*, pp. 94–95.

good work. That's why we so carefully limit the scope of its researches. . . . We don't allow it to deal with any but the most immediate problems of the moment. All other enquiries are most sedulously discouraged.

The absence of such human Machiavellian calculation makes Bernal's vision all the more dreadful. As a scientist he cannot agree to any limitation upon the scientific dynamic, even for the sake of saving science. His tyranny of mind over man is only for the purpose of a greater tyranny, until eventually both mind and man disappear into the void, a refinement to nothingness. Is this not the ultimate in nihilism? What another Baconian, Thomas Hobbes, said about mankind aptly characterizes the Bernalians: "a perpetual and restless desire of power after power, that ceaseth only in death". But in this case the finale is total annihilation.

Another aspect of Bernal's perspective is important. We have seen that he believed the good to be progress, realized through the extension and refinement of scientific control. As science evolves, so does the good. Good then is inherent in an evolutionary movement or process. This view is shared by a number of scientists who have rejected traditional ethical theories for a naturalistic position. For instance Waddington posits the idea that the criterion of the good is not external to man, but is found in human development, both organic and societal.[1] An evolutionary stage possesses capacities that "include" and "transcend" all previous stages. It has survived, it is effective, therefore, it is good—so his reasoning goes. The direction of evolution cannot help but be in the direction of the good, the better, and ultimately the best. The duty of science in this connection is to reveal the direction of evolution and by so doing to demonstrate what is good and what is bad. Julian Huxley contends that human evolution has been proceeding towards

[1] C. H. Waddington, "The Relations Between Science and Ethics", *Nature*, Vol. 148 (September 6, 1941), pp. 270–274. Also see Waddington, *Science and Ethics* (London: Allen and Unwin, 1942).

"higher levels of organization".[1] This is progress and everything that contributes to it, such as increases in knowledge,
control, autonomy, is good. Joseph Needham agrees that
this is true in biology, and extends the principle to social
evolution.[2] Communism appears historically after capitalism, exhibiting a higher degree of organization and complexity. Communism, therefore, is more progressive than
capitalism. Relatively speaking it is good, and capitalism is
bad. Oddly enough there seems to be no higher stage of
social evolution, so communism can be called the supreme
good.

There are a number of characteristics shared by all these
views, including Bernal's. First, the criterion of the good is
determined by the direction of the evolutionary process.
Second, it follows that moral value is a relative, not a static
concept. What may be good for one time and one place is
not an eternal verity. Third, since human evolution to a
great degree depends upon man's environment, the idea of
control is intimately related to the idea of the good. At the
heart of this perspective is the emphasis upon activism, movement, process. The belief in nothing but science and its
power is in itself fundamentally activistic. We are back to
the nihilism of the intellectual, and the nihilistic core of
communism—for the communist would agree with all three
of the above statements of belief.

Finally, the scientific–rationalist tradition stemming from
Bacon, shaping the thought of H. G. Wells and Sir Richard
Gregory, and finding political expression in Benthamism,
was an important factor in preparing many scientists for a
favourable reception of the ideas of communism. Professor Bernal's enthusiasm for man's conquest of nature is
essentially Baconian.[3] But the direct influence of Bacon in the

[1] T. H. Huxley and Julian Huxley, *Evolution and Ethics 1893–1943*
(London: Pilot Press, 1947), pp. 125, 230.

[2] This argument appears throughout Needham's recent writings. For
his blessing upon Waddington's ethical views see his letter to *Nature*, Vol.
148 (October 4, 1941), p. 411.

[3] The "scientific humanism" of Hogben, Bernal, and Haldane is called

British cultural heritage seems to be reinforced by the Baconian strand in Marxism. Bacon's ideas influenced the Encyclopedists, and came to Marx perhaps, as Professor Acton suggests, through Feuerbach.[1] Marx and Engels, maintains Professor Acton, were, like Bacon, fascinated by the legend of Prometheus. Bacon identified science with knowledge and knowledge with power, the conscious control of man and nature. In light of this relationship between the ideas of Bacon and Marx, it is interesting that a leading Marxist intellectual, Professor Benjamin Farrington, has written a book entitled *Francis Bacon: Philosopher of Industrial Science* (1951), that opens with a statement of its principal theme:

> The story of Francis Bacon (1561–1626) is that of a life devoted to a great idea. The idea gripped him as a boy, grew with the varied experience of his life, and occupied him on his deathbed. The idea is a commonplace today, partly realized, partly tarnished, still often misunderstood; but in his day it was a novelty. It is simply that knowledge ought to bear fruit in works, that science ought to be applicable to industry, that men ought to organize themselves as a sacred duty to improve and transform the conditions of life.[2]

Professor Farrington describes Bacon as refusing

> ... to judge knowledge by a merely external standard. It was not enough that it be logically consistent. He asked instead what it had done, how had it affected the fortunes of mankind down the ages. From this historical standpoint he proposed a new criterion of the validity of science. "Science like religion must be judged by its fruits." [3]

---

a "blend of Francis Bacon and Karl Marx" in Walter Moberly, *The Crisis in the University* (London: S.C.M. Press, 1949), p. 71.

[1] H. B. Acton, *The Illusion of the Epoch: Marxism-Leninism As a Philosophical Creed* (London: Cohen and West, 1955), p. 254.

[2] Benjamin Farrington, *Francis Bacon: Philosopher of Industrial Science* (London: Lawrence and Wishart, 1951), p. 3.

[3] *Ibid.*, p. 142.

In his popular treatise on Greek science, Professor Farrington has applied this axiom of Bacon's to the field of historical interpretation by attempting to explain the paralysis of science in the ancient world in terms of an increasing separation of science from practice.[1]

The ideas of H. G. Wells captivated many of the young scientists of the twenties, like Bernal and Haldane. His *New Worlds for Old* (1908) introduced the concept of technological planning long before the Marxists developed the idea. Two years before, he had published *A Modern Utopia* (1906), which he deemed one of the "most vital and successful" of his books.[2] Following the model of Plato's *Republic*, Wells described the scientifically organized and directed state of the future. All citizens are scientifically classified in terms of temperament, thus determining their function in society. The management of society would be in the hands of a small elite of scientists, the "Samurai". Membership in the Samurai would be voluntary, but dependent upon the passing of a series of difficult examinations. Wells tells us that the rise of the elitist parties of communism and fascism had vindicated his faith in the soundness of the idea of Samurai. His efforts to transform the Fabian Society into something akin to the Samurai failed, he confessed, one reason being that he antagonized Shaw and the Webbs by his aggressiveness. The Samurai emerged in the *New Machiavelli* (1911) as a revolutionary corps of scientists with a directive ideology. After the First World War Wells insisted "on the necessity for some such organization as my Samurai to replace the crude electoral methods of contemporary politics".[3] Wells, therefore, fascinated by science and disillusioned with conventional politics, was a pioneer popularizer of the ideas of

[1] Benjamin Farrington, *Greek Science: Its Meaning For Us*, Vol. II, "Theophrastus to Galen" (Harmondsworth, Middlesex: Penguin Books, 1949), pp. 165–166.

[2] H. G. Wells, *Experiment in Autobiography: Discoveries and Conclusions of a Very Ordinary Brain (Since 1866)* (London: Gollancz and Cresset Press, 1934), Vol. II, p. 658.

[3] *Ibid.*, Vol. II, p. 745.

applying science and reason to human affairs, of using technological planning to benefit mankind, and of establishing a
world scientific state ruled by a scientific elite. Nevertheless
he was quite unenthusiastic about Dialectical Materialism,
describing it as "pseudo-scientific", "literary", "preten-
tious", and "rhetorical". The scientific state, he affirmed,
could be established only by non-violent methods such as
education and persuasion.[1] The transition from a Wellsian
to a communist point of view could be made quite easily,
particularly if, as we have seen in the case of Bernal, communism was conceived of not as an end, but as a means for
the fulfilment of the Wellsian dream.

Another scientific-rationalist, as influential as Wells, if not
so dramatic, was his friend, collaborator, and admirer, R. G.
Gregory. A student at the Royal College of Science in the
eighteen-eighties, Gregory gained a reputation as a popularizer of scientific knowledge, writing a number of widely
used textbooks. He was active in the British Association and
in the British Scientific Guild, a brain-child of the Editor of
Nature, Sir Norman Lockyer, established in 1903 for the purpose of "applying scientific methods to public affairs". In
1915 the first of Gregory's famous editorials on science in
public affairs appeared in *Nature*, which he had assisted in
editing for twenty-two years. Becoming Editor in 1919, he
gained a highly respected and influential platform for the
dissemination of his views and for the championing of the
social relations of science movement in the thirties. After the
First World War he supported the formation of the National
Union of Scientific Workers, later to be reorganized as the
Association of Scientific Workers. Both he and Wells
sponsored *The Realist*, a scientific humanist journal edited
by Archibald Church, which survived from 1929 to 1930.
Others involved in this enterprise were Gerald Heard, J. B. S.
Haldane, and Julian Huxley. By the middle thirties, however, Gregory and Wells became worried about the rapidly
increasing number of Marxist scientists and their growing in-

[1] See letter in *Nature*, Vol. 134 (December 22, 1934), p. 972.

fluence in organizations like the Association of Scientific
Workers.[1] Ironically it was their rationalistic ideas concerning the relation of science and society that had done so much
to prepare the way for this development.

The beliefs of Wells and Gregory were an essential part
of the rationalist movement so influential in the first two decades of the twentieth century. Its exponents were devoted
partisans of science and reason. They were agnostics and religious sceptics who adopted a naturalistic approach to
philosophy and ethics. Cambridge, with its great scientific
schools, and societies such as The Heretics, was one of the
central points from which these ideas radiated. This kind
of rationalism with a Wellsian emphasis was responsible
for the "Today and Tomorrow Series" of Kegan Paul,
Trench, Truber and Company, launched in 1923 with
Haldane's *Daedalus*, originally a paper read before The
Heretics. Bernal's *The World, the Flesh and the Devil* (1929) also
appeared in this series. Most of these books rapidly glossed
over what was considered to be the present unsatisfactory
state of affairs to concentrate in great detail upon the
possibilities of a glorious scientific future.

The views of the rationalists have been propagated by a
number of groups. Foremost among them has been the
Rationalist Press Association founded in May 1899 by a free-
thinking son of a Wesleyan minister, the publisher Charles A.
Watts. The two organs of the Association, the *Rationalist
Annual* and the *Literary Guide*, have had wide circulation. A
recent statement of belief of the Association is as follows:

Rationalists take science seriously and accept the consequences of its methods in all departments of thought and
life. They believe that claims to derive some superior
knowledge—either from intuition or sacred writings—are
unacceptable. The fate of man is in his own hands and he
must expect no miracles, but so great is the power that
science has given him that civilization is at the cross-roads.

[1] According to Armytage, *op. cit.*, p. 152.

We have to choose between using that knowledge to increase human happiness and well being—which is the
Rationalist way—or using it for destruction in the service
of fanaticism and bigotry.[1]

The Association sponsors "The Thinkers' Library", published by Watts, which has sold over three million copies of
its books. In 1934 Watts also produced the first volume of its
"Library of Science and Culture", whose editor was Professor Levy. The Library was planned

> ... to present to the general reader a picture of the
> world, both of action and of thought, as science is shaping
> it. It will reveal how mankind has sought in science the
> means of satisfying its various needs; and how in turn,
> science is stimulating fresh aspirations, inspiring hopes of
> increasing mastery over the destiny of the race.[2]

The South Place Ethical Society of London, dating from the
time of John Stuart Mill, provided another important
channel of expression in its annual Conway Memorial Lectures, published by Watts. Finally, there were the "scientific humanists", a term used to describe social thinkers like
Huxley and Hogben who were influenced by Bacon, Wells,
and Marx. They were certainly not Marxists, but their ideas
about the role of science in society and the scientific organization of society were shared by the orthodox Marxists Levy,
Bernal, and Haldane.

This particular facet of British liberalism, for Wells and
the rationalists were liberals, helped to generate the social
relations of science movement and to contribute to the popularity of communism. Paradoxically, it was their ideas that

---

[1] *Rationalist Annual* (1956). Also see A. Gowans Whyte, *The Story of
the R.P.A. 1899–1949*, preface by C. D. Darlington (London: Watts,
1949). Honorary Associates of the R.P.A. have included Haldane,
Chalmers Mitchell, Julian Huxley, Wells, Levy, Childe, Joseph Needham, and Bernal.

[2] This statement appears opposite the title page in Julian Huxley,
Scientific Research and Social Needs (London: Watts, 1934).

made way for the communist anti-liberal tenets of the movement. The explanation for this strange state of affairs seems
to be that modern British liberalism was in part the legatee
of the rationalism of the Philosophic Radicals. Bentham,
like Marx, was a creature of the eighteenth-century faith in
reason, science, and progress, and like Marx he conceived the
grand project of engineering human happiness on the basis of
an axiomatic system of political truth. The general style of
approach was the same, if the substance was different. They
were both system builders, Bentham to a much more modest
extent. Of greater importance is the fact that they saw themselves as "scientific" manipulators of human material: the
one on the basis of a rational calculus of human feelings; the
other by a geometry of history. Hence, in the twentieth
century, there was a very definite affinity between the ideas
of the heirs of these two strands of the Enlightenment. The
Webbs are a classic example: the liberal Benthamites, the
social engineers *par excellence*, who ended their days as the
sympathetic interpreters of Soviet Communism. In the
hectic times of the thirties, the disillusioned liberal scientist,
who saw so many of his treasured liberal ideals shattered,
could in his desperation push aside the others and make a
fetish of science, a dogma of reason. The communist emphasis upon control and manipulation, and upon the idea of a
scientific society in which scientists would play a leading role,
touched the Achilles heel of the nihilistic scientist.[1] In a

[1] The C.P.G.B. exploited this sentiment. R. Palme Dutt in his report
to the Sixteenth National Congress in 1943 said: "The Communist Party
stands with modern Science. In contrast to the niggardly treatment of
Science at the hands of the old State and the monopolists we stand for
the fullest support and developments and facilities for scientific research,
and the fullest utilisation of the great discoveries of science in the interests of the nation. It is the scientists and the workers in alliance who
will build the new Britain." See *Unity and Victory: Report of the 16th Congress of the Communist Party, 1943* (London: C.P.G.B., 1943), p. 31.
    Another example is the appeal of Professor J. B. S. Haldane in *Why
Professional Workers Should be Communists* (London: C.P.G.B., 1945), p. 4:
"You may ask: 'If the Communists succeed in their aims, what would be
my position?' The answer is that if you are good at your job you would

world in which science alone seemed to know what it was about, communism held the hope that the rule of the scientist-king might become more than a dream.

---

have more power and more responsibility than you have now. The leading commissars in the Soviet Union, who direct great socialized industries, compared to which I.C.I. [Imperial Chemical Industries] or any of the British railways are small fry, are business executives, mostly trained as engineers. The leading scientists, writers, and artists are very important people."

PART III

BUREAUCRACY

. . . they can no longer waste time and energy in the toils of a bureaucracy which demands everything from them, from stamp licking to *Daily Worker* selling, *except* honest intellectual work; and inhibits their expression with disciplinary measures.

E. P. Thompson, "Socialism and the Intellectuals"
Universities and Left Review (Spring 1957)

Now it would be quite false to cast doubts on the genuineness of people like Gollan, Dutt, and Pollitt. They are all highly able men who have sacrificed themselves for a cause in which they believe, and they are prepared, if necessary, to be victimized on its behalf. That is not in question. The point rather is that they regard themselves as the Chosen People, the People of the Book, the personal custodians of a trust that is part of a great international movement. While the rank-and-file may argue every aspect of democracy and democratic centralism, they themselves have a loyalty much deeper than their members, or to the working class *at any given moment in history.* They are timeless, and so they and their bodyguard must always be re-elected. Democracy-cum-loyalty can always be made to work that way.

Hyman Levy, "A Marxist Party?"
New Statesman and Nation (April 27, 1957)

CHAPTER VI

WEB OF ORGANIZATION

THE DEVELOPMENT OF a mass movement from a charismatic to a bureaucratic phase as plotted by Max Weber is well illustrated by the history of British communism. From a handful of idealistic revolutionaries the C.P.G.B. has evolved into a bureaucratized organization directed by a small elite of full-time functionaries. In addition to the rigid adherence to communist orthodoxy required of the membership under this black-coat rule, each individual fulfils a strictly circumscribed and routinized role in the organization. Of all members the intellectual is perhaps subject to the greatest number of proscriptions, and of all members he is the most likely to feel uncomfortable in such bureaucratic harness.

Intellectuals may be associated with the C.P.G.B. in several ways; as open members, crypto-members, or sympathizers. The intellectuals who are open members or "card-carrying" communists belong to three different categories. A great majority are those who do not depend for a livelihood upon the Party or Party-dominated organizations. Among them are the intellectuals of great professional reputation such as Hyman Levy, Maurice Dobb, Arnold Kettle, George Thomson, and Alan Bush. A second category consists of the intellectuals who have found careers in organizations closely affiliated to the Party: Andrew Rothstein in the Society for Cultural Relations, Pat Sloan in the British Soviet Friendship Society, R. Page Arnot in the Labour Research Department, and Edgell Rickword in the publishing house of Lawrence and Wishart. An even smaller number have become professional communists: employees and leaders of the Party like R. Palme Dutt, Emile Burns, and James Klugmann.

There are no official statistics as to the number of intellectuals in the C.P.G.B. Such figures probably exist, for Moscow has always been interested in the social composition of the membership of the national communist parties. The C.P.G.B. has in the past received questionnaires for the purpose of classifying members as "Industrial Workers", "Agricultural Workers", and "Intellectuals".[1] Information upon the social composition of delegates to the National Congresses is not a reliable means of determining the number of intellectuals in the Party. Because of their small number, intellectuals would naturally be over-represented at the Congresses. Moreover, so often the data that are supplied do not distinguish between clerical workers, professional workers, and students. About all that can be said with certainty is that intellectuals constitute a small minority within the Party and that the majority of them are teachers, technicians, and scientists. What the intellectuals lack in numbers they make up in prestige and influence in the community and in the services that they render to the Party.

Crypto-members are the secret non-card-holding members of the Communist Party. They may be sympathizers whose membership the Party wishes to conceal for various reasons. Professor Haldane, closely associated with the Party from the beginning of 1937, was not known to be a member until after Mrs. Haldane had severed her relations with the Party in November 1941.[2] A short time later he was elected to the Executive Committee of the Party. Both acts were evidently devised to counter the adverse effect of her defection and her criticism of the Soviet Union. Announcement of the membership of some prominent person, a sympathizer or crypto-member, is a device used by the Party in times of crisis to

---

[1] In May 1925 the Information Department of the Comintern sent such questionnaires to the C.P.G.B., which were seized by the police in their raids in 1925; see Home Office, *Communist Papers: Documents Selected from those Obtained on the Arrest of the Communist Leaders on the 14th and 21st October, 1925*, Cmd. 2682 (London: H.M.S.O., 1926), p. 51.

[2] Charlotte Haldane, *Truth Will Out* (London: Weidenfeld and Nicolson, 1949), pp. 254–266.

offset unfavourable publicity. For example, during the recent difficulties resulting from deStalinization and the Soviet intervention in Hungary, when many communist intellectuals were openly rebelling, Hugh MacDiarmid wrote in the *Daily Worker* that he was rejoining the Party after an absence of twenty years.[1] Some intellectuals move from open to crypto-membership. After the outbreak of the last war a few occupied strategic positions in government offices, etc., providing them with the opportunity of procuring information for the Party. They were directed by the Party to refrain from engaging in Party activities, from associating with other members, and from expressing sympathy with communist policies and aims.[2] Although crypto-members in such circumstances can hardly be considered spies, they may very well end up as members of the Soviet Army Intelligence.[3] Another type of crypto-member is the sympathizer who is recruited as a possible spy.[4] Party-sponsored discussion and study groups which attract students and intellectuals are carefully watched for possible candidates. When a suitable person is discovered, he is asked to join a secret cell or group and to terminate all connections with the Party. These organizations are entirely separate from the regular Party apparatus. The members pay no dues and are given no cards. They meet for discussion and are urged to join and become active in front organizations.

The rather broad and nebulous category of communist sympathizer may be used to include anyone from certain crypto-communists to a member of the Labour Party who writes occasionally for the *Daily Worker*, or who belongs

[1] *Daily Worker*, March 28, 1957, p. 2.
[2] Douglas Hyde, *I Believed: The Autobiography of a Former British Communist* (London: Heinemann, 1950), pp. 144–147; C. H. Darke, *The Communist Technique in Britain* (London: Collins, 1953), pp. 20, 87.
[3] Alexander Foote, *Handbook for Spies* (2nd ed.; London: Museum Press, 1953), pp. 55–56, 189–190.
[4] *The Report of The Royal Commission Appointed Under Order in Council P.C. 411 of February 5, 1946* . . . (Ottawa: Controller of Stationery, 1946), pp. 69–81.

to one or more "front organizations", and generally supports
Party policies. Even occasional defenders of the Party line
are often referred to as sympathizers or "fellow-travellers".
The *Report on Organisation* of 1922 defined sympathizers as
"those who read the Party paper, vote for the Party, and are
ready to help in its work or in some phase of its work".[1]
Registers of sympathizers should be kept by the Party, the
Report continued, and every effort should be made to draw
them into the Party.[2] The Party has never admitted that it
maintains a roll of sympathizers, nor revealed any information as to their numbers. National election returns are not a
good index, for communist candidates usually contest only
a handful of seats. Sales of the *Daily Worker* are perhaps a
truer reflection of the number of sympathizers, but all sorts
of people who could not possibly be called Party members or
sympathizers buy and read the newspaper. Certainly some
of the most zealous and articulate supporters of the C.P.G.B.
and its policies have never been announced as Party members: D. N. Pritt, John Platts-Mills, Hewlett Johnson,
J. D. Bernal, J. G. Crowther, Commander Edgar Young,
Archibald Robertson, Monica Felton. The most famous
sympathizer was John Strachey, who, although he called
himself, a communist, was never an official member of the
Party. Some sympathizers are ex-Party members. Instead
of becoming anti-communists or "renegades" as the Party
calls them, they remain silent about their differences with
the Party, and continue to support its general policies. Hugh
MacDiarmid belonged to this category before he recently re-
entered the Party. Professor J. B. S. Haldane resigned from
the Party in 1950, and although he has retired from active
political controversy, he still defends much of the Party line.

[1] *Report on Organisation Presented by the Party Commission to the Annual Conference of the Communist Party of Great Britain, October 7, 1922* (London:
C.P.G.B., 1922), p. 73.
[2] This latter point was also emphasized at the Thirteenth Congress of
the C.P.G.B., held in February 1935. See *Harry Pollitt Speaks—A Call to
All Workers with the Resolutions of the XIII Party Congress* (London: C.P.G.B.,
1935), p. 69.

Sympathizers are mobilized and activated chiefly through the so-called "front organization", an invention of the propaganda genius of the Comintern, Willie Münzenberg. He conceived the front organization as an auxiliary of the communist party designed to further communist "penetration" in all spheres of endeavour. His aim was to create a satellite system of apparently "neutral" organizations around the communist party. The more organizations and the more different social groups they appeal to, the better. Many are specialized organizations of trade unionists, or youth, or women, or intellectuals. Others are heterogeneous in their membership, attracting individuals belonging to all these groups. In practice the communist orientation of the satellite organization is achieved by communist control of its bureaucratic apparatus and by the planned and concerted action of the communist fraction of its membership. As a rule the elected officers of the organization are non-communists. Communist leaders hope that by means of a vast and interlocking system of such organizations people unwilling to join the party may be enlisted to support actively one or more of its policies. In addition, the front organization can be used to influence public opinion generally, and as a reservoir for the supply of new Party members. In all these aims the front organization has been highly successful, as indicated by the history of the communist movement in the last four decades.

The famous slogan of Münzenberg, "We have to organize the intellectuals", was soon implemented after the First World War by the Comintern. In 1919 Henri Barbusse and a few friends, including Romain Rolland, Anatole France, and Magdalene Marx, established Clarté, the prototype of the front organization for intellectuals. It united writers of the allied and ex-enemy countries who were motivated by the ideal of universal brotherhood and peace. The secretary of the British section of Clarté was Douglas Goldring. Among the supporters were Charles Trevelyan, Arthur Ponsonby, and Bertrand Russell. When it became apparent to these

F

non-communists that the key Paris organization had fallen under communist influence they withdrew from the British section, which subsequently dissolved.

Clarté was followed in Britain by the endless appearance and disappearance of front organizations. The Labour Research Department and the Society for Cultural Relations established in 1924 were largely of intellectual membership and are still in existence. Many, like the Workers International Relief, the International Class War Prisoners Aid, the Friends of the Soviet Union, and the National Left Wing Movement attracted intellectuals and non-intellectuals. In the thirties a host of organizations came to life as part of the Anti-War Movement and later in connection with the Spanish Civil War. An exclusively intellectual organization was the British Section of the Writers' International instituted in February 1934 by Tom Wintringham, Edgell Rickword, John Strachey, and his sister Amabel Williams-Ellis. During the Second World War from January 1941 to January 1942 there existed "The Peoples Convention", organized and controlled by the C.P.G.B. to forward its policy under another label, because so many Britishers had been alienated by the communist "defeatist" policy. Besides regular party stalwarts, it gathered people like D. N. Pritt, Chalmers Mitchell, Beatrix Lehmann, Olaf Stapledon, Michael Redgrave, V. R. Krishna Menon, Indra Nehru, and the Reverend Stanley Evans. Perhaps the most scathing critics of this group were Victor Gollancz and John Strachey.[1] A most interesting development at this time consisted of communist efforts to penetrate the large number of auxiliary firemen, many of them intellectuals, who had volunteered for the National Fire Service. The discussion groups which were formed as a means of occupying the spare time of the firemen "tended to become demonstrations of the politics of the left".[2]

---

[1] See Victor Gollancz, ed., *The Betrayal of the Left* (London: Gollancz, 1941), pp. 151, 154–172, 276, 318–321.
[2] Stephen Spender in William Sansom *et al.*, *Jim Brady: The Story of Britain's Firemen* (London: Drummond, 1943), p. 60.

There seems to be little doubt that the Communist Party found the National Fire Service and the Fire Brigades Union an important source for members to help swell its ranks in the period from 1942 to 1943.

In the post-war period front organizations flourished as they had never done before. In respect to intellectuals the most important ones are the "Friendship Societies" and constituents of the "British Peace Movement", all proscribed by the Labour Party. Foremost among the Friendship Societies are the British–Soviet Friendship Society (B.S.F.S.) and the Society for Cultural Relations (S.C.R.). Both go back to the twenties. The first is the largest and wealthiest of the front organizations, possessing a heterogeneous membership of fifty thousand, all organized into numerous branches. The second is primarily an organization for intellectuals, divided into various cultural sections such as Education, Science, History, and Archæology. The British Peace Movement developed from the World Congress of Intellectuals for Peace held at Wroclaw, Poland, in August 1948, attended by over forty British intellectuals of whom nearly one half were Party members or sympathizers. This meeting led in 1949 to the establishment of the World Peace Committee. In the same year the British Cultural Committee for Peace, later the British Peace Committee (B.P.C.), was founded.

These organizations exhibit several common features. They all adhere faithfully to the Party Line. Their officers and executives are dominated by well-known communist sympathizers such as Pritt, Hewlett Johnson, J. D. Bernal, Monica Felton, Commander Edgar Young, and Platts-Mills, all Stalin Prize winners, except the last two. The bureaucratic functionaries of these organizations, such as Pat Sloan and Hymie Fagan of the B.S.F.S., Eleanor Fox of the S.C.R. and until recently William Wainwright of the B.P.C., are stalwart communist members. Wainwright is now head of the Central Propaganda Department of the C.P.G.B. The Friendship Societies and the B.P.C. have their own systems

of satellite organization.[1] Both systems are connected by
an interlocking directorate of communist sympathizers, the
most prominent being D. N. Pritt. He is President of the
S.C.R. and the B.P.C., an officer of several of the satellite
Friendship Societies, a member of the Bureau of the World
Peace Council, and President of the International Association
of Democratic Lawyers. His wife is Vice-President of the
National Assembly of Women, and his law partner, John
Platts-Mills, is an active officer in most of these associations.

The Association of Scientific Workers (A.Sc.W.) is hardly
a conventional front organization, yet there is evidence to
suggest that it conforms to the model. Formed after the First
World War by Cambridge scientists, and receiving the blessing of Sir Richard Gregory and *Nature*, its history has been
one of ups and downs. Membership rose from 1,059 in 1938
to 17,211 in 1946, and now stands about 11,000. The Association, always attracting the most politically radical of the
scientists, can be credited with much of the success of the
social relations of science movement. In 1946 it launched a
crusade against the sentence given to Alan Nunn May, a
member and former officer, maintaining that his breach of
the Official Secrets Act was impelled by a belief in the principle of free interchange of scientific information.[2] In 1948,
Professor Bernal in his Presidential Address attacked American imperialism, and the official policy of the Association
was highly critical of the Marshall Plan.[3] The policies of the
Soviet Union have never been criticized in the journal of

[1] The most important satellite Friendship Societies are The British–
China Friendship Association, The British Council for German De-
mocracy, The British–Czech Friendship League, The British–Polish
Friendship Society, The British–Rumanian Friendship Association, The
Committee for Friendship with Bulgaria, The British–Yugoslav Associa-
tion [Anti-Tito], The League for Democracy in Greece.

Among the satellite peace organizations are Authors' World Peace
Appeal, Artists for Peace, Musicians for Peace, Teachers for Peace,
Architects for Peace, Scientists for Peace. Also closely associated are the
National Assembly of Women and the British Youth Committee.

[2] *Scientific Worker* (June 1946), p. 26.
[3] *Scientific Worker* (June 1948), pp. 5–6, 18.

the A.Sc.W. Reviews of Lysenko's books were all favourable. The A.Sc.W. has continued its affiliation with the World Federation of Scientific Workers (W.F.S.W.) proscribed by the Labour Party.[1] Many members have objected to the political activities of the A.Sc.W. A recent example was the resignation from the Executive Committee of Mr. D. M. Cassidy, who called for an investigation into the affairs of the Association.[2] Communist sympathizers who are also active in the Friendship Societies and the B.P.C. and its satellites have tended to dominate the A.Sc.W.; and its apparatus, at least since the beginning of the war, has been in the hands of communists and sympathizers.

The C.P.G.B., in control of this network that secures support for its policies among non-communist intellectuals, has no great reason to be perturbed by the relatively small number of intellectuals who are Party members. This is a reason why today it is customary for opponents of communism to point an accusing finger at the front organizations. Yet from one standpoint they perform a definite service for British democracy. The front organization tends to prevent the complete estrangement of the communist from society by providing a point of contact with the non-communist. For many people remain in front organizations, not because they are blind to, or approve of, communist methods, but because they share views on some questions with the communist, and because they wish to influence the shaping of these views.

The C.P.G.B. has three general aims in regard to bourgeois intellectuals: to prevent them from becoming " reactionaries"; to neutralize them in the class struggle; and to win them as allies. By winning them as allies, i.e., either as sympathizers or members, the Communist Party hopes to weaken capitalism through depriving it of the support of individuals possessing the professional and technical expertise so vital

[1] J. G. Crowther is the General Secretary of the W.F.S.W. Other officers include Bernal, C. F. Powell, and W. A. Wooster.
[2] A.Sc.W. Journal (July 1955), p. 4.

for the operation of a modern industrial society. On the positive side the communists will be strengthened by the special knowledge and skills that intellectuals bring with them.[1] The communist leadership realizes that one day it may be in the position to govern, and when that day arrives it must have at its disposal loyal professional cadres of all sorts, which will be able to occupy the key positions in society. Engels was well aware of the dangers of alienating the intelligentsia, and Stalin's task of industrializing Russia was hampered by the existence of an intransigent intelligentsia.

In the twenties the newly formed Party was happy to benefit from the services of its handful of intellectuals, many of whom were experienced political activists of considerable reputation in the Labour Movement. International communism was still revolutionary and its leadership was still fluid. The talents of the intellectuals were not wasted. Colonel Malone, elected a coalition Liberal M.P. in 1918, continued as a communist until his defeat in 1922. Saklatvala and Walton Newbold won seats as Labour candidates in 1922; and in 1924 Saklatvala was re-elected as a communist, staying in the House until 1929. Ellen Wilkinson and Philips Price were unsuccessful as Labour candidates in 1923. Others entered into the work of the Party with great gusto. Page Arnot and Tom Wintringham were among the twelve British Communist leaders who in 1925 were arrested, tried and imprisoned under the "Incitement to Mutiny Act". At the local level of the party apparatus, Ellen Wilkinson was for a short time Secretary of Manchester No. 1 Branch of the C.P.G.B., and Wintringham was Secretary of the St. Pancras Branch, London, when in 1924 he became Assistant Editor of the *Workers' Weekly*. Meynell, and after him Postgate, edited the weekly paper the *Communist*, until Dutt assumed command in February 1923 of the new *Workers'*

[1] The importance of the intellectuals for the working-class is expressed in the official programme of the C.P.G.B. See *Draft Revised Text of "The British Road to Socialism"* (London: C.P.G.B., 1957), p. 14.

Weekly. Dutt also founded in April 1921 the *Labour Monthly*, which was backed by the Trinity Trust, consisting of himself, Ewer, and Page Arnot, and supported by G. D. H. Cole, Philips Price and Robert Williams. *Plebs*, the organ of the National Council of Labour Colleges, occupied the efforts of Dobb, Horrabin and his wife Winifred, and Postgate, who constituted a communist majority on the executive. Dona Torr was a translator at the Fifth Comintern Congress in 1924, and during the thirties worked at the Marx-Engels-Lenin Institute in Moscow, translating the correspondence of Marx and Engels, and the first volume of *Capital*. In addition to their activities in the L.R.D., they participated in the numerous front organizations.

Not least among the efforts of the C.P.G.B. was its role in the Indian communist movement. Here the communist intellectuals proved of exceptional merit. Indian students at the major British universities were cultivated. Clemens Dutt became the British representative in the Colonial Bureau in Paris, established by the Comintern in 1924, and then Comintern representative in India. Ralph Fox journeyed to Moscow in September 1925 to work in the Colonial Department of the Comintern, primarily on India with Roy and Goldberg. A young Cambridge communist intellectual and L.R.D. worker, Philip Sprat, went to India in 1926 to open a labour research organization, and helped to found the Indian Communist Party. Subsequently both Saklatvala and R. P. Dutt visited India to assist in the organization and establishment of the Party. Indian communism owes much to these men, and to British working-class communists like Glading, Allison, and Bradley.

After the twenties the "political" activities of the Party intellectual were curtailed. Factors accounting for this change were the entrenchment of a Stalinist bureaucracy with its natural suspicion of intellectuals, the distrust arising from the defections of the intellectuals in the twenties, and the political immaturity of the literati and scientists entering the Party. The very few doctrinal statements of the C.P.G.B.

upon the importance of theory and the role of the intellectual in the Party appeared in the thirties. The first was in connection with the controversy touched off by Freda Utley in the *Communist Review* of May 1930.[1] Miss Utley ostensibly set about to review Martin Lawrence's publication of Volume IV of the *Collected Works* of Lenin, "The Iskra Period". However, she asked the explosive question as to whether the C.P.G.B. could profit from the lesson taught by Lenin: that a socialist consciousness can only be brought to the workers from without. The duty of socialist intellectuals, we are told by Miss Utley, who paraphrases Lenin, is to provide the masses with "political knowledge" in the form of arguments, articles, pamphlets, and "live exposures". What, she asked, are the communist intellectuals doing? British communism seemed to lack "any intellectuals worthy of the name". Party intellectuals were the first to bow before the spontaneity of the masses. Despising theory and intellectuals alike, the Party leadership neglected theoretical training. Consequently the C.P.G.B. remained the weakest communist party of the advanced European countries; while in Germany, where the workers were familiar with Marxist theory, the strongest communist party had developed. "Let us cease to be a Party of amateurs," she urged; every effort must be made to acquire theoretical knowledge and understanding. The intellectuals, and not the proletarians, were the most suitably equipped for such a task. The crux of Allen Hutt's rebuttal was that Miss Utley had mechanically transferred Lenin's thought of 1902 to present-day British affairs.[2] No similarity, Hutt maintained, existed between the two situations. Great Britain had an old, politically experienced working class, but no revolu-

[1] Freda Utley, "Economism Today: the 'Iskra Period' and Ourselves", *Communist Review*, Vol. II (May 1930), pp. 196–207. Miss Utley's motives for writing this article are given in her autobiography, *Lost Illusion*, introduction by Bertrand Russell (London: Allen and Unwin: 1949), pp. 32–34.
[2] Allen Hutt, "Fundamental Questions for Our Party", *Communist Review*, Vol. II (Sept. 1930), pp. 393–400.

tionary intelligentsia; whereas just the converse was true in Tsarist Russia at the beginning of the twentieth century. Hutt believed that Miss Utley's demand for more theory was justifiable. But she had failed to emphasize the great importance of mass-work. In her rejoinder Miss Utley denied that she had neglected mass-work.[1] Far from doing this, she was trying to show that mass-work could function successfully only if it proceeded from a solid foundation of broad theoretical knowledge and training. And in reference to Hutt's contention that Russian and British conditions differed, she replied that in Britain it was all the more imperative for intellectuals to induce class consciousness in the masses, mesmerized and subdued by the propaganda and repressive agencies of capitalism.

At this point the Political Bureau of the C.P.G.B. intervened with an ultimatum to Miss Utley.[2] Agreeing with Miss Utley's observation that the C.P.G.B. suffered from the typical British contempt for theory, the Political Bureau censured her because she made "incorrect" suggestions concerning mass-work, and because she attacked the leadership of the Party, which was following the "correct" political line by attempting to improve the theoretical level of the Party. The Political Bureau then condemned her for her "offensive superiority" and pointed out that the Party was "not contemptuous of the intellectuals and does not appoint its leaders irrespective of their theoretical and practical abilities", as she charged. Knowledge of Marxist theory and the ability to apply theory to practical work were two distinct attributes, not necessarily found together. The extent to which they were conjoined in such intellectuals determined the extent to which they might contribute to the leadership of the Party. Actually, the Political Bureau ruled, Comrade

[1] Freda Utley, "Raising the Theoretical Level of the Party as a Party of Mass Work", *Communist Review*, Vol. II (October 1930), pp. 432–441.

[2] "The Theoretician of 'Left' Sectarianism and Spontaneity: The Political Bureau's Reply to Freda Utley", *Communist Review*, Vol. III (January 1931), pp. 11–19.

Utley was the one who had become the exponent of spontaneity, for she failed to realize that the activation of the masses depended upon the Party's success in penetrating factories and trade unions. Revolutionary propaganda, i.e. theoretical work, would not by itself work a miracle. Concrete agitational mass-work was also fundamental. Admittedly, the danger of lagging behind the masses, right sectarianism, was a cardinal sin, but equally as heretical was the error of Miss Utley—left sectarianism, running too far ahead of the masses.

The Political Bureau was obviously concerned with Miss Utley's outspoken attack against the authority of the Party hierarchy. However, they were also perturbed by what they recognized as the truth of her charges concerning the theoretical backwardness of the Party, and the contempt of the Party membership for theory and theoreticians. Evidence of their anxiety on this score is found in the series of articles in the *Communist Review* utilizing many of Miss Utley's arguments and repeating many of her warnings. Allan Hutt set the theme in the first of these theoretical pronouncements:

. . . our traditional and shameful theoretical level is of particular and pressing danger to us. . . . It is still, unfortunately, common enough to find among our Party membership a contempt for theory. And this attitude, unless it is determinedly and painstakingly fought to a finish, will not become less widespread with the Party growing at its present rate: rather it will become more widespread; for the large influx of new workers into the Party is bound to mean an increase in our ranks of politically untrained members, bearing in more or less strongly-marked forms the symptoms of political backwardness, that are especially characteristic of British workers. . . . How many active Party workers are there who have not heard, time and time again, Party members—and still more, workers not yet in the Party—speaking of "theory" as of some strange thing far removed from them, something in which

perhaps a handful of leading comrades might be expected
to be interested, but which was of neither interest nor
importance for the mass of the membership? How many
have not heard enthusiastic and sincere workers in the
Party speak slightingly of "theory" as of something abstract, remote from everyday life and work, something in
itself the opposite of practice; something, in fact, necessarily connoting unpracticalness? [1]

The danger of spontaneity of the Party in economic struggles,
wrote Ralph Fox a short time afterwards, substituted the
formality and emptiness of slogans for real leadership.[2]
Jack Cohen emphasized the importance of "political exposures" as a means of deepening the class consciousness of
the workers and the necessity of bringing scientific socialist
theory to the masses.[3] Adopting the position of Miss Utley,
Harry Pollitt, addressing the Fifteenth Congress of the
C.P.G.B. in 1938, affirmed that the main reason for the
Party's failure to increase its membership was the inability of
its propaganda to awaken the masses.[4]

In the midst of this discussion concerning the shortcomings
of theoretical work, R. Palme Dutt spoke authoritatively
about the role of the intellectual in the Party.[5] He warned
that bourgeois communists have to be constantly on guard
against the prejudice of their bourgeois origins, training,
and habits of thought. They must come to the proletarian

[1] Allen Hutt, "The Revolutionary Role of the Theoretical Struggle",
Communist Review, Vol. IV (February 1932), pp. 78–79.
[2] Ralph Fox, "Comrade Stalin's Letter and the C.P.G.B.", *Communist
Review*, Vol. IV (April 1932), pp. 199–207.
[3] Jack Cohen, "Critical Thoughts on Our Agitation and Propaganda",
Communist Review, Vol. IV (June 1932), pp. 292–297. Also see Idris Cox,
"The Need to Improve the Character and Content of Revolutionary
Propaganda and Agitation", *Communist Review*, Vol. IV (November
1932), pp. 549–553.
[4] *For Peace and Plenty! Report of the Fifteenth Congress of the Communist
Party of Great Britain. Held in The Town Hall, Birmingham, September 16th
to 19th, 1938* (London: C.P.G.B., 1938), p. 76.
[5] R. Palme Dutt, "Bourgeois Journalism and Our Press", *Communist
Review*, Vol. IV (July 1932), pp. 325–331.

movement "not as heaven-sent teachers of superior wisdom", but in a humble spirit, willing to learn before they teach. It is the duty of the proletariat to utilize their services and to correct their bourgeois outlook. In a later issue of the *Communist Review*, Dutt stressed the important change that was taking place among the British intellectuals.[1] Previously backward and counter-revolutionary, they had suddenly become aware of the chaos of the modern world, the bankruptcy of capitalism, the inadequacies of Democratic Socialism, and the bold revolutionary experimentation of the Soviet Union. Some of these disillusioned intellectuals had turned to fascism. Many others had found in Marxism a solution to the world's ills. In fact Marxism had established a new fashion in intellectual circles. Much of this, Dutt thought, was just a further example of bourgeois decadence. But a few intellectuals were genuinely seeking to transcend their class limitations, and to find true knowledge. These intellectuals could strengthen the communist cause, but only after a "great transformation" on their part had taken place. Quite often they came to the Party without any real experience or contact with the working-class movement. Before they could use their special talents in the service of the Party, they would have to learn to be good communists and efficient revolutionary workers. When they had succeeded in this they would then be allowed to concentrate their efforts upon serious ideological work. In other words, before the intellectual could hope to aspire to political leadership, an apprenticeship in performing the menial chores of the Party would be mandatory.

Throughout these statements it is made clear that while the C.P.G.B. welcomes intellectuals, they cannot be permitted to have an "independent" role in the Party. The vital core of the communist movement consists of the workers, whose dominance within the Party must always be assured. Communist elements from other social strata enter the Party

[1] R. Palme Dutt, "Intellectuals and Communism", *Communist Review*, Vol. IV (September 1932), pp. 421–430.

on sufferance, as it were. Bourgeois intellectuals may make very valuable auxiliaries of the working class; however, their relationship to the workers is always that of junior partners, never complete equals. The proper deportment of the party intellectual vis-à-vis the working-class member should be characterized by neither "silly adulation", nor "flippancy", nor "talking down" to him.[1] Workers are to be treated with the utmost respect, for they can claim the special endorsement of history.

Great emphasis was now placed upon the *duties* of the intellectual entering the ranks of communism. First, there was the repeated insistence that he must conform to the Party line and obey all Party directives. This was to be done with enthusiasm and vigour, never "mechanically". Second, he must participate in the ordinary routine work of the Party just like the most humble working-class novice. A long and arduous apprenticeship is necessary for all new Party members, no matter what their social origins and education, if they are to become disciplined and energetic communists. The intellectual, like the worker, must attend all branch meetings, stamp and address envelopes, put up posters, sell the *Daily Worker* and other literature on street corners, join in processions and rallies, and do all sorts of odd Party jobs. He must spend his spare time studying the communist classics, and enroll in Party classes and discussion groups. In addition to the prompt and regular payment of dues, he is expected to contribute financially as much as he can to all manner of funds and special drives. Above all he must forget that he is an intellectual, sacrifice his pride, and through self-denial, self-discipline, and humble but conscientious work become a militant fighter for communism. The rigour with which this regimen is applied to the intellectual seems to depend upon his reputation at the time that he becomes a member. Emile Burns, entering the Party in 1923, worked in the British Section of the Red International of Labour Unions (Profintern) and as an organizer of London busmen.

[1] Harry Pollitt, *Professional Workers* (London: C.P.G.B., 1946), p. 6.

David Guest and Fred Pateman went from Cambridge to the slums of Battersea. Although he had been a philosophy student in Cambridge, Maurice Cornforth became an agricultural organizer in East Anglia. Stephen Spender, on the other hand, who was well established as a leading member of the literati at the time he joined the Party, was never called upon to perform such services during his short tenure of membership. It is highly unlikely that the probationary tasks of a Haldane, for instance, could compare either in duration or in hardship with those imposed upon a young unknown, just down from Oxford or Cambridge. A Haldane would have an international professional reputation to maintain, and in the view of the Communist Party it is all-important that Party work should in no way jeopardize such a reputation. In practice, professional workers in good standing can often "buy themselves" out of the more distasteful Party chores by generous contributions to the Party treasury.

This brings us to another duty of the communist intellectual. He must maintain and increase his professional standing, setting an example for non-communist intellectuals. A primary duty of the communist scientist or artist is to be an outstanding scientist or artist. Communist intellectuals must set the highest standards, and assume leading roles in the intellectual life of the community. Their work must reflect the "nobility of communism", the "inspiration" which it brings to them. They must also take part in the work of their professional organizations and societies in order to prove the courage of their convictions to their associates. Front organizations must be joined, and an ever greater number of non-communist intellectuals drawn into them. Soviet ideas in art, science—in all cultural fields—must be defended and shown to be superior to bourgeois ideas. In his particular field the communist intellectual must attempt to demonstrate to his colleagues the value of the Marxist-Leninist approach. Wherever possible, the professional errors of reactionary intellectuals should be ruthlessly exposed. The communist intellectual, however, must never become so engrossed with political work that it interferes with his professional calling. As soon as this begins to happen, his professional standing with his non-communist fellows may very well deteriorate, and along with it the appeal of his ideology. It might also lead to a decline of his authority and prestige with the general public. Besides, an intellectual is not nearly as effective in a political capacity as a professional politician, who has spent his life at the game. So a too intensive political life on the part of a communist intellectual may actually hurt the cause rather than help it. The duty, therefore, of the communist intellectual, to excel in his vocation, and by the force of example to attract other intellectuals to the standard of communism, is in many respects the greatest service that he can render to the proletariat.

Once the communist intellectual has proved himself a dutiful and obedient auxiliary of the worker, always willing to engage in the day-to-day chores of the Party, suppressing all anarchistic and individualistic tendencies in the true Leninist style, and winning prestige for the Party by pursuing a successful professional career, he may serve two useful Party functions. He may place his special skills at the disposal of the Party, and he may engage in ideological work, becoming a Marxist-Leninist combatant in the "battle of ideas". Lawyers, economists, and scientists can advise the various Party Departments and Committees on matters of public policy, help draft reports, etc. Musicians can furnish music for Party functions, such as the annual *Daily Worker* rally in the Albert Hall. The layout of posters and the covers of pamphlets, the preparation of commemorative exhibits are all facilitated by the numerous artists in the Party. The conducting of classes and study groups, lecturing at communist week-end and summer schools are also jobs for which the intellectuals may qualify. Public lecturers are always in demand. Professor Haldane is supposed to have given about one hundred public lectures a year during the height of the war.[1] A series of public lectures was given in London in the Autumn and Winter of 1946 by leading communist intellectuals in answer to the B.B.C. broadcasts, "The Challenge of Our Time".[2] The annual Marx Memorial Lecture in London, and the John Cornford Memorial Lecture in Cambridge, both sponsored by the C.P.G.B., are often delivered by intellectuals, either Party members or sympathizers.

The most common activity of the intellectuals is the contribution of articles to the various Party organs such as the *Daily Worker*, *World News*, *Marxist Quarterly*, *Labour Monthly*, *Jewish Clarion*, *Country Standard*, and *Challenge*. John Strachey was a featured contributor to the *Daily Worker* during the thirties. Professor Haldane wrote a regular science column for the same paper, beginning on December 9, 1937, with "What Makes the Birth-rate Fall?" and ending August 9, 1950, with "They Want to Sterilize the Poor". In 1940 Haldane became Chairman of the Editorial Board of the *Daily Worker*, among whose members were Sean O'Casey, Page Arnot, Hewlett Johnson, and Beatrix Lehmann. According to Douglas Hyde the Board had neither administrative nor policy-making powers. It did, however, hold regular meetings: "Professor J. B. S. Haldane, as the Board's Chairman, would preside, taking little part in the discussion and absent-mindedly doodling in Greek as the Dean of Canterbury held forth at length".[3] Two actions of the Board did receive space in the *Daily Worker*. On one occasion it decided that the paper should take patent medicine advertisements, and some time later it signed a resolution protesting against the export ban placed upon the paper by the Ministry of Information.[4] Numerous pamphlets and books have been written by the intellectuals as part of their propaganda

[1] Peter Phillip, *Professor J. B. S. Haldane, F.R.S.* (London: Daily Worker League, n.d.), p. 7.

[2] See the collected lectures, John Lewis *et al.*, *The Communist Answer to the Challenge of Our Time*, foreword by George Thomson (London: Thames Publications, 1947).

[3] Hyde, *op. cit.*, p. 190.

[4] *Daily Worker*, May 14, 1943, p. 2; July 2, 1943, p. 1.

activities. Perhaps the best of the pamphlets were those in the "Marxism Today Series", published from 1943 to 1950 under the general editorship of Professor Benjamin Farrington, and including such contributors as Maurice Dobb, John Lewis, George Thomson, Maurice Cornforth, and Rodney Hilton.

In order to facilitate their Party work intellectuals have been organized into professional sections within the party: Scientists, Doctors, Psychologists, Writers, Musicians, Artists, Actors, Non-Professional Actors, Non-Professional Musicians, Lawyers, Teachers, Historians, and Economists. Some of these groups, such as the Scientists, may subdivide according to the interests and specialities of the members. The membership is often overlapping. Although they are organized on a national basis, under the ægis of the National Cultural Committee whose chairman is a full-time functionary and a member of the all-powerful Political Committee, in practice they are usually confined to London. A trusted old Party intellectual, such as A. L. Morton of the Historians or Alan Bush of the Musicians, may act as a sort of unofficial major-domo, apart from the elected officers, always on hand to be consulted, to advise and to warn. National meetings of the delegates from the different sections are occasionally convened, at which time they are chided and exhorted by the political and cultural leaders of the Party.

Often the groups issue their own publications or journals, like the Artists' *Realism* or the Musicians' *Music and Life*. The Historians publish a quarterly pamphlet, *Our History*, on various subjects, such as "Luddism", "The Struggle for Educational Opportunity", etc. Recently, several volumes have resulted from the activity of the groups. A product of the Economists has been John Eaton's *Political Economy: A Marxist Textbook* (1949). About two years of "collective work" on the part of the Economists, helped by the Historians and the Scientists, went into this book. John Eaton, the secretary of the group, was the author of the completed work. Another volume for which the Economists have been responsible was John Eaton's *Marx Against Keynes: A Reply to Mr. Morrison's "Socialism"* (1951). Those of the Historians Group who were greatly influenced by Dona Torr contributed essays to *Democracy and the Labour Movement: Essays in Honour of Dona Torr*, edited by John Saville of the University of Hull, and published in 1954. A second collective work of the Historians Group has been A. L. Morton's and George Tate's *The British Labour Movement 1770–1920: A History* (1956). Pamphlets, syllabuses, and bibliographies are some of the other publications of the different groups.

The groups also arrange and hold discussions, symposiums, and conferences. A symposium for the purpose of analysing and criticizing "reactionary" British writers such as T. S. Eliot, Aldous Huxley, Evelyn Waugh, and Graham Greene was organized by the Writers. The Psychologists and Teachers have critically examined the methods of mental testing used in the British educational system. An article appeared in the *Communist Review* as a result of a discussion on "Tudor Absolutism" engaged in by the sixteenth–seventeenth century section of the Historians.[1] Other discussions of the Historians have been on such topics as "Marx's theory of the increasing misery of the workers under capitalism", and "the origins of class society". To celebrate the centenary of 1848, this group set up a special committee to collect and prepare materials. These general kinds of activity characterize the work of all the professional sections.

The C.P.G.B. has not organized the intellectuals in these groups for the purpose of stimulating intellectual controversy and the exchange of ideas. They were not designed as "talking shops" for Party bohemians. The criterion used to evaluate the work of the groups is its political usefulness. All groups must "*produce concrete results useful to the Party as a whole*".[2] Whether this standard is being complied with or not

---

[1] "State and Revolution in Tudor and Stuart England", *Communist Review* (July 1948), pp. 207–214.

[2] Daphne May, "Work of the Historians' Groups", *Communist Review* (May 1949), p. 542.

is judged by the political leadership of the Party. Every effort of the intellectual must be geared to the latest development in the Party line. Still another restriction is placed upon the intellectuals. They are warned that their participation in the professional groups cannot serve as a substitute for the regular Party activity of the branch organization. The intellectual must not isolate himself from the rest of the Party by withdrawing into the specialized group. Some sort of balance between these two functions must be maintained. The danger in this tendency towards isolation in the Party, as the leadership sees it, is that organizations will be created within the party which may very well become "political" rivals of the branch and district organizations.[1] These latter groups are the "decision-making" bodies of the Party, firmly directed from the centre. In them the intellectuals can be watched and controlled because they are generally outnumbered by working-class members and Party functionaries. However, the smooth operation of the Party's bureaucratic system would be imperilled if new political centres emerged, particularly if they were completely in the hands of a group as undependable and unpredictable as the intellectuals. The consequence of such an arrangement would be the growth of a party within a party, an always threatening source of factional disruption. The attitude of the Party leadership in this matter is further evidence that the intellectuals will not be permitted to lead independent lives of their own within the Party organization.

The last important function of the Party intellectual, once he has been tried and tested, is to engage in the ideological struggle against capitalism and bourgeois culture. The professional groups provide a convenient means for thrashing out some of the problems involved in the implementation of the Party line in this sphere. General direction of the programme has been assumed by the National Cultural

[1] Since the war the Communist Party of France has also been troubled with this problem. See Laurent Casanova, *Le Parti Communiste, Les Intellectuels et La Nation* (Paris: Editions Sociales, 1949), pp. 11–12.

Committee which was founded in 1947, no doubt as part of the world-wide communist effort to intensify the ideological attack, signalled by Zhdanov's notorious purification of the Soviet cultural front. This recent British Communist ideological drive was a synchronized part of the Cold War, commencing in earnest during the first year of the Marshall Plan and extending to the end of the Korean War. The Party intellectuals and the professional groups were fully mobilized to conduct a "battle of ideas". At the First National Cultural Congress of the C.P.G.B. held in London on April 11, 1948, attended by over four hundred visitors and delegates from the cultural, scientific, and professional groups of the Party, Sam Aaronovitch raised the standard; the battle of ideas, he said,

> . . . is a class fight against the reactionary capitalist's at home. It is no less a national struggle to prevent Britain's subjection by the most powerful section of world capitalism—that of America. To win this battle in Britain means to wreck the plans of the warmongers, to make a great contribution to peace, and the forward march of mankind.[1]

Between this date and the beginning of 1955, six such cultural conferences were held, supplemented by pamphlets, books, public lectures, special Party schools.[2] The emphasis was on the threat of American economic, political, and cultural domination. Communist propaganda utilized overt nationalistic themes. The image of the nation's great cultural heritage was invoked. An insidious and barbaric fifth column of American films, comic books, professors, and cultural attachés was purported to be threatening to destroy

[1] Sam Aaronovitch, "The Communist Party and the Battle of Ideas" (Report to National Cultural Conference of the Communist Party, April 11, 1948), *Communist Review* (May 1948), p. 148.

[2] For examples of the C.P.G.B. literature of this period see the following: *The American Threat to British Culture* (London: Arena, n.d.); *Essays on Socialist Realism and the British Cultural Tradition* (London: Arena, n.d.); *Britain's Cultural Heritage* (London: Arena, n.d.).

British culture. The shrillness of the charges increased as Moscow launched its "Hate America" programme at the beginning of 1951. But after Stalin's death, and at the end of the Korean war when the thaw in the Cold War began to set in, the battle of ideas waged by British communist intellectuals appeared to wane. With the switch in the Party line, intellectuals were put to work on other ideological tasks, such as calling for greater unity with the non-communist left. Perhaps not since the Spanish War years of the thirties had they been so well organized or so active.

By such bureaucratic prescriptions the intellectual is forever reminded that he is no more than an instrument in the service of the Party and its policies. His sojourn in the Party is one of continual sufferance and perpetual probation. But how does he behave when he discovers that the "iron law of oligarchy" operates in the movement to a greater degree and in a fashion more subtle than in many bourgeois associations?

CHAPTER VII

REASONER VERSUS BUREAUCRAT

IF BUREAUCRATIC AND ideological pressure becomes
too severe the communist intellectual may decide to leave
the Party. In the history of the C.P.G.B. there have been
four occasions when intellectuals have defected in substantial numbers. The first was in the middle twenties, as a
result of the newly implemented policy of Bolshevization. A
second exodus occurred in the 1939–1940 period either because of any one of a number of reasons or because of any
combination of them; the Moscow Trials, the Nazi–Soviet
Pact, the Soviet attack upon Finland, the "imperialist war"
line. The defection of John Strachey is perhaps the best-
known example of the time. The Cold War, with its increasing demand for rigid ideological conformity, alienated many
intellectuals, among them Professor J. B. S. Haldane. The
most recent crisis followed the Twentieth Congress of the
Communist Party of the Soviet Union (February 1956).

Many of the intellectuals of the twenties forsook communism, the majority doing so before the middle of the decade.[1]
Humanitarian idealists that they were, liberal in their outlook, relishing controversy and discussion, many soon were
perturbed by the direction which the C.P.G.B. seemed to be
taking. Still rebels, they objected to the policy of Bolshevization with its emphasis upon centralization, discipline,
and conformity. They were shocked to learn how much control over the policy of the C.P.G.B. was being exerted by the
Comintern. No amount of rationalization could reconcile
them to the tactics of infiltration which began to be em-

[1] Among the intellectuals who terminated their association with communism were: Ewer, Horrabin, Malone, Mellor, Meynell, Walton Newbold, Pankhurst, Postgate, Philips Price, Utley, Wilkinson, Wintringham.
Utley and Wintringham did not leave the C.P.G.B. until the nineteen-
thirties.

REASONER VERSUS BUREAUCRAT 183

ployed by the Party. Had the Russians recognized the right of national communism to assert itself, rather than forcing its own autocratic version upon people economically and politically more advanced than themselves, the course of history might have been radically different.

At the Foundation Conference of 1920, William Mellor condemned a resolution that he believed would lead to the aggrandizement of power in the Executive. He warned the delegates that he did not think "it wise for the Communist Party at its birth to begin bureaucratizing its administration." [1] Sylvia Pankhurst refused to acquiesce in the process of centralization, and was expelled because she would not allow the C.P.G.B. to control her newspaper, the *Workers' Dreadnought*.[2] Writing in the thirties of his experience with the C.P.G.B., Raymond Postgate sharply attacked the Bolshevization Programme of the Third International, which reduced the national Communist Parties to mere "sections". The consequence was that the Parties "continually peeled portions of themselves off and threw them away, as if they had turned into onions with suicidal mania." [3] After he left the Party, Walton Newbold wrote to *Plebs*:

"Leninism", for the very reason that caused it to triumph in Russia, is in grave danger of failing miserably outside of Russia and in countries whose economic and social development have given rise to an altogether different ideology. This is all the more likely now that the disciples of the master have elevated his teachings into a veritable cult, seeking quite naturally in an appeal to this new standard of the infallible an ever ready answer to all who criticize their interpretations and their actions.[4]

---

[1] *Communist Unity Convention; London, July 31st and August 1st, 1920: Official Report* (London: C.P.G.B., 1920), p. 23.

[2] *Communist*, September 17, 1921, p. 1.

[3] Raymond Postgate, *How To Make a Revolution* (London: Hogarth Press, 1934), pp. 167, 177.

[4] *Plebs*, Vol. XVI (December 1924), p. 483.

Although Philips Price was a sympathizer and not a Party member, the C.P.G.B. did not lightly tolerate his deviation from the Party line when he was a Labour Party parliamentary candidate. His reply to this authoritarian attitude was published in the Glasgow socialist newspaper *Forward*:

> The truth is that the whole Comintern is ruled by a rigid bureaucratic machine which has, now that the revolutionary struggle is over, acquired a vested interest in propagating throughout the world the phrases and catchwords which were quite justly applicable to the world situation in the hectic days immediately following the war. It goes without saying that they are simply grotesque in the Europe of today. . . .[1]

In 1929 W. N. Ewer, no longer a Party member, wrote an article "Cross Roads" for the *Labour Monthly* in which he treated contemporary Anglo-Soviet relations as a continuation of Anglo-Tsarist relations.[2] The Editor's reaction was to treat this thesis as a heretical deviation from the party line.[3] Ewer's retort was scathing. He termed the orthodoxy of communism the "religious" or "ecclesiastical" attitude.[4] Communism was subordinated "to authoritative and infallible pronouncements"; "'deviation' becomes a moral offence" and "thought degenerates into scholasticism". The communist movement had acquired the "whole familiar apparatus of the examination of conscience, of confession, of absolution, of excommunication". Ewer was immediately

---

[1] M. Philips Price, "The Communist International and the Labour Party: A Reply to Karl Radek Suppressed by the 'Labour Monthly' ", *Forward*, Vol. XIX (May 16, 1925), p. 12.

[2] W. N. Ewer, "Cross Roads", *Labour Monthly*, Vol. XI (November 1929), pp. 671–677.

[3] "Cross Roads—A Criticism", *Labour Monthly*, Vol. XI (December 1929), pp. 757–760.

[4] W. N. Ewer, "A Reply", *Labour Monthly*, Vol. XII (January 1930), p. 43. It was followed by the italicized comments of the Editor, pp. 49–53.

denounced as a renegade, and his friendly co-existence with the C.P.G.B. was ended.

Communist intrigue for the purpose of gaining control over non-communist organizations was particularly disillusioning to the intellectuals. The L.R.D. became a communist auxiliary by such a process. Raymond Postgate describes in detail how the communist nucleus in the L.R.D., of which he was a member, so arranged the speakers and the resolutions to be proposed in the various committee meetings that its dominance was assured.[1] He concludes that this kind of "nucleing" was simply a product of Bolshevization and that by using it the C.P.G.B. alienated many who might otherwise have been loyal allies. Every effort was made by the party to capture *Plebs*. A communist majority on the executive, consisting of Postgate, Horrabin and his wife Winifred, and Dobb, seemed to guarantee the success of this aim. But in the long run only Dobb was willing to see *Plebs* become a mouthpiece for communist policy.[2] Horrabin, the Editor of *Plebs*, resigned from the C.P.G.B., because he was loath to stand by quietly while the Independent Working-Class Movement was crippled in the communist quest for power. He clearly saw that the C.P.G.B. would only keep its agreements with organizations and individuals when it served its interests to do so: "As I can't work happily with little Machiavellians of this type, I decided I should feel better outside".[3]

A field in which communist intrigue attained its zenith was in the setting up of various international organizations such as the Workers' International Relief, the International Class War Prisoners' Aid, etc. These were in reality façades for the further extension of communist influence. Walton Newbold, who had been a member of the Political Bureau of

---

[1] Postgate, *op. cit.*, pp. 178–183.

[2] Bell, *The British Communist Party, A Short History* (London: Lawrence and Wishart, 1937), p. 84.

[3] Raymond W. Postgate and J. F. Horrabin, "Trotsky's 'Comrades' ", *Plebs*, Vol. XVII (July 1925), p. 288. Part I is by Postgate and Part II by Horrabin.

the C.P.G.B. and of the Executive of the Comintern, expressed the general disgust of the intellectuals with such machinations:

> I was present at innumerable discussions concerning the tactics necessary to inveigle the Hicks and Maxton types of industrial and political leaders into movements that in the eyes of the masses commit them to Moscow, and would enable the disciplined members of the Communist Party to use them as recruiting sergeants.
>
> Gradually, the scales fell from my glamour-smitten eyes and I saw how this system of Unity Movements, Relief Committees, Class War Defence Organizations, National Minority and National Unemployed Committees all shuts, like a telescope, around the co-optive central executive of the Communist International. I saw the twin frauds of "democratic" centralism and the "united" front, not from their stucco fronts and as far off as so many of you do, but behind the scenes where the wires laced and the levers were pulled.[1]

John Strachey ended his relationship with the British Communist movement in 1940 because he seriously disagreed with the Party war line. However, he had previously been thinking about capitalism and socialism in terms that might have eventually proved difficult to reconcile with his communism. He has recently told us that in 1938 two books profoundly impressed him.[2] They were J. M. Keynes' *The General Theory of Employment, Interest and Money* (1936), and Douglas Jay's *The Socialist Case* (1936). If, as he began to believe, capitalist crises could be eliminated without basically changing the capitalist system, then there was every justification for the employment of Fabian tactics to achieve socialism, rather than the revolutionary approach of the communists.

[1] Letter by J. T. Walton Newbold, *Plebs*, Vol. XVII (June 1925), p. 247.
[2] John Strachey, *Labour's Task*, Fabian Tract No. 290 (London: Fabian Publications, 1951), pp. 1–2.

A first result of this thinking was his book *A Programme for Progress* (1940), which was written prior to the outbreak of war on September 3, 1939. Big business, Strachey affirmed, could be subjected to social control by a public policy based on Keynesian economics. Roosevelt and the New Deal had accomplished this in America, an experience from which Britain could profit. If big business could be brought to heel, and if the economic crises of capitalism could thus be eliminated, there was no reason, according to Strachey, why the capitalist economic edifice had to be destroyed by violent revolution. He argued that a properly directed social programme of a Keynesian nature could, by gradually modifying the structure of the capitalist economy, lead to socialism. He suggested such a programme consisting of six principal measures: (1) the establishment of all types of public or mixed investment and enterprise; (2) the lowering of the rate of interest to all prospective investors; (3) the redistribution of income from the rich to the poor through taxes such as death duties; (4) a system of increased pensions and social services; (5) a national and public banking system; (6) the strict public control over balance of foreign payments. For one who called himself a communist, this was, to put it mildly, a novel outlook. Maurice Dobb, in a very temperate review, felt that the book expressed a Popular Front point of view, which was perhaps inadequate to cope with the postwar situation.[1] After the war there was the danger that capitalism might use such an expansionist programme to save itself by satisfying the short-term economic demands of the masses. More outspoken and probably reflecting the official C.P.G.B. attitude to Strachey's thesis was Emile Burns, who reviewed the book for the *Daily Worker* under the title "Strachey Progresses Backwards".[2] This was Social-Democracy, not Marxism, he announced. Kingsley Martin agreed with Burns, entitling his review in the *New Statesman*, "A

[1] Maurice Dobb, "Programme for Progress", *Left News*, No. 46 (February 1940), pp. 1432–1435.
[2] *Daily Worker*, March 2, 1940, p. 4.

188   BUREAUCRACY

Social Democrat", and welcoming Strachey back to the
fold from which he had so long strayed.[1] Strachey's reply to
both was that he was still a communist.[2]

This, very briefly, was Strachey's theoretical postion when
one month later he denounced the Party line in regard to
the war. At least in retrospect, his gradual deviation since
1938 from an orthodox Party viewpoint would appear to
have made a final break with communism inevitable. All
that was now needed to effect it was some action of the Party
that would make a mockery of everything that he had so
wholeheartedly fought for during the thirties. The parting
of the ways came in the Spring of 1940, when the Party line
began to identify Soviet, and hence communist, interests with
a total Nazi victory over Britain, France, and Norway.[3]
Originally he had been quite willing to accept the Nazi–
Soviet Pact. This was merely a temporary compromise with
fascism that could easily be defended on expediential
grounds. Likewise he had not hesitated over the Party line
of the Autumn of 1939: that the war was a struggle between
Nazi and British imperialism. The way out, he agreed at that
time, was not the victory of either side, but for the people of
both nations to force their governments to declare peace, and
to establish true peoples' democracies.[4] What he was asked
to do in the Spring of 1940 was not to support a compromise
with fascism, but a capitulation to all that was evil, even as
he was beginning to realize how socialism might be achieved
within the framework of democracy in the capitalist countries.
He was deeply concerned over the consequences to the allies
of a defeat at the hands of Hitler, as the Party did not seem
to be:

[1] Kingsley Martin, "A Social Democrat". *New Statesman and Nation*,
Vol. XIX, New Series (March 30, 1940), p. 436.

[2] *Daily Worker*, March 11, 1940, p. 3; letter to *New Statesman and Nation*,
Vol. XIX, New Series (April 6, 1940), p. 462.

[3] See John Strachey, letter to *New Statesman and Nation*, Vol. XIX, New
Series (April 27, 1940), p. 559; John Strachey, "The C.P. Line—Now",
Left News, No. 50 (July 1940), pp. 1498–1499.

[4] John Strachey, "The War", *Left News*, No. 44 (December 1939), pp.
1409–1411.

. . . every line written in the *Daily Worker* drives me to the conviction that those controlling the *Daily Worker* are prepared, for the sake of what they consider to be the interests of the Soviet Union, to give way to Hitler to any extent, and that they are utterly irresponsible as to the consequences to the British people of such unlimited giving way. So long as that remains the case I, and, it seems, almost everybody else in the country, can have nothing to do with them, however much we, like all sane people, "do not want the war", and however much we may agree with them as to the general character of the war.[1]

Letters to the *New Statesman* condemning Strachey were written by William Rust, the Editor of the *Daily Worker*, and Christopher Hill.[2] Strachey later contributed to *The Betrayal of the Left* (1941) edited by Victor Gollancz, a volume highly critical of communist policy. He also rejoined the Labour Party. Not since the nineteen-twenties had such a distinguished intellectual forsaken communism in such a public fashion. Conformity to the Party Line at the cost of his own intellectual and moral integrity was a price that John Strachey was not willing to pay. But as a host of intellectuals have discovered, honesty is a virtue least esteemed by the communists.

Professor Haldane was not outwardly affected by the zigzags of the Party line during the Second World War. Even his wife's defection did not shake his loyalty. But Haldane, like Strachey, and other intellectuals in the Party, possessed a sensitive point which if touched by communist orthodoxy would cause him to rebel. His pressure point was his scientific activity. When the Party, as part of the ideological campaign of the Cold War, began to lay down a correct line in genetics, Haldane refused to conform and resigned from the

[1] John Strachey, letter to *New Statesman and Nation*, Vol. XIX, New Series (April 27, 1940), p. 559.
[2] William Rust, letter to *New Statesman and Nation*, Vol. XIX, New Series (May 4, 1940), pp. 588–589; Christopher Hill, letter to *New Statesman and Nation*, vol. XIX, New Series (May 18, 1940), p. 644.

Party. As long as Lysenkoism was confined to the Soviet Union, Haldane was willing to overlook it. It was a different matter, however, when Lysenkoism became part of the policy of the C.P.G.B., and his own scientific probity was at stake.

In November 1948 Haldane discussed Lysenko in his weekly science article for the *Daily Worker*, generally praising him, but taking issue with him upon a number of specific points.[1] Later in the same month he participated with several outstanding British geneticists in a B.B.C. broadcast about Soviet genetics. Although the others did not hesitate to declare Lysenko a charlatan, Haldane was as non-committal as possible, defending Lysenko, yet disagreeing with him.[2] By this time it must have been fairly evident to the C.P.G.B. leaders that Haldane was attempting to straddle the fence. This of course, from their standpoint, was an unsatisfactory state of affairs. Within the privacy of the Party Haldane was much less compromising. At a number of meetings of Party geneticists and scientists, with Burns or Cornforth officiating, he refused to accept Lysenkoism, and most of the other communist geneticists followed suit.[3] He even wrote a point-by-point critique of a *Daily Worker* "Educational Commentary" defending Lysenko, cyclostyling and distributing it within the Party. Since Haldane and the communist geneticists had rebelled against the line, the C.P.G.B. had to resort to two unknown non-geneticists as "scientific" spokesmen for Lysenkoism: an agricultural plant breeder, James Fyfe; and a botanist, Alan Morton—both of whom appeared with books defending Lysenko and the Party line.[4] The star scien-

[1] J. B. S. Haldane, "Lysenko and Darwin", *Daily Worker* (November 1, 1948), p. 2.

[2] A detailed analysis of Haldane's remarks on this occasion is given in John Langdon-Davies' *Russia Puts the Clock Back: A Study of Soviet Science and Some British Scientists*, foreword by Sir Henry Dale (London: Gollancz, 1949), pp. 86–120.

[3] As reported in Gabriel A. Almond, *The Appeals of Communism* (Princeton: Princeton University Press, 1954), pp. 314—316.

[4] See James Fyfe, *Lysenko is Right* (London: Lawrence and Wishart, 1950); Alan G. Morton, *Soviet Genetics* (London: Lawrence and Wishart, 1951).

tist of British Communism became J. D. Bernal, who gave
his blessing to Lysenkoism, while Haldane's name appeared
with less frequency in the *Daily Worker*. His position in the
controversy was clarified, at least to the public, by an article
in the *Modern Quarterly* of the Summer of 1949, in which he
complained

> . . . that wholly unjustifiable attacks have been made on
> my profession, and one of the most important lessons which
> I have learned as a Marxist is the duty of supporting my
> fellow workers. We are not infallible, but we certainly do
> not hold many of the opinions which are attributed to us.[1]

Reviewing John Langdon-Davies' *Russia Puts the Clock Back*
for the *Daily Worker*, Haldane criticized the author's handling of the genetics controversy, but he also hit Lysenko:
"Unfortunately I think he has gone a great deal too far and
rejected a lot of sound biology along with the nonsense." [2]
By the end of 1950 the leadership of the C.P.G.B. had
managed to enforce the Lysenkoist line. After more than a
year, British Communist scientists on April 30, 1950, passed
a resolution giving unqualified support to Lysenkoism. Haldane, whose last article in the *Daily Worker* was on August 9,
1950, withdrew from its Editorial Board. The Sunday newspapers of November 12 carried reports that he had resigned
from the Party, which he denied in a characteristic statement:

> Professor Haldane considers that a very bad precedent
> would be established if university teachers were expected to
> state their membership or otherwise of political organiza-
> tions when requested to do so by newspapers.
>
> He also considers that, when suffering from a broken
> leg (Pott's fracture of malleolus), he was under no obliga-
> tion to ascend the staircase to answer a telephone call from

[1] J. B. S. Haldane, "In Defence of Genetics", *Modern Quarterly*, Vol.
IV, New Series (Summer 1949), p. 202.
[2] J. B. S. Haldane, "Nonsense about Lysenko", *Daily Worker*, November 14, 1950, p. 1.

a newspaper (the *Sunday Pictorial*) which refused to state the subject under discussion.

He has not read the various statements made about him in newspapers and leaves it to their readers to speculate as to their truth or otherwise.

For the guidance of such readers, he remarks that in view of the experiences of 1914–1918 and 1939–1945, he regards the rearmament of Germany as a suicidal policy for Britain, and that, as a doubtless old-fashioned believer in such notions as honour, he regards the wholesale massacre of civilians, whether by atom bomb or otherwise, as unworthy of a civilized people.

In this respect he is in full agreement with the policy of the Communist Party.[1]

The newspaper reports, however, had been correct despite Haldane's evasions. He had resigned from the Party, although there was never any official announcement. The nearest approach was a statement six years afterwards in the Polish Government newspaper *Życie Warszawy* that he had left the C.P.G.B. "because of Stalinist interference in Science . . . he could not reconcile himself to the dogma of the infallibility of authorities outside the field of science in solving the problems of science . . . ".[2] Haldane's only reply to this was that "the report was not entirely correct". About the same time, after two years of criticism, Lysenko was relieved of all duties as President of the All-Union Academy of Agricultural Sciences; and began to conduct extensive experiments with fertilizers. An organ of the Communist Party of the Soviet Union, *Party Life*, accused him and his colleagues of being responsible for crop failures in Siberia, and of "adjusting facts to fit their hypotheses".[3] The verdict of the C.P.G.B. delegation that visited the Soviet Union in the Autumn of 1956 appears to be conclusive: "For ten years it was impossible to carry out genuinely scientific work in the

[1] *Daily Worker*, November 14, 1950, p. 1.
[2] Quoted and reported in *The Times*, April 7, 1956, p. 4.
[3] *The Times*, April 10, 1956, p. 10; May 29, 1956, p. 10.

field of genetics".[1] Once again the Soviet line had changed, and once again the subservience of the C.P.G.B. had been proven. The penalty for this rigid adherence to the orthodoxy of Soviet communism, and for the suppression of divergences within the Party, was the loss of Professor Haldane, and some of its other leading members.

Unlike Strachey, Haldane left the communist movement without making a forthright assertion of his points of difference with the Party. Because of his reputation, and because he showed no tendencies of becoming a "renegade", the Party let him go quietly. Never publicly or unequivocally denouncing Lysenkoism, he yet remained unconvinced that "mutation is a highly adaptive process", but denied Lysenko was either always right, or always wrong.[2] Dropping out of active politics, he nevertheless continued as a sympathizer to support many of the policies of the Party. He is an active member of Scientists for Peace, and a very occasional contributor to the *Daily Worker*. In November 1955 he gave the fifth of the communist-sponsored John Cornford Memorial Lectures in Cambridge. Fascinated by India and its attempt at large-scale economic planning and disgusted with Great Britain, Haldane has resigned from the faculty of University College, London, and has emigrated to India with his wife, Dr. Helen Spurway, where they plan to work together in the India Statistical Office of Calcutta. Haldane explained that he wanted "to live in a free country where there are no foreign troops based all over the place".[3] The Suez affair, which he described in terms of "the mass murders at Port Said", was also a decisive factor in his decision.[4]

Strachey and Haldane deserted communism over matters that personally concerned them. At the time of their

[1] "British Communists in the Soviet Union (3): The Changes Since Stalin", *World News*, Vol. IV (January 19, 1957), p. 39. Professor Hyman Levy was a member of this delegation.

[2] J. B. S. Haldane, *The Biochemistry of Genetics* (London: Allen and Unwin, 1954), pp. 16, 88, 96, 98, 116–117.

[3] *The Times*, July 25, 1957, p. 7.

[4] *The Times*, November 21, 1956, p. 6.

G

defection, neither had called attention to the basic issue under-lying their grievances. Both had focused upon a particular instance and had neglected the universal. The crux of their respective disputes with the C.P.G.B. was their refusal to obey the demand for absolute conformity in word, thought, and deed made by an entrenched bureaucracy subservient to Moscow. The significance of the party rebellion oc-curring in the period from 1956 to 1957 is that criticism was concentrated upon this main issue from the very beginning of the crisis. Contention was directly concerned with the problems of intra-party democracy, of freedom of discussion and criticism, and of responsible party government. More-over, the attack was launched by intellectuals while they were still members of the Party. The valiant attempt to wage the fight against the tyranny of bureaucracy was made from *within* the Party. In degree at least, this was something uni-que in the history of the C.P.G.B. The criticism directed against the bureaucrats of Bolshevization in the twenties was similar, but less extensive and less intensive.

In 1956 an unprecedented ferment occurred among the intellectuals of the C.P.G.B. in reaction to events that took place in the communist world from the beginning of the year. First there was the "dethronement of Stalin" and the official revelations of his bureaucratic and terroristic reign which were made at the Twentieth Party Congress of the Communist Party of the Soviet Union (C.P.S.U.) in Febru-ary 1956. The impact of this event alone was enough to start the British Communist intellectuals upon their ques-tioning course. But the victorious stand of Gomulka in Poland against the Stalinists, and the courageous uprising of the Hungarian people, and its bloody suppression by the intervention of the Soviet armed forces transformed the mood of uneasy questioning into one of open revolt, especi-ally when the C.P.G.B. leadership continued to mouth the rationalizations of the Kremlin. The crisis in the Party was still further exacerbated by the strange disappearance or "exile" of Professor George Lukacs of Hungary, and by the arrest in East Germany and sentencing to ten years' imprisonment of Professor Wolfgang Harich, who as a "reforming" communist had unsuccessfully led a movement within the East German Communist party to overthrow the Ulbricht regime. In order to understand how these happenings affected the C.P.G.B. and its intellectuals, certain developments must be examined: (1) the publishing of the unofficial Party "opposition journal", *The Reasoner*; (2) the general situation in the C.P.G.B. caused by the Hungarian uprising; (3) the Minority Report of the Commission on Inner Party Democracy; (4) the controversy over a letter published by C.P.G.B. intellectuals in the non-communist press; (5) the emergence of a new wave of anti-intellectualism in the Party; (6) the Twenty-Fifth (Special) Congress of the C.P.G.B.

The first noticeable consequence of the Twentieth Congress of the C.P.S.U. in the British Communist movement was the discussion that took place in the letter columns of the *Daily Worker* in March 1956 just prior to the Twenty-Fourth National Congress of the C.P.G.B. Between February 29 and March 29, 1956, nearly sixty letters on the subject appeared in the *Daily Worker*. About one-third were pro-Stalin, one-half of these being written by women. The other two-thirds of the letters were critical either of Stalin, of the U.S.S.R., or of the C.P.G.B. and its leaders. Approximately one-tenth of the total number of letters were written by individuals who could be identified as Party intellectuals. All, with the exception of one by Pat Sloan, General Secretary of the British-Soviet Friendship Society, were, in varying degrees, critical of the communist record.[1]

It was not until some time after the holding of the British Congress that the intellectuals returned to the fray, with an obvious determination to thrash out the whole problem of

[1] The letters by intellectuals appeared in the *Daily Worker* upon the following dates: March 12, 1956 (Rodney Hilton, Pat Sloan); March 21, 1956 (Maurice Dobb, Ronald L. Meek); March 23, 1956 (Maurice Cornforth); March 27, 1956 (Bridget and Christopher Hill); March 29, 1956 (John Lewis).

Party democracy and the past performance of communism. Their letters began to appear in the official discussion in *World News*. John Saville of the University of Hull wrote that unless the leaders of the C.P.G.B. frankly admitted that many of the policies of the C.P.S.U. had been wrong, and unless they explained why they had supported them despite their being incorrect, they and the whole Party would stand discredited in the British Labour movement.[1] The "political honesty" of the C.P.G.B. "as a political party" was at stake. Calling for the widespread and genuine discussion of various problems of theory and practice, he decried the fact that in recent years the Party and its membership had become increasingly conformist. Taking up where Saville had finished, Edward Thompson of Leeds University, author of a recent study of William Morris, pointed to the decline of controversy within the Party. "Criticism and self-criticism" was nothing more than a "jargonized" form of Party controversy that was limited to the terms defined by the leadership. He continued in a vein reminiscent of W. N. Ewer's retort to the Editor of the *Labour Monthly* more than a quarter century before:

> Holy Church in medieval times also encouraged disputations on the dogma of the priesthood. But woe to those heretics who were unmasked as having acted for many years as agents of the Devil!
>
> The aim of controversy is more fundamental: it is to arrive at truth out of the clash of opposing views. This is the first meaning of dialectics.[2]

How much of British Communism, he wondered, was foreign in inspiration and conception, dogma out of touch with British conditions? The Assistant General Secretary of the C.P.G.B., George Mathews, replied to Thompson in an

---

[1] John Saville, letter to *World News*, Vol. III (May 19, 1956), p. 314.
[2] Edward Thompson, "Winter Wheat in Omsk", *World News*, Vol. III (June 30, 1956), p. 408.

article entitled "A Caricature of Our Party".[1] Controversy and discussion, he admitted, were needed for the sake of Party unity, but they must be in the "spirit of Marxism", aimed at achieving unity. He complained that Thompson viewed controversy as an end in itself. Weeks later several letters were published reprehending Mathews. Why was it necessary, admonished Bridget and Christopher Hill, for an *official* reply to Thompson, who was merely participating in the discussion?[2] Why must the Party membership always be told what to think by the leadership? Why did the leadership always identify criticism of itself with criticism of the Party? Rodney Hilton, who was disturbed by the "impermissably censorious tone" of Mathews, felt that if the Party leadership asked for discussion, it should not reject it as soon as it was practised, on the grounds that the unity of the Party might be threatened.[3]

Frustrated in their attempts to conduct any serious discussion in the Party press, and perceiving that the leadership would not tolerate independent and critical thinking, Saville and Thompson produced the first number of their unofficial communist journal, *The Reasoner*, in the latter part of July 1956.[4] The keynote of this unique venture was set by the quotation from Marx that appeared on the title page: "To leave error unrefuted is to encourage intellectual immorality". The editors proposed to use the journal as a forum for the discussion of "questions of fundamental

[1] George Mathews, "A Caricature of Our Party", *World News*, Vol. III (June 30, 1956), pp. 409–410. Thompson's reply to Mathews sent to *World News* was rejected upon the grounds that there was no space to publish it because of the great number of other contributions. Hence Thompson published the reply in *The Reasoner*. See E. P. Thompson, "Reply to George Mathews", *The Reasoner*, No. 1 (July 1956), pp. 11–15.

[2] Bridget and Christopher Hill, letter to *World News*, Vol. III (August 18, 1956), pp. 524–525.

[3] Rodney Hilton, letter to *World News*, Vol. III (September 1, 1956), pp. 552–553.

[4] For a detailed statement as to why *The Reasoner* was published, see "Statement of the Editors", *The Reasoner*, No. 3 (November 1956), pp. 37–44.

principle, aim, and strategy".[1] Contributors to *The Reasoner*, which ceased publication with the third number in November, included Ronald L. Meek, Doris Lessing, Hyman Levy, Rodney Hilton; three former members of the staff of the *Daily Worker*, Sheila Lynd, Derek Kartun, and Gabriel; and Professor G. D. H. Cole. Perhaps the most interesting remarks were made by Professor Levy in the September number, and by "P. H." of Sheffield in the final number. Prior to his article in *The Reasoner*, Professor Levy had objected in the *Jewish Clarion* to an editorial that had all too lightly treated the extermination of Jewish intellectuals in the Soviet Union: "As fighters for Socialism WE EXPECT NOT ONLY LEADERSHIP ON ECONOMIC MATTERS, BUT HONESTY AND FRANKNESS ON MORAL RIGHTS AND HUMAN INJUSTICE".[2] His article in *The Reasoner* declared that Marxism, originally an unorthodoxy, had, since its establishment and institutionalization, sought to exclude all unorthodoxy. He continued by asking the question:

> How can an unorthodox party leave no room for unorthodoxy within its own ranks, and expect to survive without doing violence to its best values, to its imagination, and therefore finally to its own integrity? To a scientific body integrity is its very life-blood.[3]

As if in answer to Professor Levy's question, "P. H." of Sheffield commented that

> ... the whole Communist world has taken over from Russia a system of organisation which is democratic not in the sense of involving rule by the members, but rule by an elite sprung from the members, and that conditions are so dissimilar in England from those ruling in the past in Russia that steps must be taken to develop a new theory of

[1] "Why We Are Publishing", *The Reasoner*, No. 1 (July 1956), p. 1.
[2] Hyman Levy, "Blot on the History of Socialism", *Jewish Clarion*, No. 9, New Series (July–August 1956), p. 2.
[3] Hyman Levy, "The Place of Unorthodoxy in Marxism", *The Reasoner*, No. 2 (September 1956), p. 14.

organisation. . . . All organisation tends to lead to oligarchical control. There are technical and other factors which make for this, but with the passage of time, the growth in membership and the degree of centralism, this tendency becomes more pronounced.[1]

The C.P.G.B. leadership naturally became "gravely concerned" over the publication of *The Reasoner*.[2] On September 5, 1956 the Editors, refusing a Political Committee request to cease publication, continued with the second number. To a second request their reply was the same, although they promised that the third number in November would be the last. A third warning with a hint of disciplinary action likewise went unheeded. Finally, after the publication of the last number on November 7, which called upon the Executive Committee of the C.P.G.B. to repudiate the Soviet intervention in Hungary and to demand the withdrawal of Soviet troops, the Executive Committee proposed to suspend Saville and Thompson from the Party for three months, and to review their position at the end of that time.[3] Both men, seeing that their fight from within the Party was hopeless, resigned from the Party. In their contest with the Editors of *The Reasoner*, the Executive Committee claimed that the Party Rules gave them the authority to prohibit independent publication by Party members. Since there is no specific rule granting them this power, the Executive Committee relied on Rule 27, which allows them to interpret the other rules as they see fit. However, their decision to contest the publication of *The Reasoner* was in essence political rather than legal, for the *Labour Monthly* was an independent publication whose editor, R. Palme Dutt, also happened to be a member of the Executive Committee. His views, however, coincided with the Party line, and those of

---

[1] "P. H.", "On Democratic Centralism", *The Reasoner*, No. 3 (November 1956), pp. 14–15.

[2] "Communist Party Executive Committee Statement on 'The Reasoner' ", *World News*, Vol. III (September 22, 1956), p. 600.

[3] *Daily Worker*, November 15, 1956, p. 1.

the Editors of *The Reasoner* did not. Hence, as Saville and
Thompson pointed out, there was one law for the members
of the Party leadership and another for the rank and
file.[1]

Thompson's parting shot at the leadership of British Communism was to accuse them of the Stalinist mode of thought.
By refusing to dissociate themselves from the Soviet intervention in Hungary, they had clearly demonstrated that they
had learned nothing from the past errors of the Party. They
were still Stalinists at heart. There followed a damning
critique of Stalinism:

> Stalinism is socialist theory and practice which has lost
> the ingredient of humanity. The Stalinist mode of thought
> is not that of dialectical materialism, but mechanical
> idealism. . . . Stalinism is Leninism turned into stone. . . .
> Instead of commencing with facts, social reality, Stalinist
> theory starts with the idea, the text, the axiom: facts, in-
> stitutions, people, must be brought to conform to the idea.
> . . . Stalinist analysis, at its most degenerate, becomes a
> scholastic exercise, the search for "formulations" "correct"
> in relation to text but not to life.[2]

Thompson and Saville and other ex-Communists have
organized a new movement for the discussion of Marxist
problems, the Socialist Forum, and are now publishing *The
New Reasoner*.

The Hungarian uprising and the intervention of the Soviet
armed forces accelerated and solidified the discontent within
the C.P.G.B. Never perhaps in its history had the Party
experienced a crisis of such serious proportions. Between
the Twenty-Fourth Party Congress and the end of the year
the average circulation of the *Daily Worker* had fallen from

[1] "Statement of the Editors", *The Reasoner*, No. 3 (November 1956),
p. 41.
[2] E. P. Thompson, "Through The Smoke of Budapest", *The Reasoner*,
No. 3 (November 1956), Supplement 6.

77,000 to 68,400.[1] John Gollan, General Secretary of the Party, stated on a television programme of December 10, 1956, that he expected the membership to fall by about 30%.[2] The figures released on February 27, 1957, after the normal registration period of eight weeks, proved that he was too pessimistic. Party membership had decreased from 33,959 at the time of the Twenty-Fourth Congress to 26,742, a loss of 21%.[3]

After the C.P.G.B. officially sanctioned Soviet intervention in a statement of November 4, 1956, many prominent communists either resigned or protested. Among the Trades Union leaders who left the Party were: R. B. Seabrook, an area organizer for the United Shop, Distributive and Allied Workers; John Horner, General Secretary, and Jack Grahl, Assistant General Secretary of the Fire Brigades Union; Les Cannon, Education Officer and Member of the Executive Committee of the Electrical Trades Union; Alec Moffat, a District Secretary of the National Union of Mineworkers, and brother of Abe Moffat, the communist President of the Scottish Miners. Nearly a quarter of the thirty members of the Editorial staff of the *Daily Worker* resigned their positions in protest, including: Gabriel (James Friell), the cartoonist for twenty years; Malcolm MacEwen, the Features Editor; and Derek Kartun, the Foreign Editor.[4] Peter Fryer, the *Daily Worker's* reporter in Budapest, whose frank reports were suppressed by the paper, resigned from the staff on November 16, and was later expelled from the Party for publishing a book, *Hungarian Tragedy*, in which he attempted to present the true facts about the revolt. It was reported in *The Times* that the Oxford University Communist Club had dissolved.[5]

---

[1] Edward Crankshaw, "A Minority Report on the Party Crisis", *Observer* (January 27, 1957), p. 1. According to *Tribune*, April 19, 1957, p. 3, the circulation of the *Daily Worker* in 1957 had slumped to 57,000.

[2] *Daily Worker*, December 11, 1956, p. 1.

[3] *World News*, Vol. 4 (March 9, 1957), p. 149.

[4] By May 1957 there had been thirteen resignations from the staff of the *Daily Worker*; see *Newsletter*, Vol. I (May 10, 1957), p. 2.

[5] *The Times*, November 10, 1956, p. 4.

The Communist Society of the London School of Economics vehemently protested against the Party line. Unity Theatre, a communist-supported organization, staged a "living newspaper" of events in Hungary and Suez, "World on Edge", in which the presentation on Hungary deviated considerably from the Party line. The telegram of protest sent by the Authors' World Peace Appeal to the Union of Soviet Writers was signed by a number of well-known British Communist writers.

Letters in the *Daily Worker* and the *New Statesman*, written singly or jointly by almost forty Party intellectuals, were critical of the Party line, some only mildly, others outspokenly, but none fully backing it.[1] The only intellectuals who unqualifiedly supported the Party line in the press were not members, but sympathizers: D. N. Pritt, Edgar P. Young, Hewlett Johnson, and Archibald Robertson.[2] Some of the intellectuals who are publicly known to have resigned from the Party, either at the time of the Hungarian uprising or shortly after the first of the year, are Edward P. Thompson, John Saville, Doris Lessing, Ronald L. Meek, Randall Swingler, Rodney Hilton, Rutland Boughton, the composer, and Len Doherty, the working-class author of *A Miner's Sons*. Christopher Hill, the Balliol historian, followed them, but not until after the Twenty-Fifth (Special) National Congress of April 1957.

The crisis in the C.P.G.B. was further aggravated by the Report of the Commission on Inner Party Democracy, made available to the public in January 1957. As a result of the discussion at the Twenty-Fourth National Congress, the Executive Committee appointed this Commission. Probably in reaction to *The Reasoner* and the general turmoil within the

[1] See *Daily Worker*, November 9, 1956, p. 2; November 12, 1956, p. 2; November 14, 1956, p. 2; November 15, 1956, p. 2; November 19, 1956, p. 2; November 22, 1956, p. 2; November 23, 1956, p. 2. *New Statesman and Nation*, Vol. III; November 17, 1956, p. 625; December 1, 1956, p. 701.

[2] See *Daily Worker*, November 9, 1956, p. 2; November 13, 1956, p. 2; *The Times*, November 13, 1956, p. 5.

Party, the membership of the Commission was enlarged and made more representative in July 1956, and a discussion upon inner party democracy was opened in *World News* in September. The Commission held eleven meetings, totalling more than fifty hours, between September 11 and December 6, 1956. The majority report, signed by twelve members of whom three had reservations, was accepted by the Executive Committee. The minority report was drawn up by Christopher Hill, Peter Cadogan, a Cambridge school-teacher and local Party Secretary, and Malcolm MacEwen, who had resigned as Features Editor of the *Daily Worker* while still a member of the Commission. It was this minority report and its rejection by the Executive Committee that further provoked discontent within the Party.

The basic thesis of the minority report was that democracy and unity must be combined so that neither would be impaired.[1] The authors believed that without democracy the optimum unity could never be achieved. Party unity depended upon a common belief of the membership in the aims and ideals of communism. Unless this belief was permitted to thrive and grow strong through free and democratic discussion, unity would be imperilled. Genuine unity characterized by a fighting Party morale could never be realized, the minority contended, by iron discipline and dictatorial control from the top down. The proposals of the majority report would "perpetuate the bureaucratic centralism that has had such disastrous results in Eastern Europe".[2]

The minority report, therefore, criticized the entrenchment of the Party bureaucracy and advocated measures that would free the Party from its oligarchical and irresponsible control. It began by calling attention to the composition and procedure of the Commission. Ten of the fifteen members were full-time Party workers, five being members of the Executive Committee. Among the five remaining members, one

[1] *Report to the Executive Committee by the Commission on Inner Party Democracy, December 1956* (London: C.P.G.B., 1957), p. 45.
[2] *Ibid.*, p. 46.

was an employee of the *Daily Worker*. Hence only four members of the Commission were not financially dependent upon the Party. Clearly, those who had a vital stake in the preservation of the Party, as it was presently constituted and organized, controlled the Commission. The minority report implied that the majority report had been railroaded through the Commission.

Central to the criticism of the minority was the question of the status of the Political Committee. Although it was generally considered a committee subordinate to the Executive Committee, it appeared

> . . . to wield very large powers, which are nowhere defined. It is clearly far superior in status to an advisory or working committee. It appears to exercise real control over the Party press, plays a major role in the selection of the recommended list for the new Executive Committee, controls the Party apparatus, and issues important political statements. It appears to be a policy-making body in between the two-monthly meetings of the Executive Committee. It consists exclusively of full-time professional political workers, and we are told that its time of meeting (Thursday mornings) frustrated attempts that had been made to include industrial or professional workers or trade union officials in it. While the Party must have a day-to-day leadership, there seems to be a danger here of excessive concentration of power in a small body of full-time political workers, that can be harmful to inner-Party democracy, and weaken the real authority and status of the elected executive.[1]

Not only did the minority charge that the Political Committee controlled the Executive Committee, but also that it dominated the election of the new Executive Committees at the Party Congress. A final accusation directed towards the

[1] *Report to the Executive Committee by the Commission on Inner Party Democracy, December 1956* (London: C.P.G.B., 1957), pp. 50–51.

Party hierarchy was its subservience to Soviet policy, a subservience that had disastrous consequences for the Party:

> A growing minority believe that the uncritical support given by the Executive Committee to Soviet policy divides, discredits, and isolates the Party, identifies Communism in the minds of British people with the denial of personal freedom and with certain indefensible policies, and renders ineffective the Party's efforts to combat anti-Soviet tendencies.[1]

Full independence from the Communist Party of the Soviet Union must be the aim of British Communism.

A second important and closely related theme of the minority report was the need for freedom of expression for all members of the C.P.G.B. The reason for this was contained in an eloquent plea that derived from John Stuart Mill's argument in the *Essay on Liberty*:

> Communism's greatest strength is, or should be, the truth. Without access to the truth communists cannot take the right decisions. Truth is a weapon in our hands, but truth cannot be dissected into those parts which are helpful to our cause, and therefore publishable, and those parts which are harmful, and must therefore be suppressed. Truth has to be taken as a whole, and the more damaging truth may be, the more necessary it is to know it, if mistakes are to be put right, and injustices undone.[2]

But unless, the report asserted, there is freedom of discussion, of the right of the minority to express its views, the truth can never be ascertained and acted upon. Nothing can be published in the Party press, the *Daily Worker*, *World News*, *Labour Monthly*, and the *Modern Quarterly* without approval of the Executive Committee. The ban on *The Reasoner* showed that the Party leadership feared any independent thinking

---

[1] *Report to the Executive Committee by the Commission on Inner Party Democracy, December 1956* (London: C.P.G.B., 1957), pp. 58–59.
[2] *Ibid.*, p. 51.

by the membership. Until this situation is rectified, the minority report declared, until the individual member is in a position to freely express his views without fear of recrimination, Party policy would not be based upon the truth, and hence would be essentially unsound policy.

One result of this unprecedented appeal for democracy and responsible government within the Party was a meeting held by 110 communist dissenters in Holborn Hall, January 24, 1957.[1] The leaders of this meeting were Dennis Swinnerton, his wife Jane Swinnerton, and Leslie Sewell, all of whom had long and faithfully served the communist cause. For all intents and purposes, the platform of these rebels was the minority report. They demanded democratization of the Party, the removal of the present Executive Committee, which was opposed to all change, and the independence of the C.P.G.B. from the C.P.S.U. Several weeks later Mrs. Swinnerton stated that she had not renewed her membership card because "We don't like 'thought control', or brute force, or repression, all of which the C.P. purports to fight, but in reality uses".[2] Writing in the *Observer*, her husband condemned the fates of Wolfgang Harich and George Lukacs, and urged communists to withdraw from the Party, applying "some of the concern which has been previously reserved for the 'victims of American injustice' to the cause of Harich and other victims of Communist repression."[3]

No doubt another result of the minority report and its effect upon the membership was the self-criticism of the *Draft Political Resolution* adopted by the Executive Committee for discussion at the Special Party Congress to be held at Easter. It contained what amounted to an admission, mild though it was, of the charges of the minority report. Leading committees of the Party had neglected discussion of principles upon which policy decisions had been taken.

[1] *Tribune*, February 1, 1957, p. 9.

[2] Letter to *New Statesman and Nation*, Vol. LIII (February 16, 1957), p. 203. The letter was also published in the *Tribune*, February 15, 1957, p. 11.

[3] Letter to *Observer*, April 7, 1957, p. 12.

REASONER VERSUS BUREAUCRAT

There had not been enough discussion and controversy throughout the Party upon matters of policy. A "big gap" had existed between the Executive Committee, and the Branches. Sufficient regard had not been paid to the views of rank-and-file members, nor had their suggestions been adopted. The general response of the Party leadership to criticism had been inadequate. Finally, the resolution affirmed that "there has been a tendency to understress democracy and overstress centralism". Whether the Executive Committee will actually seek to remedy this situation only time will tell. So far, although there has been a certain relaxation in the limits placed upon discussion, there is no evidence that the bureaucracy is loosening its grip upon the Party.

That the leaders of the C.P.G.B. had learned little from the events of 1956 is shown by their reaction to a letter signed by a number of communist intellectuals that was published in the *Tribune* and the *New Statesman*.[1] The letter, which according to the writers had been refused publication by the *Daily Worker*, condemned the Soviet action in Hungary and the British Executive Committee's uncritical support of it. For the past dozen years, it declared, the political analyses of the C.P.G.B. had been based upon "a false presentation of the facts". If the C.P.G.B. expected to make any headway in the British Labour Movement, it would have to repudiate all its past errors and those of current Soviet policy. The Political Committee replied almost immediately with a statement in *World News*.[2] A short history of the letter was given with an explanation as to why it was not published in the *Daily Worker*. The Editor of the *Daily Worker*, who had

[1] *Tribune*, November 30, 1956, p. 3; *New Statesman and Nation*, Vol. LII (December 1, 1956), p. 701. The signers were Chimen Abramsky, E. J. Hobsbawm, Hyman Levy, Robert Browning, Paul Hogarth, Jack Lindsay, Henry Collins, George Houston, Hugh MacDiarmid, Christopher Hill, V. G. Kiernan, Ronald L. Meek, R. H. Hilton, Doris Lessing, E. A. Thompson (*sic*).
[2] "Statement of the Political Committee of the Communist Party", *World News*, Vol. III (December 8, 1956), p. 781.

received the letter on November 20, 1956, from Christopher Hill, acting on behalf of the signers, got in touch with the Political Committee. Afterwards he wrote Hill that the Political Committee objected to such a nation-wide collection of signatures. Letters of protest were usually signed by members of the same locality or place of work. Hence this letter would set an entirely new precedent. There would, however, be no objection to publishing such letters over individual signatures. The political content of the letter, he emphasized, was not at issue. Hill's answer to the Editor was that this letter would set no precedent since a similar letter signed by a number of Party members throughout the country had in fact been published in the *Daily Worker* of November 15. However, the Political Committee pointed out that the letter to which Hill referred was of a non-controversial nature urging communists to remain in the Party. The letter that Hill had been responsible for sending "represented a political platform in conflict with the policy of the Party, for which signatures had been collected outside the democratic machinery of the Party". Actually, the Political Committee had contradicted itself. The political content of the letter and the right to freely express it within the Party were the only things at stake.

The debate touched off by the Political Committee's statement lasted for three months. Professor Levy in a brief letter to *World News* protested that the signers of the letter were in no way a "faction", but that the conduct of the Political Committee was forcing them to become one.[1] A week later, George Mathews, the Assistant General Secretary of the C.P.G.B., ignoring the advice of Professor Levy, renewed the attack on behalf of the Political Committee.[2] He labelled the letter as both "negative" and "defeatist". By concentrating "exclusively on the past mistakes", of the Party, it constituted a direct attack upon the Party. The re-

[1] Hyman Levy, letter to *World News*, Vol. IV (January 5, 1957), p. 13.
[2] George Mathews, "Lessons of a Letter", *World News*, Vol. IV (January 12, 1957), pp. 24–26, 32.

cord of international communism for the past twelve years was not solely one of error, as the letter would seem to indicate, but also one of great accomplishment, such as the winning of seven hundred million people to the cause of socialism. Mathew's implication was that the few mistakes were trivial compared to such overwhelming victories. He concluded with an attack upon the writers as intellectuals:

> The comrades who signed it are, many of them, members of long standing, who have done good work for the Party and the working-class movement. If they have put their names to a letter so redolent of a petty-bourgeois outlook, so remote from a working-class approach, so bankrupt of positive content, it is certainly not only their responsibility that they should have arrived at this position.
>
> The Party leadership must accept its share of responsibility for not appreciating sufficiently that such comrades have special problems, are subjected to different influences from those which face comrades in the factories, and need special help from the Party.
>
> The Party regards the work of these comrades as an important contribution to its efforts on behalf of tl.e British working class. But just as it needs the intellectual ;, so they need the Party. They need the sense of discipline which it can give them. They need its help in combating petty-bourgeois ideas. They need the understanding which it can give them that the Party is bigger than any individual or group of individuals, however distinguished.
>
> *Only if this lesson is learnt as a result of recent events, will any good at all come out of an action harmful to the Party and to the working class.*

Letters from Christopher Hill and Eric Hobsbawm followed.[1] Professor Levy wrote an impassioned article in which he deplored the leaders' lack of moral courage over the revelations of the Twentieth Congress of the C.P.S.U.[2] He revealed

[1] *World News*, Vol. IV (January 26, 1957), pp. 61–63.
[2] Hyman Levy, "Lessons of an Article", *World News*, Vol. IV (March 2, 1957), pp. 138–139.

that his first impulse upon reading Mathews' diatribe "was to go straight to King Street and to tear up my Party card publicly". "Why," he exclaimed, "did Mathews deliberately misrepresent the motives of the writers?"

> To discredit us in the eyes of those who did not know us personally? Or was it intended to teach "those intellectuals" a lesson? A lesson in bad Marxism? Or to drive a wedge between so-called intellectuals and non-intellectuals in the Party?

At stake in the controversy were

> . . . the qualities of genuineness and honesty essential, as I see it, to a scientific Marxist in the pursuit of the cause of socialism . . . *the whole principle of democratic centralism is here involved*. That principle in the last resort depends for its functioning on the genuineness and honesty of the Centre *vis-à-vis* the members, and the alertness and frankness of the members *vis-à-vis* the Centre.

John Gollan, the General Secretary, next entered the debate, repeating much of Mathews' argument.[1] The letter was not published in the Party press because factions would not be tolerated. Like Mathews, he concluded by attempting to put the Party intellectuals in their place, and although disclaiming any intention of intellectual-baiting, at the same time he reminded them of their subordinate role in the working-class movement.

The "anti-intellectual" features of the articles by Mathews and Gollan were by no means isolated instances, for since Harry Pollitt had remarked at the closed session of the Twenty-Fourth Party Congress that only the Party intellectuals were disturbed by Khrushchev's revelations, there seemed to be a general trend in this direction. An increasing number of slurs upon the Party intellectuals had appeared

---

[1] John Gollan, "The Cause of the Party is Socialism", *World News*, Vol. IV (March 9, 1956), pp. 154–156.

in *World News*.[1] Other members of the Party besides Professor Levy had noticed the trend and had cautioned the Party against it.[2] One letter to *World News* suggested that there was a tendency for the Party membership to split into those demanding greater democracy and freedom of discussion—the intellectuals—and those supporting unity and centralism—the working-class members.[3] It would be the intellectuals, the writer believed, who would have to make the greatest adjustment if they were to remain within the Party, because in the communist movement there must be limitations upon freedom for the sake of militant action.

The Executive Committee's *Draft Political Resolution* of February 1957 evidently had in mind Lenin's criticism of bourgeois intellectuals in the Party, when it referred to the "right opportunist and liquidationist outlook" as the chief danger developing within the C.P.G.B.[4] Joan Simon, the wife of Brian Simon of the University of Leicester, took her cue from this passage of the Resolution by quoting Lenin that in times of crisis certain Party intellectuals unconsciously act as "purveyors of bourgeois ideas which corrupt the class consciousness of the proletariat . . .".[5] This, she argued, was exactly what the intellectuals were now doing in the C.P.G.B.:

> Clearly it is politically necessary to establish that the people concerned are intellectuals because we have got to recognize this negative propaganda for what it is. Equally

---

[1] See the following letters in *World News*, Vol. IV: Geoff Laxton, February 9, 1957, p. 90; Doug. Adam, February 9, 1957, pp. 93–94; Frank Jackson, February 16, 1957, p. 111; J. Gamble, March 16, 1957, p. 172.

[2] For example see: Doris Lessing, "A Letter to the Editors", *The Reasoner*, No. 2 (September 1956), p. 11; John Lewis, "Questions of Theory", *World News Discussion Supplement*, No. 1 (January 26, 1957), p. 19; Lipman Kessel, letter to *World News*, Vol. IV (February 23, 1957), p. 126; J. Lyons, letter to *World News*, Vol. IV (March 16, 1957), p. 174.

[3] Ron Bellamy, letter to *World News*, Vol. IV (October 20, 1956), p. 467.

[4] Executive Committee of the C.P.G.B., *Draft Political Resolution* (London: C.P.G.B., 1957), p. 17.

[5] Joan Simon, letter to *World News*, Vol. IV (February 23, 1957), pp. 125–126.

clearly the Executive Committee would be failing in its fundamental duty if it failed to condemn it and to show that it has nothing in common with Communist criticism.

Such reasoning was further applied by Geoff Laxton, who used Lenin as an authority to brand the minority report of Hill, Cadogan, and MacEwen as the product of bourgeois intellectuals, still bourgeois in outlook despite their association with the Party.[1] Thus the latent anti-intellectualism of the Party had come to the fore to aid the Political Committee in suppressing the rebellion. Moreover, the ruling oligarchy had gained a useful weapon for its protection in the future. All who might demand democratic reforms within the Party could be denounced as still suffering from bourgeois illusions. Much the same rationalization was once used in Russia to defend the Stalinist dictatorship.

The leadership at the Twenty-Fifth (Special) National Congress, which was convened on Good Friday, April 19, 1957 in Hammersmith Town Hall for the purpose of considering the Report of the Commission on Inner Party Democracy, *The Draft Political Resolution* and the revision of Party policy in *The British Road to Socialism*, was obviously impatient with the idealistic reasoners. Hyman Levy still vigorously attacked the leadership.[2] Christopher Hill was not so outspoken, although he left little illusion as to his position.[3] It was the task of Arnold Kettle of the Executive Committee and Andrew Rothstein to rebuke the intellectuals officially. Kettle stated that there was no question of "contempt for intellectuals" in the Party, but emphasized that there could be no "special status" given to them.[4] The cardinal sin of *The Reasoner* and the cause of the leadership's condemnation of the letter in the *New Statesman* was "the immodest parading of conscience, of moral superiority,

---

[1] Geoff Laxton, letter to *World News*, Vol. IV (March 23, 1957), pp. 188–189.

[2] Levy's complete speech is given in *Tribune*, April 26, 1957, p. 5.

[3] As reported in *World News*, Vol. 4 (May 18, 1957), pp. 317–318.

[4] *World News*, Vol. 4 (May 4, 1957), p. 279.

which some of our middle-class intellectuals have gone in for. . . ." Truth and morality, he implied, was a function of the judgment of the leadership and not of the reasoning of the individual member: "the doing of the necessary right thing at each particular moment of struggle is a higher principle than that of subjective sincerity . . .". This was precisely the canon of truth and morality that the intellectuals in Great Britain and elsewhere in the communist world had objected to. Their position was expressed by Howard Fast's plea to the Soviet writer, Boris Polevoi: "But has it ever been dishonourable to follow the dictates of one's own conscience?" [1] This was a principle that Party stalwarts failed to appreciate. Andrew Rothstein, invoking the early history of Bolshevism, scorned these amateurs of revolution:

> The struggle was particularly violent in Russia in 1907 to 1911, when triumphant reaction was making a counter-offensive after the defeat of the first revolution.
>
> In those years, tens of thousands of workers left the Party of Marxism because, Comrade Levy, they were bewildered and confused by groups of backboneless and spineless intellectuals who had turned in upon their own emotions and frustrations (loud interruptions) to rend the Party instead of using their capabilities to rally the workers around it (more interruptions).[2]

Rothstein was interrupted by a delegate from the floor, John McLoughlin, the communist shop steward who had provoked the recent unofficial strike at Briggs Motor Bodies. He shouted "You are the enemy, you lying old swine." [3] But the bureaucrats had won the day. The reasoners were given the choice of worshipping the idol of unreason or of leaving. Any hopes they cherished that British communism might become more than a dogmatic revelation from on high were shattered.

[1] As quoted in Harrison E. Salisbury, "Writers in the Shadow of Communism", *New York Times Magazine* (June 9, 1957), p. 33. Fast had resigned from the C.P.U.S.A. at the beginning of the year.

[2] *Daily Worker*, April 23, 1957, p. 3.

[3] As quoted in *Tribune*, April 26, 1957, p. 5.

CONCLUSION

CHAPTER VIII

CONCLUSION

THE RECENT HAPPENINGS in the C.P.G.B. are in many respects a repetition of the experiences of the intellectuals in the nineteen-twenties who revolted against the policy of Bolshevization. The criticisms that are now being aimed at the oligarchic leadership of the Party are the same that bourgeois students of communism have been voicing for years. The analyses of the nature of the organization of political movements of Robert Michels and Max Weber antedate the Russian Revolution. Yet why can the communist intellectual never seem to profit, whether from the experience of intellectuals who were formerly in the Party, or from the investigations of great students of politics and society? Why must he discover from his own painful experience how communism can make the life of an intellectual a torment? Communism is an experience of an extremely intense personal nature. Some intellectuals accept the communist mode of life, others reject it. Why is this? What mental adjustment and transformation is necessary if the intellectual is to become a loyal member of the Party? Can any generalized statement be made about this experience?

The pattern of thought and outlook of the intellectual changes as he is gradually integrated into the Party. First his adherence to the Party line is required. This he finds much more difficult than the worker, whose whole life (as Lenin saw) is usually one of rather sombre conformity. The intellectual is much more at home with theoretical problems and abstract ideas than the average worker. Hence he tends to be more sensitive to changes in the Party line, and to be more fully aware of their implications. But there is a more important reason why conformity to the Party line is difficult for the intellectual. When he enters the Party, he is

deeply committed to certain values that stand outside the
Party and the Party line. As a scientist his fundamental allegiance is to truth; as an artist he is committed to beauty.
Since the trusted Party member can have only one supreme
value, loyalty to the Party and a belief in Marxism-Leninism, to which all other values must be subordinated, there
immediately arises the problem of the conflict of values for
the intellectual. An important conflict, for example between
truth and Party loyalty, may not occur for some time. When
it does, the intellectual may attempt to compromise, maintaining some sort of uneasy equilibrium of values. Such a
state of co-existence is neither a stable nor a happy one.
Sooner or later a decision must be made as to which values
will dominate. If after repeated breakdowns of this co-
existence an extremely sharp conflict arises, the intellectual
like Strachey or Haldane may reject the Party. The longer
he remains in the Party and persists in a life of compromise,
the more probable will be his eventual surrender to the Party
values. This is particularly true if his livelihood comes to
depend upon the Party or a Party-sponsored organization.

As a newcomer to communism the intellectual may look
upon an act or particular policy of the Party as an end in itself, designed to benefit mankind here and now, to increase
social justice. He still views men as individuals, and thinks
of their welfare in the present. After he has remained in the
Party for any great length of time, he may begin to notice
that the policies which he had once espoused in his early
days of membership have since been rejected, and perhaps
even replaced by those of an opposite and conflicting nature.
Often the new programme may appear less beneficial to the
masses than the old one. What happens now to the ideals
concerning the good of the masses, about which he was
originally so anxious? How does he become reconciled to
the change in line? He gradually learns that when a communist speaks of the good of mankind he usually thinks of it
in terms of the future. Not until the goal of the world communist commonwealth has been achieved will social justice

be established. An act of the Communist Party can never
be judged by its immediate consequences, but by the contribution that it makes towards this ultimate goal. The intellectual who accepts this approach begins increasingly to
focus his attention upon the future to the neglect of the
present. Since the communist millennium exists only as a
dim constellation of ideas and ideals, and since he views the
present in terms of this abstraction, reality itself becomes no
more than a series of highly stylized abstractions, usually in
blacks and whites. The details, the particularity and in-
dividuality of the acts and actors of the present scene are
blurred in the intellectual's cognition. The abstraction of
the present in terms of an abstraction of the future profoundly influences his action. If the present is considered
important only as an avenue to the future, then the main
task is one of clearing the way, of removing everybody
and everything that may impede the inevitable march of
history. Human life, feeling, sentiment, traditional values
are of little consequence. Nothing possesses a value in
itself, but only as it stands in relation to the future commonwealth.

Here again a communist intellectual is confronted with a
conflict of values. Must he jettison the values that he has so
long cherished, by subjecting them to a vague dream of the
future? Must he cause men to suffer in the present for the
sake of the idea that human suffering will be eliminated
eventually, or prostitute his reason in the hope that by so doing reason one day will rule the earth? The intellectual
may baulk at this, particularly when his professional values
or interests are at stake. Haldane was able to accept up to a
certain point the doctrine that the end justifies the means,
but when he was told that he must compromise his concept
of scientific truth by completely accepting Lysenkoism and
repudiating classical genetics, he could no longer remain a
communist. Every Party intellectual has a breaking point
beyond which he will not go. If he has no such point, he has
ceased to be an intellectual. It might almost be said that the

raison d'être of the C.P.G.B. is the search for the breaking-point of every intellectual in its midst.

The intellectual who manages to survive a number of Party crises must make one more adjustment before achieving the state of mind of a Dutt or a Burns. Since the criterion of thought and action is its usefulness to the cause of communism, who is to be judge? The answer is simply that judgment must be rendered by those best qualified to use Marxism-Leninism to analyse the present situation, and to put into practice the results of their analysis. By definition these can only be the present leaders of international communism, particularly those who preside over the world's first socialist republic, the Soviet Union. Once the intellectual begins to believe that all actions and pronouncements of the communist hierarchy are for the ultimate interest of mankind, he has secured himself against all possible changes in the Party line. He becomes a faithful member of the Party, accepting with unquestioning obedience all Party directives. At this moment he ceases to be an intellectual, a creator of ideas, and becomes a retailer of the ideas of others and a manufacturer of slogans. He no longer searches for the truth; he begins with the truth as revealed in the pronouncements of the Party leaders. It is his job to juggle with words, facts, and ideas so as to support this truth. The communist intellectual is an ideologist whose function is to manipulate and persuade. When he becomes a good communist, one above all reproach, and thereby ceases to be an intellectual, he is often a member of the body of black-coats, who are either paid functionaries of the Party or of Party-supported organizations. He thereby gains a material as well as a spiritual stake in the Party. It is now too late to retreat. Having ceased to be an intellectual, he becomes a communist bureaucrat.

Only a handful of the many intellectuals who have been associated with the C.P.G.B. have sacrificed their intellect in such a conclusive fashion. R. Palme Dutt and Emile Burns are representative of this minority. Both were men of exceptional

talent with promising futures. The more brilliant of the
two, Dutt, who might have won a reputation as a student
of international politics, instead became the pontifical ideologue of the British Communist bureaucracy and the scholas-
tic rationalizer of the Kremlin's decrees. His rise in the
Party was immediate and spectacular. He has been a member of the Executive Committee since 1922. Burns rose to
be the Party's technician of propaganda and "chief whip"
among intellectuals. Unlike Dutt his participation at the
lower echelons of Party activity was long and arduous. He
knows what it is to sell the Party newspaper on the street
corner and to be an agitator and organizer among the
workers. The writings of these two bureaucrats have been
facile exegeses of the Party line, lacking intellectual depth.
Their Marxist analyses of society have been reflections of the
thinking of others, not provocative contributions such as
those of a Caudwell or a Lukacs. As good communists and
prudent men of power, they have made the necessary adjust-
ments to each of the many ideological zigzags of the Kremlin.
Survival in the rough and tumble of communist politics is a
sign of manipulative prowess rather than intellectual integrity.

The case of James Klugmann is not so widely known. He
was an undergraduate and research student during the early
thirties at Trinity College, Cambridge, where he belonged
to the communist coterie that included David Guest,
Maurice Cornforth, John Cornford, Guy Burgess, Charles
Madge, and Fred Pateman. His sister, Kitty, married Cornforth, who has become a Party black-coat and ideological
overseer. Tom Driberg describes the student Klugmann as
"an able literary historian" who urged Burgess to join the
Party.[1] After entering the British Army in 1940 Klugmann
was assigned to Brigadier Fitzroy Maclean's Military Mission to the Yugoslav Partisans. As a Major he was General
Staff Officer II in the rear Headquarters Staff of this unit.

[1] Tom Driberg, *Guy Burgess: A Portrait with Background* (London:
Weidenfeld and Nicolson, 1956), p. 18.

He left the Army after hostilities to accept the position of Principal Executive Assistant to the Chief of the UNRRA Mission in Yugoslavia. Since 1952 he has been a member of the Executive Committee of the C.P.G.B., Head of the Central Education Department, and until the recent Twenty-Fifth Congress a member of the all-powerful Political Committee.

In the summer of 1948 Klugmann found himself in the predicament that sooner or later every communist intellectual experiences. It came in the form of the expulsion of Yugoslavia from the Cominform and the Kremlin's assault upon Tito. The dilemma confronting Klugmann was whether or not he should follow the Party line and turn against those whom he had aided during the war and who in turn had befriended him. Should he denounce those whose post-war experiment in social and economic reconstruction he had championed so enthusiastically? This was the supreme test of his life: of his faith in communism, of his intellectual integrity, of his moral courage. He chose, what certainly could not have been the easy way, to prove himself a steadfast communist by denouncing the object of his past ardour. His excoriation of Yugoslav communism, *From Trotsky to Tito*, was published in 1951. Testimony of what he now accepted as the ultimate criterion of thought and action is given by the following passage:

> Those of us, like myself, who in the early stage were deceived by the manœuvres of the Titoites, can well understand the gratitude that we owe, and that, indeed, the peoples of all countries owe, to the wisdom of the warnings given by the Communist Party of the Soviet Union. Indeed we only have to think what might have happened if the Communist Information Bureau, on Soviet initiative, had not warned and had not unmasked the plots of the Tito gang, to understand the debt of all progressive people to the Soviet Communists.[1]

[1] James Klugmann, *From Trotsky to Tito* (London: Lawrence and Wishart, 1951), p. 202.

He was rewarded the following year with a promotion to the top of the Party hierarchy. But fate had not finished with Klugmann. The Soviet line changed and Tito was welcomed back to the communist fraternity. *From Trotsky to Tito* was withdrawn from circulation by the C.P.G.B. In Stalinist Russia Klugmann would have paid with his head; in the C.P.G.B. he evidently only received a slight demotion. What did Klugmann think? Had he indeed become the Spartan communist? Communist politics, like bourgeois politics, is fraught with tragic undertones.

If the intellectual becomes a Party leader, he participates in the formulation of the Party line. He is at last a judge of the correct communist action and thought. At this, the final stage in his bureaucratization, his perspective again changes. He begins to identify his own interests as a member of the bureaucratic elite with the interest of the communist movement. Any threat or challenge to his position and to his own security becomes a threat to communism itself. The longer he remains in the seat of power the more firmly he becomes attached to this identification. The status quo within the movement together with his position in it must be preserved at all costs. This is the ideology that binds him to his fellow bureaucrats and that stamps his outlook. This is the state of mind that extends throughout the Party bureaucracy down to the lower levels. Any great change in the movement, threatening radically to alter it, may imperil their offices. More pressure for change from below results in more unity at the top in opposition to it. Every stratagem is employed to put down the challenge. Their struggle for survival is facilitated by the nature of communism, with its emphasis upon monolithism and democratic centralism. All these "counter-revolutionary" actions of the elite are in the name of saving the revolution.

The intellectuals, who recently have revolted against the Party bureaucracy, may complain that the intellectuals among the present leaders do not understand what they are asking. This may not be quite true. The rebels are the intellectuals who have reached the breaking-point in the bureaucratizing process. They protest against thought control, intellectual dishonesty, undemocratic procedures that hamper free discussion, and irresponsible leadership, etc. They make these criticisms in the hope that if something is done about them, the movement will be strengthened and win a greater following among the British masses. Those to whom they make their plea turn a deaf ear. They are no longer intellectuals or workers, but bureaucrats. What, after all, is the essential difference between a Harry Pollitt and a Palme Dutt, a John Gollan and an Emile Burns, a George Mathews and a James Klugmann? They are all "good communists" and nothing more. Their patterns of thought are basically the same despite the fact that one is an ex-boiler-maker and another a Balliol honours graduate. Power, even in the most limited sense, has left its imprint. They are the complete masters in their tiny parish of true believers. Like all holders of power, they seek to suppress dissension in order to retain their power. Objectively speaking their critics may well be right. The changes that they propose might lead to a swelling of Party ranks. British communism might become a potent political force instead of a trouble-making propaganda sect. But such a consequence might also mean an end to the careers of the present leaders and to the comfortable routines that they have made for themselves. Formerly radical, vigorous, and imaginative, now they are none of these things. They have grown conservative defending revolution. They preside over a system that has bureaucratized all thought and action. As a consequence, the intellectual who enters the Party, the philosopher who would be king, may cease to be a philosopher, and will seldom be a king.

A fundamental question remains. Intellectuals are generally inclined to political apathy. In times of acute crisis a cause such as communism that is basically the antithesis of politics attracts many intellectuals, particularly the literati and the scientists. Is this pure coincidence, or do the poet and the physicist share some common predisposition that renders them the most apolitical of an apolitical species? Scientific invention seems to be the consequence of the same sort of creative process as literary invention. In order to describe the psychology of mathematical invention the French mathematician, Jacques Hadamard, resorts to such expressions as "act of discovery", "illumination", "poetic inspiration", "poetic emotion", "sense of scientific beauty".[1] Henri Poincaré calls our attention to the importance of the "sieve" of "æsthetic sensibility" in scientific discovery.[2] The creative imagination of the great poet like Auden would seem to be analogous to that of the great scientist like Haldane. At least no great gulf separates them. Or to put it another way, the creative imagination of poet and scientist are different aspects of the same mode of activity. Creative minds of a high level of ability are concerned with grasping the essence of reality. They seek the universal in the particular, the poet through metaphor, the scientist by mathematics. The microcosms of the artist and scientist are ordered and harmonious abstractions of the macrocosm of activity. Theirs is an attempt to leap from the Platonic cave of the particular into the world of understanding.

Aristotle in the *Poetics* might have been speaking of politics when he compared history to poetry.

> . . . poetry is a more philosophical and a more excellent thing than history: for poetry is chiefly conversant about general truth, history about particular.

To the creative thinker political activity is concerned with the superficial, the relative, and the temporal, of much less significance than the universal with which he is occupied. A political "solution" of a problem is never a solution, but always a temporary expedient, an attempt to achieve the

[1] Jacques Hadamard, *An Essay on the Psychology of Invention in the Mathematical Field* (Princeton: Princeton University Press, 1949), pp. 10, 17–19, 31.

[2] Henri Poincaré, *Science and Method*, trans. by Francis Maitland; preface by Bertrand Russell (New York: Dover, 1952), pp. 59–60.

H

possible, a *modus vivendi*. The political answer to any question is never definitive, but inconclusive and vacillating. Instead of the doctrinal certainty and positive action of communism, politics offers only uncertainty and incoherence, compromise and conciliation, the oscillation of retreat from nowhere and advance to nowhere. Politics makes a virtue of everything that poet and scientist struggle to transcend, for the quest for beauty and truth brooks no compromise, no conciliation, no vacillation. Politicians seldom act, they appear to talk a talk that is just talk—an incessant stream of platitudes and empty slogans. The image of the politician in the creative imagination tends to be that of the astute manipulator, a broker of power, the pathetically gauche middle-man who buys ideas cheaply and sells demagogy dearly—at the cost of social well-being itself. Politics is no better than a dirty word, a synonym for dishonesty, corruption, superstition, and stupidity—all that is ugly and irrational in society. Politics is a "pulsing pusillanimous rigmarole" to C. H. Waddington, a world in which advancement and success depend upon guile, string-pulling, and shady deals. As viewed by the creative artist or scientist, politics is entirely irreconcilable with their values, a distinctly second-rate activity, something perhaps to be tolerated, but never to be pursued.

Few great creative artists have been concerned with depicting political activity. Plato and Marx sought to eliminate it from their vision of the harmonious social order. The absence of a great novel or poem about political activity is further evidence of this attitude. If one versifies Herodotus the result is still history, not poetry. This opinion of Aristotle characterized the outlook of the modern artist. In the graphic arts the politician is usually presented as an ignoble creature at the centre of all that is chaotic and ugly. The satire and the caricature are practically the only media used for his portrayal. One thinks of Hogarth and Daumier, of Ronald Searle in *Punch*, and the bitterness of painters of the left like George Grosz. An important element in Sir Herbert Read's anarchism and the late Wyndham Lewis' search for a *dux* is a disgust with the banality of politics. Perhaps something of the enchantment of André Malraux with the Bergsonian Charles de Gaulle is that he sees a fellow artist guided by intuition who rises above politics to create a new order of things in France.[1] Hence the typical response of the artist is usually to withdraw from the world of politics, to ignore it and often to condemn it.

A scientist's passionate confidence in the power of science often leads to a self-assured and even condescending attitude towards the layman, in some respect reminiscent of the way in which the ardent religionist views the non-believer. Areas of endeavour that have not been penetrated by science are looked upon as heathen lands, to which the true gospel, and the one way of life, must be brought. Pausing in his concern for the world of nature, the scientist is acutely conscious of the upheavals continuously plaguing humanity, the "irrational" social institutions, and the misery and privation of mankind. He concludes that all these maladies can be cured by the universal healing power of science. If scientists, or at least scientifically trained administrators, armed with the latest methods and techniques of the natural sciences, would replace the superstitious and irrational fumblings of the politicians, the present gloomy chapter of history would shortly be ended. The emergent society would be characterized by the beauty and rationality of a well-ordered scientific explanation. So by their admiration of the universal order of things, poet and scientist are joined in opposition to politics.

Marx, creative genius that he was, with his vision of a future human fellowship, sought to reconcile thought with action by subjecting the latter to the precision and symmetry of an axiomatic science. His ideal was the new man in whom thought and action achieved some sort of Platonic

[1] See Jean Gaulmier, *Anthologie de Gaulle* (Beyrouth: Editions France-Levant, 1943), pp. 18–25. The author is indebted to Dr. George Stolz of New York City for calling his attention to these suggestive early ideas of General de Gaulle.

unity. According to the theory of Lenin the Communist Party was to be a harmonious whole of thought and action rendered possible by the proper kind of organization. Rational organization would destroy all distinction between mental and physical labour, first in the Party, and then in the communist republic. But one factor of immense importance was neglected in this perspective of the communist fathers. Action and thought, to be successful, must be organized. How is organization controlled and prevented from becoming a tyrant over both action and thought? Where was the regulator, the equivalent of Platonic justice, which would check and balance organization, thought, and action? Was organization itself intended to assume this role? If this was the intention, it was a grievous miscalculation. For the disciplined routine and hierarchical relationships demanded by Bolshevik organization do not produce favourable conditions for nourishing the spontaneity, the imagination, and the bold, independent creativeness so necessary for action as well as thought. This is true to a slighter degree of any kind of organization. Indeed, the man of organization differs from the man of thought and the man of action. He is the keeper of records, the staff officer, the business manager—in short, the bureaucrat, so vital for the complexities of a modern life of action, yet so dangerous if allowed to operate without restraints. Uncontrolled bureaucracy, particularly when it is rapidly expanding, may cease to function as a vehicle for the effective blending of thought and action, and become the master, forcing thought and action to become its minions in the struggle for survival and in the quest for greater power. Proof that a bureaucratic despotism can grow and flourish, at least as easily in a communist state as in any other kind, is found in the recent Soviet disclosures of the iniquities of the Stalinist dictatorship. Had the communist fathers given theoretical and practical attention, proportionate to their consuming interest in economics, to the oligarchical tendencies in organization, world communism might be a truly democratic movement.

CONCLUSION 229

Directed by Stalin, the bureaucratic apparatus of the Soviet state eliminated all men of independent thought and action. The new Soviet hero was the man of organization. The standard of thought and action was the preservation of the bureaucracy. Thought and action formed the protective screen of the Soviet elite. Thought was reduced to the rationalizations of Agit-Prop, and action to the terror of the O.G.P.U. A horde of black-coats, like beetles out of some Kafkaesque fantasy, descended upon Soviet society and despoiled international communism.

The philosopher-king as conceived by Plato and Marx was the man of creative imagination, the seeker after truth. He was supposed to act in the light of the *summum bonum* to save society from the political brokers of the market place. So it came as a shock to many intellectuals to discover that the communist party, inspired by the vision of Marx, was ruled not by workers-cum-philosophers but by the most artful of politicians. Understanding remained the thrall of power; Prometheus, the creature of Zeus.

SELECTED REFERENCES

SELECTED REFERENCES

1. *Documents*

In addition to the many official publications of the Communist International and the C.P.G.B., including reports of Congresses, etc., the following two volumes contain useful information.

Canada. *The Report of the Royal Commission Appointed Under Order in Council P. C. 411 of February 5, 1946 to Investigate the Facts Relating to and the Circumstances Surrounding the Communications by Public Officials and Other Persons in Positions of Trust of Secret and Confidential Information to Agents of a Foreign Power. June 27, 1946.* Ottawa: Controller of Stationery, 1946. 733 pp.

Great Britain. Home Office. *Communist Papers: Documents Selected from those Obtained on the Arrest of the Communist Leaders on the 14th and 21st October, 1925.* Cmd. 2682. London: H.M.S.O., 1926. 126 pp.

2. *Newspapers and Periodicals*

Adelphi, Communist, Communist International, Communist Review, Daily Worker, Discussion, Folios of New Writing, Forward, International Press Correspondence, Lansbury's Labour Weekly, Left News, Left Review, Manchester Guardian, Modern Quarterly, Nature, Newsletter, New Statesman and Nation, New Verse, Plebs, Reasoner, Student Vanguard, Sunday Worker, The Times, Tribune, World News, Workers' Life, Workers' Weekly.

3. *Books and Pamphlets*

Aaronovitch, Sam, *et al. The American Threat to British Culture.* London: Arena, n.d. 56 pp.

Acton, H. B. *The Illusion of the Epoch: Marxism-Leninism as a Philosophical Creed.* London: Cohen and West, 1955. 278 pp.

Adams, Mary, ed. *Science in the Changing World.* London: Allen and Unwin, 1933. 286 pp.

Almond, Gabriel A. *The Appeals of Communism.* Princeton: Princeton University Press, 1954. 415 pp.

Annan, Nöel. "The Intellectual Aristocracy", in J. H. Plumb, ed., *Studies in Social History: A Tribute to G. M. Trevelyan.* London: Longmans, 1955. pp. 243–287.

Arendt, Hannah. *The Burden of Our Time*. London: Secker and Warburg, 1951. 477 pp.

Armytage, W. H. G. *Sir Richard Gregory: His Life and Work*. London: Macmillan, 1957. 241 pp.

Arnot, R. Page. *Forging the Weapon: The Struggle of the Labour Monthly, 1921–1941*. London: Labour Monthly, n.d. No pagination.

—— *History of the Labour Research Department*. London: Labour Research Department, 1926. 62 pp.

—— *Twenty Years: The Policy of the Communist Party of Great Britain from its Foundation July 31st, 1920*. London: Lawrence and Wishart, 1940. 80 pp.

Ashley, M. P., and C. T. Saunders. *Red Oxford: A History of the Growth of Socialism in the University of Oxford*. Oxford: Oxford University Labour Club, 1933 (2nd ed.). 46 pp.

Association of Scientific Workers. *Planning of Science: Report of Proceedings of the Open Conference Held at Caxton Hall January 30th–31st, 1943*. London: A.Sc.W., 1943. 127 pp.

Auden, W. H. and Christopher Isherwood. *Journey to a War*. London: Faber and Faber, 1939. 301 pp.

—— and Louis MacNeice. *Letters from Iceland*. London: Faber and Faber, 1937. 269 pp.

Baker, John R. *Science and the Planned State*. London: Allen and Unwin, 1945. 120 pp.

—— *The Scientific Life*. London: Allen and Unwin, 1942. 154 pp.

Barbusse, Henri. *Lettre aux intellectuels*. Rome: Casa ed. Rossegna internazionale, 1921. 105 pp.

—— *Manifeste aux intellectuels*. Paris: Les Ecrivains Reunis, 1927. 45 pp.

Barefoot, Brian, and Tom Cottrell. *Two Politicians in Search of a Party*. London: Quality Press, 1949. 192 pp.

Bell, Tom. *The British Communist Party; A Short History*. London: Lawrence and Wishart, 1937. 201 pp.

—— *Pioneering Days*. London: Lawrence and Wishart, 1941. 316 pp.

Bell, Quentin, ed. *Julian Bell: Essays, Poems and Letters*. Foreword by J. M. Keynes. London: Hogarth Press, 1938. 396 pp.

Benda, Julien. *The Great Betrayal*. Trans. by Richard Aldington. London: Routledge, 1928. 188 pp.

Bernal, J. D. *The Freedom of Necessity*. London: Routledge and Kegan Paul, 1949. 437 pp.

Bernal, J. D. *The Social Function of Science.* London: Routledge, 1939. 482 pp.

—— *The World, The Flesh and The Devil: An Enquiry into the Future of the Three Enemies of the Rational Soul.* London: Kegan Paul, Trench, Trubner, 1929. 96 pp.

Briffault, Robert. *Breakdown; The Collapse of Traditional Civilization.* London: Gollancz, 1935. 288 pp.

Britain Without Capitalists: A Study of What Industry in a Soviet Britain Could Achieve. By a Group of Economists, Scientists, and Technicians. London: Lawrence and Wishart, 1936. 474 pp.

Brown, Alec. *The Fate of the Middle Classes.* London: Gollancz, 1936. 288 pp.

Burns, Emile. *What is Marxism?* London: Gollancz, 1939. 94 pp.

Calder-Marshall, Arthur. *The Changing Scene.* London: Chapman and Hall, 1937. 271 pp.

—— *The Magic of My Youth.* London: Hart-Davis, 1951. 226 pp.

Carr, Richard Comyns, ed. *Red Rags: Essays of Hate from Oxford.* London: Chapman and Hall, 1933. 291 pp.

Casanova, Laurent. *Le Parti Communiste, Les Intellectuels et La Nation.* Paris: Editions Sociales, 1949. 141 pp.

Caudwell, Christopher. *Further Studies in a Dying Culture.* Edited by Edgell Rickword. London: The Bodley Head, 1949. 256 pp.

—— *Illusion and Reality: A Study of the Sources of Poetry.* London: Macmillan, 1937. 351 pp.

—— *Studies in a Dying Culture.* Introduction by John Strachey. London: The Bodley Head, 1938. 228 pp.

Charques, R. D. *Contemporary Literature and Social Revolution.* London: Secker, 1933. 195 pp.

Clark, F. LeGros, ed. *National Fitness: A Brief Essay on Contemporary Britain.* Foreword by Maj.-Gen. Sir Robert McCarrison. London: Macmillan, 1938. 222 pp.

Cockburn, Claud. *In Time of Trouble: An Autobiography.* London: Hart-Davis, 1956. 264 pp.

Cole, G. D. H. *A History of the Labour Party from 1914.* London: Routledge and Kegan Paul, 1948. 516 pp.

—— *A History of Socialist Thought.* Vol I, "Socialist Thought; the Forerunners 1789–1850", 346 pp. Vol. II, "Socialist Thought; Marxism and Anarchism 1850–1890", 482 pp. Vol. III, "The Second International 1889–1914", in two parts, 1043 pp. London: Macmillan, 1953–1956.

Cole, G. D. H. *The Next Ten Years in British Social and Economic Policy*. London: Macmillan, 1929. 459 pp.

—— *A Short History of the British Working Class Movement, 1789–1947*. London: Allen and Unwin, 1948 (rev. ed.). 500 pp.

—— *Studies in Class Structure*. London: Routledge and Kegan Paul, 1955. 195 pp.

—— *What Marx Really Meant*. London: Gollancz, 1943. 317 pp.

Cole, Margaret. *Beatrice Webb*. London: Longmans, 1945. 197 pp.

—— *Beatrice Webb's Diaries, 1912–1924*. Introduction by Lord Beveridge. London: Longmans, 1952. 272 pp.

—— *Growing Up Into Revolution*. London: Longmans, 1949. 224 pp.

—— ed. *The Webbs and Their World*. London: Muller, 1949. 304 pp.

Collard, Dudley. *Soviet Justice, and the Trial of Radek and Others*. Introduction by D. N. Pritt. London: Gollancz, 1937. 208 pp.

Crossman, R. H. S., ed. *The God that Failed*. New York: Bantam Books, 1954 (rev. ed.). 277 pp.

Crowther, J. G. *The Social Relations of Science*. London: Macmillan, 1941. 665 pp.

—— *Soviet Science*. London: Kegan Paul, Trench, Trubner, 1936. 342 pp.

Dark, Sidney, ed. *Conrad Noel: An Autobiography; With a Memoir of his Childhood by a Cousin and Tributes* by Kingsley Martin, Harry Roberts, and Richard Church. London: Dent, 1945. 136 pp.

Darke, C. H. ("Bob"). *The Communist Technique in Britain*. London: Collins, 1953. 160 pp.

Dataller, Roger. *A Pitman Looks at Oxford*. London: Dent, 1933. 205 pp.

Deane, Herbert A. *The Political Ideas of Harold J. Laski*. New York: Columbia University Press, 1953. 370 pp.

Dobb, Maurice. *Marx as an Economist*. Marxism Today Series. London: Lawrence and Wishart, 1943. 32 pp.

—— *On Marxism To-Day*. London: Hogarth Press, 1932. 48 pp.

—— *Russia To-Day and To-Morrow*. London: Hogarth Press, 1930. 48 pp.

Driberg, Tom. *Guy Burgess: A Portrait with Background*. London: Weidenfeld and Nicolson, 1956. 124 pp.

Dutt, R. Palme. *Fascism and Social Revolution*. London: Lawrence, 1934. 296 pp.

Dutt, R. Palme. *The Political and Social Doctrine of Communism.* London: Hogarth Press, 1938. 144 pp.

Eaton, John. *Marx against Keynes: A Reply to Mr. Morrison's "Socialism".* London: Lawrence and Wishart, 1951. 142 pp.

—— *Political Economy: A Marxist Textbook.* London: Lawrence and Wishart (rev. ed.), 1952. 235 pp.

Fainsod, Merle. *How Russia is Ruled.* Cambridge: Harvard University Press, 1953. 575 pp.

Farrington, Benjamin. *Francis Bacon: Philosopher of Industrial Science.* London: Lawrence and Wishart, 1951. 198 pp.

—— *Greek Science: Its Meaning for Us.* Vol. II, "Theophrastus to Galen". Harmondsworth, Middlesex: Penguin Books, 1949. 181 pp.

Fyfe, James. *Lysenko is Right.* London: Lawrence and Wishart, 1950. 65 pp.

Gallacher, William. *The Case for Communism.* Harmondsworth, Middlesex: Penguin Books, 1949. 208 pp.

—— *The Chosen Few: A Sketch of Men and Events in Parliament.* Foreword by Reg Bishop. London: Lawrence and Wishart, 1940. 231 pp.

—— *Revolt on the Clyde: An Autobiography.* London: Lawrence and Wishart, 1936. 301 pp.

—— *"Rise Like Lions".* London: Lawrence and Wishart, 1951. 253 pp.

—— *The Rolling of the Thunder.* London: Lawrence and Wishart, 1947. 229 pp.

Gollancz, Victor, ed. *The Betrayal of the Left.* London: Gollancz, 1941. 324 pp.

—— *My Dear Timothy: An Autobiographical Letter to His Grandson.* London: Gollancz, 1952. 439 pp.

—— *More for Timothy; Being the Second Instalment of an Autobiographical Letter to His Grandson.* London: Gollancz, 1953. 390 pp.

Gorer, Geoffrey. *Nobody Talks Politics; A Satire with an Appendix on Our Political Intelligentsia.* London: Joseph, 1936. 221 pp.

Graves, Robert, and Alan Hodge. *The Long Week-End: A Social History of Great Britain 1918–1939.* London: Faber and Faber, 1940. 472 pp.

Grigson, Geoffrey. *The Crest on the Silver: An Autobiography.* London: Cresset Press, 1950. 234 pp.

Guest, David. *A Text Book of Dialectical Materialism.* Edited by T. A. Jackson. London: Lawrence and Wishart, 1939. 110 pp.

Haden-Guest, Carmel, ed. *David Guest: A Scientist Fights for Freedom* (1911–1938). London: Lawrence and Wishart, 1939. 256 pp.

Haldane, Charlotte. *Truth Will Out.* London: Weidenfeld and Nicolson, 1949. 339 pp.

Haldane, J. B. S. *A Banned Broadcast and Other Essays.* London: Chatto and Windus, 1946. 258 pp.

—— *The Biochemistry of Genetics.* London: Allen and Unwin, 1954. 144 pp.

—— *Daedalus or Science and the Future.* London: Kegan Paul, Trench, Trench, Trubner, 1924. 93 pp.

—— *Everything Has a History.* London: Allen and Unwin, 1951. 292 pp.

—— *Heredity and Politics.* London: Allen and Unwin, 1938. 185 pp.

—— *Human Biology and Politics.* The Norman Lockyer Lecture: 10th Annual, Nov. 28, 1934, Hall of the Goldsmith's Company, London. London: The British Science Guild, n.d. 23 pp.

—— *The Inequality of Man and Other Essays.* London: Chatto and Windus, 1932. 295 pp.

—— *The Marxist Philosophy.* Ninth Annual Haldane Memorial Lecture. May 24, 1938. Birkbeck College. 20 pp.

—— *The Marxist Philosophy and the Sciences.* London: Allen and Unwin, 1938. 183 pp.

—— *Possible Worlds and Other Essays.* London: Chatto and Windus, 1927. 312 pp.

—— *Science Advances.* London: Allen and Unwin, 1947. 253 pp.

—— *Science and Ethics.* Conway Memorial Lecture. London: Watts, 1928. 46 pp.

—— *Science and Everyday Life.* London: Lawrence and Wishart, 1939. 284 pp.

—— *Science in Peace and War.* London: Lawrence and Wishart, 229 pp.

—— *Why Professional Workers Should be Communists.* London: C.P.G.B., 1945. 4 pp.

Hall, Sir Daniel, *et al. The Frustration of Science.* Foreword by Frederick Soddy. London: Allen and Unwin, 1935. 144 pp.

Harris, H. Wilson, ed. *Christianity and Communism.* Oxford: Blackwell, 1937. 77 pp.

Harrisson, Thomas Harnett. *Letter to Oxford.* Wyck, Gloucestershire: Reynold Bray, The Hate Press, 1933. 98 pp.

Hilton, Rodney. *Communism and Liberty*. Marxism Today Series. London: Lawrence and Wishart, 1950. 32 pp.

—— et al. *Essays on Socialist Realism and the British Cultural Tradition*. London: Arena, n.d. 86 pp.

Hogben, Lancelot. *Dangerous Thoughts*. London: Allen and Unwin, 1939. 283 pp.

—— *The New Authoritarianism*. Conway Memorial Lecture delivered at Conway Hall, Red Lion Square, London, W.C.1, on March 22, 1949. Foreword by Professor F. A. E. Grew, F.R.S. London: Watts, 1949. 44 pp.

—— *The Retreat from Reason*. Conway Memorial Lecture delivered at Conway Hall, Red Lion Square, London, W.C.1, on May 20, 1936. Chairman's Introductory Address by Julian Huxley. London: Watts, 1936. 83 pp.

Hunt, R. N. Carew. *Marxism Past and Present*. London: Bles, 1954. 180 pp.

—— *The Theory and Practice of Communism*. London: Bles, 1957 (5th rev. ed.). 286 pp.

Hutt, Allen. *The Condition of the Working Class in Britain*. Introduction by Harry Pollitt. London: Lawrence, 1933. 272 pp.

—— *The Final Crisis*. London: Gollancz, 1935. 288 pp.

—— *The Post-War History of the British Working Class*. Foreword by Harold J. Laski. New York: Coward-McCann, 1938. 274 pp.

Huxley, Julian. *If I Were Dictator*. London: Methuen, 1934. 122 pp.

—— *Scientific Research and Social Needs*. London: Watts, 1934. 287 pp.

Hyde, Douglas. *I Believed: The Autobiography of a Former British Communist*. London: Heinemann, 1950. 303 pp.

Isherwood, Christopher. *Lions and Shadows: An Education in the Twenties*. London: Methuen, 1953. 312 pp.

Jackson, T. A. *Dialectics: The Logic of Marxism, and its Critics—An Essay in Exploration*. London: Lawrence and Wishart, 1936. 648 pp.

—— *Solo Trumpet: Some Memories of Socialist Agitation and Propaganda*. London: Lawrence and Wishart, 1953. 166 pp.

Jameson, Storm. *Civil Journey*. London: Cassell, 1939. 327 pp.

—— *No Time Like the Present*. London: Cassell, 1933. 238 pp.

Joad, C. E. M., and John Strachey. *After-Dinner Philosophy*. London: Routledge, 1926. 137 pp.

Johnson, Hewlett. *Marxism and the Individual*. London: Lawrence and Wishart, 1943. 32 pp.

—— *The Socialist Sixth of the World*. London: Gollancz, 1939. 384 pp.

—— *Soviet Strength: Its Source and Challenge*. London: Muller, 1942. 154 pp.

—— *Soviet Success*. London: Hutchinson, n.d. 285 pp.

Kemp, Harry, Laura Riding, *et al. The Left Heresy in Literature and Life*. London: Methuen, 1939. 270 pp.

Klingender, F. D. *The Condition of Clerical Labour in Britain*. Preface by W. J. Brown. London: Lawrence, 1935. 117 pp.

Klugmann, James. *From Trotsky to Tito*. London: Lawrence and Wishart, 1951. 204 pp.

Koestler, Arthur, *et al. The Challenge of Our Time*. London: Percival Marshall, 1948. 78 pp.

Langdon-Davies, John. *Russia Puts the Clock Back: A Study of Soviet Science and Some British Scientists*. Foreword by Sir Henry Dale. London: Gollancz, 1949. 160 pp.

Left Review. *Authors Take Sides on the Spanish War*. London: Left Review, 1937. No pagination.

Lehmann, John. *New Writing in Europe*. Harmondsworth, Middlesex: Penguin Books, 1940. 158 pp.

—— *The Whispering Gallery: Autobiography I*. London: Longmans, 1955. 342 pp.

——, T. A. Jackson, C. Day Lewis, eds. *Ralph Fox: A Writer in Arms*. London: Lawrence and Wishart, 1937. 252 pp.

Levy, Hyman. *A Philosophy for Modern Man*. London: Gollancz, 1938. 287 pp.

—— *Science in an Irrational Society*. Conway Memorial Lecture, delivered at Conway Hall, Red Lion Square, London, W.C.1, on April 25, 1934. Chairman's Introduction by J. B. S. Haldane. London: Watts, 1934. 82 pp.

—— *Social Thinking*. London: Cobbett Press, 1945. 174 pp.

—— *Thinking*. London: Newnes, n.d. 22 pp.

—— *The Universe of Science*. London: Watts, 1932. 224 pp.

—— *The Web of Thought and Action*. London: Watts, 1934. 238 pp.

——, John Macmurray, Ralph Fox, R. Page Arnot, J. D. Bernal, and E. F. Carritt. *Aspects of Dialectical Materialism*. London: Watts, 1934. 154 pp.

Lewis, C. Day. *A Hope for Poetry*. Oxford: Blackwell, 1934. 78 pp.

Lewis, C. Day, ed. *The Mind in Chains: Socialism and the Cultural Revolution*. London: Muller, 1937. 256 pp.

Lewis, John, Karl Polanyi, Donald K. Kitchin, eds. *Christianity and the Social Revolution*. London: Gollancz, 1935. 526 pp.

Lindsay, Jack. *After the Thirties: the Novel in Britain and its Future*. London: Lawrence and Wishart, 1956. 239 pp.

Macmurray, John. *The Philosophy of Communism*. London: Faber and Faber, 1933. 96 pp.

—— *Creative Society: A Study of the Relation of Christianity to Communism*. London: Student Christian Movement Press, 1935. 196 pp.

Madge, Charles and Tom Harrisson *Mass Observation*. Foreword by Professor Julian Huxley. "Mass-Observation Series" No. One. London: Muller, 1937. 64 pp.

Martin, Kingsley. *Harold Laski (1893–1950): A Biographical Memoir*. London: Gollancz, 1953. 287 pp.

Mirsky, Dmitri. *The Intelligentsia of Great Britain*. Trans. by Alec Brown. London: Gollancz, 1935. 237 pp.

Mitchell, Sir Peter Chalmers. *My Fill of Days*. London: Faber and Faber, 1937. 440 pp.

Mitchison, Naomi. *The Moral Basis of Politics*. London: Constable, 1938. 376 pp.

Montefiore, Dora B. *From a Victorian to a Modern*. London: Archer, 1927. 222 pp.

Morton, A. L., and George Tate. *The British Labour Movement 1770–1920: A History*. London: Lawrence and Wishart, 1956. 313 pp.

Mowat, Charles Loch. *Britain Between the Wars, 1918–1940*. London: Methuen, 1955. 694 pp.

Muggeridge, Malcolm. *The Thirties: 1930–1940 in Great Britain*. London: Hamish Hamilton, 1940. 327 pp.

Murphy, J. T., ed. *New Horizons*. London: The Bodley Head, 1941. 352 pp.

Murry, John Middleton. *The Defence of Democracy*. London: Cape, 1939. 315 pp.

—— *The Necessity of Communism*. London: Cape, 1932. 136 pp.

Needham, Joseph. *History is on our Side: A Contribution to Political, Religious, and Scientific Faith*. London: Allen and Unwin, 1946. 226 pp.

—— Integrative Levels: *A Revaluation of the Idea of Progress*. The Herbert Spencer Lecture. Oxford: Clarendon Press, 1937. 59 pp.

Needham, Joseph. *Time, The Refreshing River*. Essays and Addresses, 1932–1942. London: Allen and Unwin, 1943. 280 pp.

—— and David E. Green, eds. *Perspectives in Biochemistry: Thirty-one Essays Presented to Sir Frederick Gowland Hopkins by Past and Present Members of His Laboratory.* Cambridge: University Press, 1937. 361 pp.

Pelling, Henry. *America and the British Left: From Bright to Bevan.* London: Black, 1956. 174 pp.

—— *The British Communist Party: A Historical Profile.* London: Black, 1958. 204 pp.

Phillip, Peter. *Professor J. B. S. Haldane, F.R.S.* London: Daily Worker League, n.d. 8 pp.

Polanyi, Michael. *The Contempt of Freedom: The Russian Experiment and After.* London: Watts, 1940. 116 pp.

—— *The Logic of Liberty: Reflections and Rejoinders.* London: Routledge and Kegan Paul, 1951. 206 pp.

—— *Personal Knowledge: Towards a Post-Critical Philosophy.* London: Routledge and Kegan Paul, 1958. 428 pp.

—— *Pure and Applied Science and their Appropriate Forms of Organization.* Occasional Pamphlet No. 14. Oxford: Society for Freedom in Science, Dec. 1953. 13 pp.

—— *Rights and Duties of Science.* Occasional Pamphlet No. 2. Oxford: Society for Freedom in Science, June 1945. 18 pp.

—— *Science, Faith and Society.* University of Durham, Riddell Memorial Lectures. London: Oxford University Press, 1946. 80 pp.

Pollitt, Harry. *Professional Workers.* London: C.P.G.B., 1946. 12 pp.

—— *Serving My Time: An Apprenticeship to Politics.* London: Lawrence and Wishart, 1940. 292 pp.

Postgate, Raymond. *How to Make a Revolution.* London: Hogarth Press, 1934. 199 pp.

Pritt, D. N. *The Zinoviev Trial.* London: Gollancz, 1936. 39 pp.

Ralphs, Lincoln, ed. *Young Minds for Old: Fourteen Young University Writers on Modern Problems.* London: Muller, 1936. 225 pp.

Rickword, Edgell. *War and Culture: The Decline of Culture under Capitalism.* No. 6, Peace Library. London: C.P.G.B., n.d. 14 pp.

Roberts, Michael, ed. *New Country: Prose and Poetry by the Authors of New Signatures.* London: Hogarth Press, 1933. 256 pp.

Roberts, Michael, ed. *New Signatures: Poems by Several Hands.* London: Hogarth Press, 1932. 103 pp.

Romilly, Giles, and Esmond Romilly. *Out of Bounds.* London: Hamish Hamilton, 1935. 309 pp.

Rowse, A. L. *Politics and the Younger Generation.* London: Faber and Faber, 1931. 303 pp.

Rust, William. *Britons in Spain: The History of the British Battalion of the XVth International Brigade.* London: Lawrence and Wishart, 1939. 212 pp.

Saville, John, ed. *Democracy and the Labour Movement: Essays in Honour of Dona Torr.* London: Lawrence and Wishart, 1954. 275 pp.

Science at the Cross Roads: Papers Presented to the International Congress of the History of Science and Technology held in London from June 29th to July 3rd, 1931, by the Delegates of the U.S.S.R. London: Kniga (England) Ltd., 1931. Each paper paginated separately.

Simon, Brian. *A Student's View of the Universities.* Preface by Sir John Stopford. London: Longmans, 1943. 142 pp.

Sloan, Pat, ed. *John Cornford: A Memoir.* London: Cape, 1938. 252 pp.

—— *Russia without Illusions.* Preface by Beatrice Webb. London: Muller, 1938. 268 pp.

—— *Soviet Democracy.* London: Gollancz, 1937. 288 pp.

Sommerfield, John. *Volunteer in Spain.* London: Lawrence and Wishart, 1937. 159 pp.

Spender, Stephen. *The Creative Element: A Study of Vision, Despair and Orthodoxy among some Modern Writers.* London: Hamish Hamilton, 1953. 199 pp.

—— *The Destructive Element: A Study of Modern Writers and Beliefs.* London: Cape, 1935. 284 pp.

—— *Forward From Liberalism.* London: Gollancz, 1937. 295 pp.

—— *World Within World: The Autobiography of Stephen Spender.* London: Hamish Hamilton, 1951. 349 pp.

Spender, Stephen, and John Lehmann, eds. *Poems for Spain.* London: Hogarth Press, 1939. 108 pp.

Strachey, John. *The Banks for the People.* London: Gollancz, 1940. 77 pp.

—— *The Coming Struggle for Power.* London: Gollancz, 1932. 299 pp.

—— *Contemporary Capitalism.* London: Gollancz, 1956. 302 pp.

—— *A Faith to Fight For.* London: Gollancz, 1941. 156 pp.

—— *Federalism or Socialism?* London: Gollancz, 1940. 283 pp.

Strachey, John. *The Frontiers*. London: Gollancz, 1952. 222 pp.

—— *Hope in America*. New York: Modern Age Books, 1938. 215 pp.

—— ed. Karl Marx, *Capital*. Abridged with introduction by Strachey. London: Nelson, 1936. 376 pp.

—— *The Menace of Fascism*. London: Gollancz, 1933. 280 pp.

—— *The Nature of the Capitalist Crisis*. London: Gollancz, 1935. 384 pp.

—— *Post D: Some Experiences of an Air Raid Warden*. London: Gollancz, 1941. 135 pp.

—— *A Programme for Progress*. London: Gollancz, 1940. 352 pp.

—— *Revolution by Reason: An Account of the Financial Proposals Submitted to the Labour Movement by Mr. Oswald Mosley*. London: Parsons, 1925. 256 pp.

—— *The Theory and Practice of Socialism*. London: Gollancz, 1936. 488 pp.

—— *What Are We To Do?* London: Gollancz, 1938. 398 pp.

—— *Why You Should Be a Socialist*. London: Gollancz, 1938. 96 pp.

—— *Workers' Control in the Russian Mining Industry*. Foreword by A. J. Cook. London: The New Leader, 1928. 48 pp.

Thompson, Edward P. *William Morris, Romantic to Revolutionary*. London: Lawrence and Wishart, 1955. 908 pp.

Thomson, George. *Marxism and Poetry*. Marxism Today Series. London: Lawrence and Wishart, 1945. 64 pp.

—— *et al. Britain's Cultural Heritage*. London: Arena, n.d. 64 pp.

Towster, Julian. *Political Power in the U.S.S.R. 1917–1947; the Theory and Structure of Government in the Soviet State*. Introduction by Quincy Wright. New York: Oxford University Press, 1948. 443 pp.

Toynbee, Philip. *Friends Apart: A Memoir of Esmond Romilly and Jaspar Ridley in the Thirties*. London: MacGibbon and Kee, 1954. 189 pp.

Utley, Freda. *Lost Illusion*. Introduction by Bertrand Russell. London: Allen and Unwin, 1949. 237 pp.

Waddington, C. H., ed. *Science and Ethics*. London: Allen and Unwin, 1942. 144 pp.

—— *The Scientific Attitude*. Harmondsworth, Middlesex: Penguin Books, 1941. 128 pp.

—— *The Scientific Attitude*. West Drayton, Middlesex: Penguin Books, 1948 (2nd ed.). 175 pp.

Webb, Sidney and Beatrice Webb. *Soviet Communism: A New Civilization?* London: Longmans, 1935. 2 vols.

Webb, Sidney and Beatrice Webb. *Soviet Communism: A New Civilization.* London: Longmans, 1937 (2nd ed.). 2 vols.

Wells, H. G. *Experiment In Autobiography: Discoveries and Conclusions of a Very Ordinary Brain (Since 1866).* London: Gollancz and Cresset Press, 1934. 2 vols.

Wertheimer, Egon. *Portrait of the Labour Party.* Translated from the German. London: Putnam, 1929. 328 pp.

West, Alick. *Crisis and Criticism.* London: Lawrence and Wishart, 1937. 199 pp.

Whyte, A. Gowans. *The Story of the R.P.A. 1899–1949.* Preface by C. D. Darlington. London: Watts, 1949. 105 pp.

Wintringham, Thomas Henry. *English Captain.* London: Faber and Faber, 1939. 333 pp.

Young, Allan, John Strachey, W. J. Brown, and Aneurin Bevan. *A National Policy: An Account of the Emergency Programme Advanced by Sir Oswald Mosley, M.P.* London: Macmillan, 1931. 63 pp.

INDEX

Jaurès, J. L., 15
Jay, Douglas, 69, 186
Jerrold, Douglas, 54
Jewish Clarion, 176, 198
Joad, C. E. M., 59, 99
Johnson, Hewlett, 79 n., 160, 163, 176, 202
Joyce, James, 101

Kalinin, M. I., 21
Kamenev, L. B., 19, 24
Kapitza, Soviet physicist, 87
Kartun, Derek, 198, 201
Kautsky, Karl, 15
Kemp, Harry, 72
Kenny, Rowland, 77
Kettle, Arnold, 27, 79 n., 84, 85 n., 157, 212–13
Keynes, J. M., 41, 72–3, 100, 106–7, 186
Khrushchev, N. S., 30, 210
Kiernan, V. G., 79 n., 84, 85 n.
Klingender, F. D., 79 n.
Klugmann, James, 27, 79 n., 157, 224; education, 83 n., 84, 85 n., 86; career, 221–3
Knox, Bernard, 79 n., 84
Koestler, Arthur, 55, 96, 130
Krassin, L. B., 24
Krestinsky, 19
Krishna Menon, V. R., 162

Labour Monthly, 167, 176, 184, 196, 199, 205
Labour Party, British: recent emergence of intellectuals as leaders of, 15; membership (1920, 1922), 23; Labour Government of 1929–31, 39; secession of I.L.P. from, 39; accused of inaction, 107; proscribes Friendship Societies, 163, 165
Labour Research Department, 77–9, 162
Langdon-Davies, John, 79 n., 80, 84, 191
Lansbury, George, 60, 77
Laski, Harold J., 43, 46–7, 61–2, 73, 129
Lassalle, Ferdinand, 15
Laval, Pierre, 40
Lawrence, D. H., 119
Laxton, Geoff, 212

Layton, Sir Walter, 53
League of the Kingdom of God, 65
Leavis, F. R., 72
Lee, Jennie, 73
Left Book Club, 60–3
Left Book News (later *Left News*), 61, 63
Left Review, 58–9, 70, 113
Legal Marxists, 16
Lehmann, Beatrix, 79 n., 162, 176
Lehmann, John, 39, 41, 59–60, 80–1, 83–4, 85 n., 102, 104
Lenin, V. I., 15, 20, 22, 26, 45, 212, 217, 225, 228; his "anti-intellectualism", 17–18, 211
Lennox-Boyd, A., 54
Lesser, Sam, 56 n.
Lessing, Doris, 198, 202
Levy, Professor Hyman, 79 n., 127, 129, 136–7, 157, 198, 208–12
Levy, Paul, 21
Lewis, C. Day, 38, 41, 53, 55, 72, 79 n., 80 and n., 84, 97, 102–3, 108
Lewis, J., 28
Lewis, Rev. Dr. John, 61, 63, 66–7, 79 n., 177, 223
Lewis, Wyndham, 54, 226
Liberalism, 80–1
Liebknecht, K., 15
Lilley, S., 79 n., 84
Lindemann, F. A. (Lord Cherwell), 129
Lindsay, Jack, 79 n., 157
Literary Guide, 148
Literature: magazines and reviews of the 1930's, 57–60; the Left Book Club, 60–3; alleged to be under communist control in the 1930's, 73; dominant writers of late 19th and early 20th centuries, 97; appearance of new group of writers, c. 1925, 97; and the new political consciousness, 97–105; nihilism of the writers, 106 ff.
Lockyer, Sir Norman, 147
London Magazine, 80
London School of Economics, radical societies at, 51, 202
Longuet, 15
Lovestone, Jay, 21, 47
Lukacs, Professor George, 194, 206, 221

182, 185, 218; antecedents, 82;
education, 83–4, 85 n.; career
and intellectual development,
113–17; severs relationship with
communist movement, 186–9,
193–4
Student Labour Federation, 52
Student Vanguard, 38, 51
Suez incident, 193
Swingler, Randall, 202
Swingler, Raymond, 79 n.
Swinnerton, Dennis and Jane, 206
Synge, R. L. M., 79 n., 80 n., 82,
83 n., 84, 85 n.

Tanner, Jack, 27 n.
Tansley, A. G., 135
Tate, George, 79 n., 84, 178
Thalmann, E., 21
"Thinkers' Library", 149
Thomas, Dylan, 70
Thompson, Edward, 196–7, 199–
200, 202
Thomson, Professor George, 27,
79 n., 84, 85 n., 88, 157, 177
Thorez, M., 21
Thornycroft, Christopher, 56 n.
Times, The, 54
Tito, Marshal, 222–3
Tizard, Sir Henry, 129
"Today and Tomorrow Series",
148
Tomalin, Miles, 56 n.
Torr, Dona, 75 n., 76 n., 77, 167, 178
Tours, Congress of, 22
Toynbee, Arnold, 81
Toynbee, Philip, 55, 79 n., 80 *and
n.*, 81, 83 n., 84
Traill, R., 56 n.
Trevelyan, Charles, 161
Tribune, 207
Trotsky, Leon, 15, 18–20, 50
Turner, W. J., 70 n., 71

Unemployment, in 1930's, 37–8
Unity Theatre, 202
United States, abandons Gold
Standard, 40. *See also* Commu-
nist Party
Universities: radical organizations
in, 51–3; fascism in, 53; intel-
lectuals educated at, 84–90
Upward, Edward, 38, 79 n., 84,
112

Us, 63
Utley, Freda, 75 n., 76 n., 168–71,
182 n.

Vandervelde, 15
Verschoyle, Derek, 70 n.
Viewpoint (later *Left Review*), 58
Voigt, F. A., 50
Voroshilov, K. Y., 21

Waddington, C. H., 79 n., 83 n.,
84, 88, 226; *The Scientific Atti-
tude*, 132–3
Wainwright, William, 163
Wall Street crash, 39
Walpole, Sir Hugh, 97
Wanderer, The, 57
Warner, Rex, 38, 79 n., 80, 84,
108
Watts, Charles A., 148
Waugh, Alec, 70 n.
Waugh, Evelyn, 54, 70 n., 178
Webb, Beatrice, 24, 43–5, 75, 77,
146, 150
Webb, Sidney, 43–5, 77, 146, 150
Weber, Max, 157, 214, 217
Week, The, 54, 58
Wells, H. G., 70 n., 73, 129–30,
144, 146–9
West, Rebecca, 59
West, Vita Sackville, 70 n., 71
Whitaker, Malachi, 70 n.
Whitehead, A. N., 99
Whittaker, Peter, 56 n.
Wilkinson, Ellen, 75 n., 76 n., 77,
79, 166, 182 n.
Williams, Rhys J., 57
Williams, Robert, 167
Williams-Ellis, Amabel, 58, 162
Wintringham, Tom, 56 n., 57–9,
75 n., 76 *and n.*, 79 n., 83 n.,
85 n., 162, 166, 182 n.
Wittgenstein, Ludwig, 99–100
Wolfe, Bertram, 47
Wood, Dr. Alex, 87
Woolf, Leonard, 48, 59, 100, 104
Woolf, Virginia, 96–101, 107
Wooster, Nora and W. A., 79 n.,
84
Workers Dreadnought, 183
Workers International Relief, 162,
185
Workers Socialist Federation (*later
the* British Communist Party), 22